The Nature—Nurture Debate

Essential Readings in Developmental Psychology

Series Editors: Darwin Muir and Alan Slater

Queen's University, Kingston, Ontario, and the *University of Exeter*

In this brand new series of nine books, Darwin Muir and Alan Slater, together with a team of expert editors, bring together selections of readings illustrating important methodological, empirical, and theoretical issues in the area of developmental psychology. Volumes in the series and their editors are detailed below:

- Infant Development *Darwin Muir and Alan Slater*
- Childhood Social Development *Wendy Craig*
- Childhood Cognitive Development *Kang Lee*
- Adolescent Development *Gerald Adams*
- The Psychology of Aging *William Gekoski*
- The Nature–Nurture Debate *Steven Ceci and Wendy Williams*
- Educational Attainment *Charles Desforges*
- Language Development *Elizabeth Bates and Michael Tomasello*
- Developmental Disorders *Darwin Muir, Alan Slater, Wendy Williams, and Steven Ceci*

Each of the books is introduced by the volume editor with a rationale behind the chosen papers. Each reading is then introduced and contextualized within the individual subject debate as well as within the wider context of developmental psychology. A selection of further reading is also assigned, making each volume an ideal teaching resource for both classroom and individual study settings.

The Nature–Nurture Debate
The Essential Readings

Edited by Stephen J. Ceci and Wendy M. Williams

First published 1999

2 4 6 8 10 9 7 5 3 1

Blackwell Publishers Ltd
108 Cowley Road
Oxford OX4 1JF
UK

Blackwell Publishers Inc.
350 Main Street
Malden, Massachusetts 02148
USA

British Library Cataloguing in Publication Data

A CIP catalogue record for this book is available from the British Library.

Library of Congress Cataloging-in-Publication Data

The nature-nurture debate : the essential readings / edited by Stephen
J. Ceci and Wendy M. Williams.
     p.   cm. — (Essential readings in developmental psychology)
Includes bibliographical references and index.
ISBN 0-631-21738-X (alk. paper). — ISBN 0-631-21739-8 (pbk. :
alk. paper)
     1. Nature and nurture.   I. Ceci, Stephen J.   II. Williams, Wendy
M. (Wendy Melissa), 1960–   .   III. Series.
BF341.N39   1999
155.7—dc21   99-16941
                                                                         CIP

Typeset in 10½ on 13 pt Photina
by Best-set Typesetter Ltd., Hong Kong
Printed in Great Britain by T J International, Cornwall.

This book is printed on acid-free paper

Contents

Acknowledgments

The editors and publishers wish to thank the following for permission to use copyright material:

Academic Press for Craig T. Ramey and Sharon Landesman Ramey, Prevention of intellectual disabilities: early interventions to improve cognitive development. *Preventative Medicine*, *27* (1998) 224–32. Copyright © 1998 by American Health Foundation and Academic Press;

The American Association for the Advancement of Science for Thomas J. Bouchard, Jr., Genes, environment and personality, *Science*, *264* (June 1994) 1700–1. Copyright © 1994 The American Association for the Advancement of Science;

American Medical Association for Milton Diamond and H. Keith Sigmundson, Sex reassignment at birth, *Pediatric and Adolescent Medicine*, 151 (1997) 298–304. Copyright © 1997 American Medical Association; and Matti O. Huttunen and Pakka Niskanen, Prenatal loss of father and psychiatric disorders, *General Psychiatry*, *35* (1978) 429–31. Copyright © 1978 American Medical Association;

American Psychological Association for K. Anders Ericsson and Neil Charness, Expert performance, *American Psychologist*, *49*:8 (August

1994) 725–47. Copyright © 1994 American Psychological Association; and Stephen J. Ceci, Schooling and intelligence, *Psychological Science Agenda* (Sept/Oct 1992) 7–9. Copyright © 1992 American Psychological Association;

The British Psychological Society for Ann Clarke and Alan Clarke, Early experience and the life path, *The Psychologist* (Sept 1998) 433–6;

Cambridge University Press for Michael J.A. Howe, Jane W. Davidson and John A. Sloboda, Innate talents: reality or myth?, *Behavioural and Brain Sciences*, *21* (1998) pp. 399–407; and Michael Rutter et al. Developmental catch-up and deficit, following adoption and severe global early privation, *Journal of Child Psychology and Psychiatry*, *39*(40) (1988) pp. 465–76;

Neil Charness for Figure 1 from N. Charness, Search in chess: age and skill differences, *Journal of Experimental Psychology: Human Perception and Performance*, *7* (1981) 469, included in K. Anders Ericsson and Neil Charness, Expert performance, *American Psychologist*, 49:8 (August 1994) pp. 725–47. Copyright © 1994 American Psychological Association;

Discover Magazine for Jared Diamond, 'War Babies', *Discover* (Dec 1990) 70–75. Copyright © Jared Diamond 1990;

Elsevier Science for Figure 5 from N. Charness and E.A. Bosman, Expertise and aging: life in the lab, in *Aging and Cognition: Knowledge Organization and Utilization*, ed., T.H. Hess (1990) 358, included in K. Anders Ericsson and Neil Charness, Expert performance, *American Psychologist*, 49:8 (August 1994) 725–47. Copyright © 1994 American Psychological Association;

Judith Rich Harris for How to succeed in childhood, *Wilson Quarterly*, 23:1 (Winter 1999) 30–37;

Scientific American, Inc. for Robert Plomin and John C. DeFries, The genetics of cognitive abilities and disabilities, *Scientific American* (May 1988) 62–9. Copyright © 1998 by Scientific American, Inc;

John Wiley & Sons Ltd on behalf of the Ciba Foundation for adapted Figures 3 and 4 from K.A. Ericsson, R.Th. Krampe and S. Heizmann, Can we create gifted people? in *The Origins and Development of High Ability* (1993) 222–49, included in K. Anders Ericsson and Neil Charness, Expert performance, *American Psychologist*, 49:8 (August 1994) 725–47. Copyright © 1994 American Psychological Association.

Every effort has been made to trace the copyright holders but if any have been inadvertently overlooked the publishers will be pleased to make the necessary arrangement at the first opportunity.

Introduction
Born vs. Made: Nature–Nurture in the New Millennium

Stephen J. Ceci and Wendy M. Williams

When we were invited by the series editors, Alan Slater and Darwin Muir, to compile a volume of classic papers on the nature–nurture dispute, we felt like children in a candy shop. There is so much good research on one side or the other (as well as in between), we felt sure our sole difficulty would be deciding among a surfeit of excellent candidates for inclusion in this volume. We were wrong. The reason is not that there were few excellent articles on this debate, but that most of the existing articles were inaccessible to readers lacking ample statistical, biological, and psychological training. To evaluate such articles requires knowledge of multivariate statistics and many sub-areas of psychological and biological science.

Our solution to this problem was to choose articles that have made substantial contributions, yet are understandable to students with limited backgrounds in psychology, if they are accompanied by prefaces written by us. Using these two criteria (i.e., important contributions and accessible if accompanied by prefaces), we were able to whittle down a very large set of potential articles to a mere few hundred. Further whittling was accomplished by invoking a third criterion: we would not include articles that have been refuted or called into doubt by subsequent research. (This latter point is the reason we eventually abandoned our original title for this volume "Classic Contributions to the Nature–Nurture Debate" – because many of the classic papers, especially those written during the first half of the twentieth century, have now been refuted.) Once we excluded classic papers that have been called in question, we were left with a manageable number for inclusion in this volume. Our fourth criterion allowed us to finalize the selection: this major concern is that the articles should reflect the dynamic and changing nature of the subject, and the current "state of the art." Thus, 12 of the 14 articles have been published in the 1990s, with half appearing since 1995.

As you go through the readings in this volume there are three things that you should bear in mind. First, these readings span many areas of developmental psychology. Several of them are about the respective contributions of genes and environments to intellectual growth. Others have to do with gender development and how biology and ecology exert their respective influences. Still others deal with the forces of nature and nurture in producing pathologies such as schizophrenia and mental retardation. And still others are concerned with the roles that parents and peers play in socializing children – and the implications of this research for broader claims about the respective influences of nature and nurture. In short, the debate over how genes and environments shape human development is not confined to questions of IQ scores; it has implications for virtually every aspect of human character and competence. We tried to reflect this broad expanse in the articles we selected for inclusion.

The second point to bear in mind when reading this volume is that studies may appear contradictory but the contradiction may be more illusory than real. This is particularly the case when comparing studies that focus on *averages* or means with studies that focus on *variances* or differences among individuals. For example, studies that demonstrate huge elevations in IQ scores of children over what might be expected on the basis of their biological mothers' IQ scores may be perfectly compatible with other studies that claim high heritability for IQ (Ceci, 1996). (The concept of heritability is discussed below.) The former studies are concerned with changes in average scores while heritability studies are based on variability among scores. There is nothing inconsistent about saying that a trait is both highly changeable and highly heritable. This point is so basic, yet important, that an example is worth pondering.

This distinction between means and variances is nicely illustrated by a famous study carried out in 1949 by Skodak and Skeels. (Subsequently, researchers criticized this study for its methodology and assumptions. Still, it serves us well to make the distinction between means and variances.) Skodak and Skeels demonstrated massive IQ gains as a function of the environment. In their study, a group of mothers who gave their offspring up for adoption had a mean IQ of 85.7. The children themselves were tested during early adolescence and found to have an average IQ of 107, fully 21.5 points superior to their biological mothers.

Although Skodak and Skeels found these massive IQ gains over what might be expected from the biological mothers' IQs – therefore clearly indicating environmental influences – they also found a correlation between the children's IQs and their biological (natural) mothers' IQs. That is, the brighter biological mothers' children had higher IQs than the children of biological mothers who had lower IQs, even though neither group was reared by their biological mothers. In all cases, however, the adoptive children's IQs, as mentioned earlier, were much higher in absolute terms than that of their biological mothers. Thus, the correlation between the biological mothers' IQs and their children's IQs is a clear indication of genetic influence, while the raised absolute IQs are a clear indication of environmental effects.

The point we are trying to make is that even when the heritability of a trait (abbreviated h^2) is extremely high, as it is for height, the environment still can exert a very powerful influence. Consider, for example, the surge in the heights of second-generation Japanese children who were raised in the US. The heritability (h^2) among this group was over 0.90, meaning that American-reared sons of tall Japanese fathers tended to be both taller than American-reared sons of short Japanese fathers, and, more importantly, taller than the sons of tall Japanese fathers who were reared in Japan. The American-reared offspring were over five inches taller than they would have been if they had been reared in Japan (Greulich, 1957). Along these same lines, Tanner (1962) showed that both American and British teenagers were a half-foot taller, on average, than their predecessors a century earlier. Finally, Angoff (1988) reported that the heights of young adult males in Japan were raised by about three and a half inches since the end of World War II, an enormous gain in such a brief period of time. If something as highly heritable as height can fluctuate so dramatically in such a relatively short period of time, then surely traits like intelligence, personality, and musical ability can be altered, too.

Explaining the Concept of Heritability

The concept of heritability is one of the most controversial in psychology (see Hirsch, 1997, for a review of debatable assumptions). In the simplest form, *heritability refers to the portion of variability in a trait (such as intelligence) that results from differences in heredity.* Put somewhat more precisely, heritability (or h^2) is the genotypic variance (i.e., variations in genetic make-up of individuals) divided by the phenotypic variance (variations between individuals in their physical and psychological characteristics, such as differences in IQ scores, which are determined by both genetic *and* environmental factors). Thus, when researchers write about heritability they are making claims about the relative degrees to which genes and the environment influence variation among individuals in the expression of a trait.

Geneticists make clear that heritability is affected by characteristics of the population as well as the trait being measured. Within the same population, heritability will differ depending on which trait is being measured (e.g., higher for IQ than for most aspects of personality). Heritability will also differ for the same trait (e.g., IQ) when it is assessed in different populations.

An interesting thesis is that heritability will tend to be higher in a good environment than in a poor one, because the former provides the necessary resources for the biological potential to be realized. After all, what good is having a great potential for acquiring Russian if the schools you attend do not teach foreign languages? Similarly, having a good potential for intelligence may be of limited use if you are reared in an environment lacking intellectual resources.

A seemingly counterintuitive dictum is that heritability rises as the environment becomes more equal across individuals. In other words, if everyone was raised in the same great environment, then any differences among them would have to result from non-environmental factors, most notably biological differences. Thus, making the environment equal for everyone will serve to increase heritability (h^2). But herein lies the rub: at the same time as equating the environment increased h^2, it would probably reduce the magnitude of differences observed. High h^2 would co-occur with small differences among people. Please bear this in mind when thinking and reading about the concept of heritability; elevations in h^2 are not the same thing as increases in the absolute magnitude of the trait being assessed. If all children were given the very best environment possible, they would probably end up differing much less than they would if some had been given the worst possible environment. But at the same time, h² would rise because although the total variability in the trait has decreased, the only possible source of such differences is genes.

Estimating Heritability: A Statistical Calculation

Let's return to the Skeels and Skodak study mentioned above. Is a 21.5-point increase in the adopted children's mean IQ over their biological mothers' IQs compatible with a very high heritability, say 0.7, that is 70 percent of the differences being genetically determined? Can IQ be so heritable if it is so changeable? The answer to both questions is "yes," and the reasoning is similar to that discussed earlier for changes across generations in height. That is, a particular trait, such as IQ, will consistently show changes in the direction of environmental changes (sometimes called "environmental drift"), but the rank ordering of the individuals remains as one would expect on the basis of genetic differences between them. It may be that a full understanding of this point requires some statistical reasoning. This is given below. We suggest that readers skip this section if they are not interested in how this is accomplished, or if they have limited statistical training.

The 21.5-point gain over biological mothers' mean IQ *is* consistent with a heritability as high as 0.7. You can see this if you carry out a statistical procedure called "regressing parental IQ on their offspring." First, make the assumption that some degree of assortive mating occurs. This means that people tend to choose partners who resemble themselves on IQ, personality, and physical appearances; i.e., "likes mate with likes" to a certain extent. Because of assortive mating, the biological fathers probably had IQs that were similar to but slightly higher than the biological mothers' IQs, and our best guess is that their IQs were around 94.5.[1]

Thus, if the biological mothers of the Skodak and Skeels children had an average IQ of 85.7 and the biological fathers' average IQ was estimated to be 94.5, then parental midpoint average IQ would have been 90.1 (85.7 + 94.5 ÷ 2).

To determine whether the children's 21.5-point IQ gain is consistent with a heritability as high as 0.7, we can regress IQ by simply adding the population mean for IQ (100) to the product of heritability, say, 0.7 (which is abbreviated h^2) × the parental midpoint IQ, minus the mean population IQ:

$$\text{estimated IQ of offspring (assuming } h^2 \text{ is } 0.7)$$
$$= \text{IQ population} + h^2 \times (\text{IQ midpoint} - \text{IQ population}), \text{ or}$$
$$100 + 0.7\,(90.1 - 100) = 93.0$$

So, we expect that the children of mothers with an average IQ of 85.7 would have an average IQ of 93.0, not 85.7. But this is still 14 points below the 107 IQ that they scored in adolescence. Doesn't this imply that heritability as high as 0.7 is incompatible with these data? No, because 93 is the IQ that would be expected if children's IQs were 100 percent determined by genes, that is, if h^2 were 1.0, as opposed to 0.7 or 70 percent determined by genes. It turns out that the difference between the IQ expected on the basis of 100 percent heritability (93) and the observed IQ of 107 is well within a heritability as high as 0.7. Here is why.

The homes in which the Skeels and Skodak children were raised were far above average, with the heads of the adoptive households usually working as professionals. How much above average these family environments were is hard to gauge, but it seems reasonable to suppose that they were between one and two standard deviations (SDs) above the population average. So let us take the superior adoptive homes to be 1.5 SDs above the population mean for 1949. How much of an increment ought that produce to the expected IQ of 93? This is a straightforward calculation: Since the standard deviation (SD) of the IQ test was 15 or 16 (let us be conservative and say it was only 15), the total variation to be explained is 15 squared, or 225. Thus, the proportion of the total IQ variance that may be due to non-genetic sources (environment plus any measurement error) is the reciprocal of h^2 multiplied by total variance, or

$$0.3 \times 225 = 92.0$$

To get the amount of enhancement due to being in a professional environment, take the square root of this value, or $\sqrt{92} = 9.6$ and multiply it by the degree to which these adoptive homes were above the population mean in affluence for 1949, which we already estimated to be 1.5 SDs. Since $1.5 \times 9.6 = 14.4$, we expect that even with an heritability (h^2) as high as 0.7, children reared in 1.5 SD superior homes would be expected to have an average IQ of almost exactly what was observed. And if the higher standard deviation for the IQ test was used (i.e., 16 rather than 15), the amount of enhancement due to environment would be higher still and compatible with a heritability even higher than 0.7.

The point of this exercise is not to argue that biology is unimportant in determining IQ or that the concept of heritability is useless, but to demonstrate that it is hard to imagine environmental influences on IQ gains that are incompatible with even very high heritability claims. So, keep in mind that IQ gains are about means or averages, while heritability estimates are based on variances or differences. (This exercise should also make it clear that if we are interested in promoting human potential, even quite high values of h^2 still leave plenty of room for environmental enhancement.)

A Few Final Points

Four final points to bear in mind when reading the papers in this volume are that: (1) heritability estimates require making a number of assumptions that need to be kept in mind (e.g., a trait will always regress toward the population mean; mothers will mate with fathers who tend to resemble them in a trait such as IQ); (2) nearly all responsible researchers agree that human traits are jointly determined by both nature and nurture, though they may disagree about the relative contributions of each; (3) not all biological influences on development are genetic; some are prenatal chemicals (hormones), others are viruses and infections. As seen in some of the following papers, these biological influences can be critical features of the intrauterine environment that can be mistaken for genetic influences; and (4) heritability estimates are highly situational: they are descriptions of the relative contributions of genes and environments to the expression of a trait in a specific group, place, and time. Such estimates tell us nothing about the relative contributions if the group, place, or time is changed. This is why there is a wide range of heritability estimates for various traits, depending on the country, time, and group measured.

The battle today seems more over the specific genetic and environmental mechanisms than over whether genes or environments matter. Recent work in quantitative trait loci (Chorney et al., 1998) and proximal processes (Bronfenbrenner and Ceci, 1994) are suggestive, though far from definitive, illustrations of the way that biology and ecology combine to produce human proclivities.

Notes

1   But since there must be some creep or regression toward the mean of 100, the fathers' IQs must be closer to the population mean of 100 than were the biological mothers' IQs, given the mothers' low scores. (Note, however, that if the mother's IQs had been over 100, then the fathers' IQs would have had to creep downward toward the population mean of 100 and, as a result, be lower than the mothers' IQs.) There is some historical evidence to assume that assortive mating for Skodak and Skeels's families was 0.39. So, we would expect the biological fathers to have IQs around 94.5 – the population mean of 100 minus 0.39× the difference between the mothers' mean IQ and the population mean. Symbolically, this can be phrased as:

$$\text{Biological father's estimated IQ} = 100 - (0.39 \times 14.3) = 94.5$$

References

Angoff, W. H. (1988). The nature–nurture debate, aptitudes, and group differences. *American Psychologist, 43,* 713–20.

Bronfenbrenner, U. and Ceci, S. J. (1994). Nature–nurture in developmental perspective: a bioecological theory. *Psychological Review, 101,* 568–86.

Ceci, S. J. (1996). *On Intelligence: A Bioecological Treatise on Intellectual Development.* Cambridge, MA: Harvard University Press.

Chorney, M. J., Chorney, K., Seese, N., Owen, M. J., Daniels, J., McGuffin, P., Thompson, L. A., Detterman, D. K., Benbow, C. P., Lubinski, D., Eley, T. C., and Plomin, R. (1998). A quantitative trait locus (QTL) associated with cognitive ability in children *Psychological Science, 9,* 159–66.

Greulich, W. W. (1957). A comparison of the physical growth and development of American-born and Japanese children. *American Journal of Physical Anthropology, 15,* 489–515.

Hirsch, J. (1997). Some history of heredity-vs-environment, genetic inferiority at Harvard, and the (incredible) Bell Curve. *Genetica, 99,* 207–24.

Skodak, M. and Skeels, H. M. (1949). A follow-up study of 100 adopted children. *Journal of Genetic Psychology, 75,* 85–125.

Tanner, J. M. (1962). *Growth at Adolescence: With a General Consideration of the Effects of Heredity and Environmental Factors Upon Growth and Maturation from Birth to Maturity.* 2nd edition. Springfield, IL: C. C. Thomas.

Part I

Fetal Influences on Later Development

War Babies

Introduction

This article reports fascinating results from an "experiment of nature." In this report we get a glimpse into one of the best-documented analyses of the impact of severe malnutrition on later development. Pregnant women facing the brunt of the Nazi siege of the Netherlands during the final seven months of World War II were reduced to near starvation. Some of these pregnant women miscarried. But if they successfully gave birth, their offspring appeared unremarkable after a period of catch-up growth. At age 18 when tested for military service, those males who were gestated by starving mothers seemed no different than their better-nourished peers on a battery of mental tests. Thus, if they survived, they were unscathed.

However, the children of the Nazi siege are now over 50 years old, and many have children of their own – the grandchildren of the pregnant women of 1944. It turns out that even girls who had themselves been normal weight at birth nevertheless went on to have babies of their own (i.e., grandchildren of the starved women) who were either underweight or grew into small adults. In other words, the grandmothers of these small women gave birth to babies who were normal size, but who nevertheless passed on the effects of starvation to the next generation's offspring, a sort of "sleeper effect."

Diamond offers some evolutionary speculations for these results. But for us, the most important point is to show that nature and nurture work in tandem, and often quite mysteriously, to exert their influence. Starvation had different effects depending on two timing issues: (1) when it occurred during pregnancy, and (2) which generation was studied. Concerning the former, it often was the case that when the brunt of the famine occurred during the first trimester of pregnancy, the baby's birth weight was unaffected, whereas when starvation occurred later during pregnancy, the baby was underweight. Concerning the latter, there are effects that may not be detected in the first generation of offspring that nevertheless emerge in a later generation. In short, timing is crucial when considering the interplay between biology and ecology.

Further reading

Stein, Z. and Susser, M. (1976). Prenatal nutrition and mental competence. In J. D. Lloyd-Still (ed.), *Malnutrition and Intellectual Development*. Littleton, MA: Publishing Sciences Group.

ONE

War Babies

Jared Diamond

It is easy to write now that each person got 400 calories a day. In prac-
tice it was quite another thing. . . . People sought food everywhere in the
streets and the surrounding countryside. Anything edible was picked up
in this way, and they were lucky who found a potato or two or a handful
of greens. . . . People dropped from exhaustion in the streets and many
died there. Often people were so fatigued that they were unable to return
home, before curfew; so they hid in barns or elsewhere to sleep and there
died. . . . Older people, who lacked the strength to go searching for food,
stayed at home in bed and died.
                    Famine and Human Development: The Dutch Hunger
                                               Winter of 1944–1945

Among the homey images I recall from my wife's pregnancy are the
bigger-than-usual milk cartons in the refrigerator and her vitamin
bottles on the kitchen counter. To our generation the value of good
nutrition for pregnant women seems obvious. But what makes us so
sure? After all, we can't run experiments on people to prove it. Starving
hundreds of pregnant women and then comparing their kids with well-
nourished cousins would be absolutely unthinkable.

Yet such an inhuman experiment was indeed once conducted. By
imposing a famine on part of the population of the Netherlands during
the last seven months of World War II, the Nazis effectively reduced
40,000 pregnant women to starvation. These cruel circumstances
resulted in a study of the effects of prenatal nutrition that was grimly
well-designed, complete with a control group: while these women were
starving, other mothers-to-be in the same society were eating comparatively healthy rations.

Years later, when the babies who survived had grown into adults, epidemiologists could distinguish the different effects of prenatal and postnatal nutrition; they could even discern the effects of malnutrition at different stages of pregnancy, for at the time the famine took hold, some women were further along in their pregnancy than others. Even now we are still learning what toll was exacted by the events of 45 years ago. Only recently have researchers learned that the famine's effects reached far beyond its immediate victims: now that girls born to the starved Dutch women have grown up and had children of their own, it's become apparent that some of these children too are marked by the deprivations suffered years earlier by their grandmothers!

Today we accept without question that proper nutrition is important for maintaining our health as adults and even more important for the development of our children. The evidence seems most persuasive when we look at the malnourished Third World and see shorter life spans, lowered resistance to disease, and high infant mortalities. But even in the industrialized world we can readily see the positive effects of a good diet. For one thing, today's adults tend to be taller than their parents; the difference approaches six inches in Japan. On average, too, people who are poor, with comparatively limited access to food, are shorter and less healthy than their wealthier countrymen. Moreover, it is not just physical health that seems to be at risk. Many tests of mental function suggest that poor nutrition in childhood may affect learning ability throughout life.

One might speculate that if we are so susceptible to the effects of poor nutrition as children, we must be especially sensitive to those effects while we're still in the womb, when our brain and body are forming. And, indeed, many studies have shown an association between poor nutrition, low weight at birth, and poor physical and mental performance later on. Yet it's not easy to prove that inadequate prenatal nutrition itself is the culprit. Sadly, babies poorly nourished in the womb are likely to be poorly nourished after birth as well. Furthermore, diet may not be the only thing influencing their health. Access to medical care, schooling, and stimulation outside school may play a part.

Figuring out just how big a role prenatal malnutrition plays in this miserable chain of events, then, is difficult at best. But the starvation in the Nazi-occupied Netherlands nearly half a century ago offers some thought-provoking answers.

The Dutch tragedy was the result of one of the most controversial decisions of World War II. After the Allied forces invaded Normandy and liberated France in the summer of 1944, our generals debated two strategies for completing Germany's defeat: to advance northeastward from France into Germany's Ruhr industrial region or to push eastward into the Saar. Had all our resources been concentrated on a single strategy, either might have succeeded. In fact both advances were attempted at once, and both ground to a standstill.

The northern advance hinged on the famous Battle of Arnhem, which inspired the film *A Bridge Too Far*. On September 17, 1944, British paratroops were dropped on the Dutch city of Arnhem to take command of a crucial bridge over the Rhine; other Allied forces, meanwhile, tried to join them from the south. Dutch railroad workers courageously called a general strike to impede the Nazis' efforts to bring up reinforcements. But stiff Nazi resistance forced the Allies to retreat, on September 25, after heavy losses. The Allies then shifted their military effort away from the Netherlands, most of which remained under German occupation until May 1945.

In retaliation for the Dutch strike an embargo on transport in the Netherlands, including transport of food, was ordered by the notorious Nazi Reichskommissar Seyss-Inquart, later tried and hanged at Nuremberg. The predictable result of the embargo, which began in October 1944, was a famine that became progressively worse as stored food supplies were exhausted and that was not lifted until the Netherlands was liberated the following spring. Because an unusually severe winter hampered relief efforts, the famine became known as the Dutch Hunger Winter.

Intake dropped as low as 400 calories a day, down from an already-reduced daily ration of 1,500 calories. Still, some people were better off than others. The hunger was milder in the farming regions of the north and south; it was most severe in the large industrial cities of the west, such as Amsterdam, Rotterdam, and The Hague. Those people with enough strength went to the countryside to seek food, including tulip bulbs, in the fields. The hunger was also somewhat selective by social class: people of higher socioeconomic status were able to use money, property, and influence to obtain additional food.

Altogether 10,000 people starved to death, and malnutrition contributed to the deaths of countless others. Adults in the famine cities who survived lost, on average, 15 to 20 percent of their body weight.

Some women weighed less at the end of their pregnancy than at its inception.

When the Allies finally liberated the Netherlands in early May 1945, they rushed in food, and conditions quickly improved. But by then 40,000 fetuses had been subjected to the hardships of famine. Depending on their date of conception, these babies were exposed at various stages of gestation, for periods as long as seven months. For example, babies conceived in April 1944 and born in early January 1945 were exposed to the starvation just in the last trimester of pregnancy; those conceived in February 1945 and born in November 1945 were exposed only in the first trimester. Babies unlucky enough to be conceived in August 1944 and born in May 1945 spent their entire second and third trimesters inside increasingly malnourished mothers.

In the late 1960s four researchers at Columbia University School of Public Health – Zena Stein, Mervyn Susser, Gerhart Saenger, and Francis Marolla, all of whom had studied malnutrition in urban ghettos – realized that much might be learned from the now-grown babies of the Dutch Hunger Winter. The outcomes of pregnancies in the stricken cities of the west could be compared with those in towns to the north or south, outside the worst-hit area. In addition, the results of pregnancies during the famine could be compared with those that occurred before and after it.

Hospital records and birth registries yielded statistics on the health of the wartime mothers and their newborns. And at least for the boys, follow-up information on those same children as young adults could be extracted from the records of the Dutch military draft system. Virtually all boys at age 19 were called up for an exam that recorded their height and weight, medical history, results of mental-performance tests, level of schooling completed, and father's occupation; the latter served as a rough indicator of socioeconomic status.

These studies provided some important insights, the first of which concerned the famine's effect on fertility. During the winter of 1944 conceptions quickly declined to one-third the normal level. This suggests that the women's fertility became impaired as their fat reserves, already depleted due to reduced wartime rations, were rapidly used up. The decline was more pronounced for wives of manual workers than of non-manual workers, presumably because the former had less means to buy their way out of starvation.

The Dutch results agree with other evidence that body weight affects our reproductive physiology. Women in German concentration camps often ceased to menstruate (while low sperm counts and impotence were common among male inmates). Moreover, studies have shown that girls begin menstruating earlier in well-fed industrialized nations than in underfed Third World countries. The same trend applies to the present generation of American women compared with their less well nourished grandmothers. All these pieces of evidence suggest that a woman's fertility is dependent on having sufficient body weight to support conception.

Among the famine babies themselves, the most obvious effects were seen in those who were exposed during the last trimester, which is normally the period when a fetus undergoes its most rapid weight gain: these babies had markedly lower average birth weights (6 pounds 10 ounces) than those born before the famine began (7 pounds 6 ounces). Starvation during the third trimester also resulted in babies who were born slightly shorter and with smaller head circumferences, indicating slightly slower than normal growth of the bones and brain. But the main impact was to retard the growth of muscle and fat.

The prefamine pregnancies had taken place while wartime rations still hovered around 1,500 daily calories – meager for a pregnant woman, who normally requires 2,500 calories a day. Medical records showed that these expectant mothers lost weight themselves but were able to maintain a normal birth weight for their babies. Once rations dropped below 1,500 calories, however, babies began to share the impact. And eventually, as the famine wore on and severe starvation struck, all further weight loss was suffered by the baby rather than the mother. Birth weight recovered quickly when food supplies improved, though: babies born three months after the famine's end had normal weights.

Both during and right after the Hunger Winter there was a sharp rise in infant deaths in the Netherlands' hard-hit cities. For babies exposed to famine only in the first trimester, the rate of stillbirth nearly doubled. Those babies had been conceived just three months before the famine's end, and so they in fact completed most of their gestation inside mothers who were relatively well nourished. Yet malnutrition during those first three months had evidently planted a slow-fuse time bomb that went off at birth.

Still greater, however, was the effect on babies exposed during the second, and especially the third, trimesters. Those babies had a higher-than-normal death rate in their first week of life, and the rate continued to climb until they were at least three months old. Some of these babies died of malnutrition itself, others succumbed to normal childhood infections to which they had lowered resistance. Fortunately, once the famine babies reached the age of one year, their increased risk of death disappeared.

Let's now see how the babies who survived the perils of birth and early infancy were faring 19 years later, when the boys were called up for the draft. In many respects these young men were similar to any others their age. Their height, for example, showed all the usual effects of socioeconomic factors, including family size and diet: sons of manual workers averaged nearly an inch shorter than sons of wealthier fathers, children from families with many mouths to feed were shorter than only children, and later-born sons were shorter than first-born sons. The common thread is that children who have access to less food end up shorter. But postnatal, rather than prenatal, nutrition was the culprit here. If you picked any given group – say, sons of manual workers – the young men whose mothers were starved during pregnancy were no shorter than their peers.

Records from the Dutch draft exams also allowed the Columbia researchers to see if poor nutrition in pregnancy might cause lasting mental deficits as well as physical ones. Experiments with rats had shown that offspring of mothers that are starved in pregnancy end up with fewer-than-normal brain cells and learning disabilities. So when the researchers compared the grown-up famine babies' performance on tests of mental proficiency with the performance of those who had received better prenatal nourishment, they expected to find poorer scores for those who had been starved during gestation.

No such result was forthcoming. The draft exam, which included tests of verbal, arithmetic, clerical, and mechanical skills, clearly showed the effects of social environment, which were parallel to the physical effects already mentioned – thus, sons of manual laborers, sons from large families, and sons born late into a family of several children tended to score below other young men. But no effect whatsoever could be attributed to prenatal starvation. One possible explanation is that our brain has enough extra cells to preserve mental function even if some of our cells are lost. At any rate, whatever effects can be attributed to nutrition must be due to nutrition after birth, not before it.

This, then, was the good news, such as it was. Those starved children who made it to adulthood were no worse off than their better-nourished counterparts. However, the medical records of the male famine babies who never made it to a draft physical did reveal one consequence of prenatal starvation – and it was sobering. Fetuses exposed to famine during their first three months in the womb were twice as likely as others to have defects of the central nervous system, such as spina bifida (in which the spine fails to close properly) and hydrocephalus (a related condition, characterized by fluid accumulating in the brain). The birth defects, it now appears, almost certainly arose from starvation during the first trimester, when the nervous system was being laid down.

Just how did a lack of food have such a dire result? Animal experiments have raised the suspicion that such defects can arise from a deficiency of the B vitamin folic acid early in pregnancy. A year ago this finding was confirmed for humans in a study of 22,776 pregnant women in Boston. Babies born to mothers who took multivitamins including folic acid during the first six weeks of pregnancy had a nearly fourfold lower frequency of central nervous system defects than did babies born to women who did not take such supplements. Brands of multivitamins that lacked folic acid, or multivitamins taken only after the seventh week of pregnancy, offered no protection.

All the results from the Dutch famine studies that I've discussed so far describe the effects of starvation on mothers and their children. But recent findings have raised disturbing questions about the famine's effect on a third generation. By now the famine babies are 45 or 46, and most of the girls have long since had children of their own; the "girls" themselves are women at the end of their reproductive careers. More than 100 of these women happened to have had their babies in the same Amsterdam hospital in which they themselves were born, which makes for an easy comparison of birth records. An examination of those records has revealed something very odd: it turns out that those women who were themselves fetuses in their first and second trimester during the Dutch Hunger Winter gave birth to underweight babies. That is, the babies were somehow affected by the starvation of their grandmothers many decades earlier.

This result might have been easier to understand if the mothers themselves had been underweight at birth or were small as adults. Neither was true. Recall that starvation in the first or second trimester produced babies with normal birth weights. Only third-trimester starvation led to small babies. Yet, paradoxically, when these small babies later became mothers, they gave birth to normal-size babies. It was the women who were themselves normal size at birth who became mothers of underweight infants.

Somehow the grandmothers' suffering programmed their children in utero so that the grandchildren would be affected. This astonishing result will undoubtedly inspire experiments aimed at identifying the still-unknown cellular mechanism. But what is indisputable is that the Dutch famine left its harsh imprint on at least three generations.

From the perspective of evolutionary biology, the famine posed to the bodies of pregnant mothers an agonizing dilemma. What would you do in a situation threatening both your life and your child's life if anything you did to help one would hurt the other? Think quickly: If you see a car about to crash head-on into your car, do you throw yourself in front of your child sitting strapped in the seat beside you or do you try to protect yourself instead? Now let's make the choice more agonizing: What if your child's subsequent survival hinges on your own? You've all heard the airlines' standard safety announcement that in the event of a loss of cabin pressure, place the oxygen mask on yourself first, *then* place the mask on your child. In that situation, you have to help yourself first, because you'll be in no state to help your child if you are unconscious.

Similarly a mother starving in the Netherlands in 1944 was forced to unconsciously "choose" whether to devote the few available calories to her own body or to her fetus. This is a classic example of a conflict between two genetically related individuals. Natural selection favors the individual who passes on his or her genes to the most descendants. The genetic interests of the fetus are served by saving itself, and hence we evolve as fetuses to be parasites on our mother, commandeering her nutrients as efficiently as possible. But the mother's genetic interests are served by passing her genes to offspring. She gains nothing if her nutritional sacrifices kill not only herself but her child. Perhaps she would be best off, from an evolutionary point of view, if she sacrificed that fetus and tried again later. Yet there is no certainty that she will have another chance later.

The outcome of the Dutch famine indicates that natural selection struck a compromise. When the famine began, a mother's body at first accepted the full brunt, losing weight while preserving the weight of the fetus. In the next stage of famine both the fetus and the mother shared the hardship. In the last stage all weight loss came at the expense of the fetus, because any more weight loss by the mother would have threatened the mother's survival and thereby the survival of her child.

These pregnant women had no say in how their body allocated its precious resources, of course. Natural selection proceeded along its inexorable journey oblivious to any human agony or ethical dilemma. To ask whether the decisions it made were wise, whether they were somehow the "right" decisions, is irrelevant. The choices were arrived at in accordance with the cold logic of evolution and nothing more.

But what about the decisions that created such cruel conditions in the first place? What about the reasoning that even today, in the guise of wartime expediency, can compel one group of people to consciously impose starvation on another and thus scar the lives of unborn generations? For that matter, what about the reduction of social programs in our own society that might subject untold numbers of children, both before and after birth, to the dangers of malnutrition simply by failing to ensure proper nourishment for them and their mothers? The lessons of the Dutch Hunger Winter are there for the learning. We can ignore them only at our children's, and our grandchildren's, expense.

Prenatal Loss of Father and Psychiatric Disorders

Introduction

Of the myriad factors that could influence the developing fetus, none has been the object of more speculation than maternal stress. When a pregnant woman experiences stress, her adrenal glands become active, secreting hormones. Because these hormones can cross the placenta and cause vasoconstriction (narrowing of vessel walls) and oxygen depletion, it is possible that prenatal stress can lead to physical changes in the fetus.

In this article, two Finnish physicians examined the records of over 300 Finnish citizens whose fathers died either before they were born or within the year following their birth. They wanted to know whether the stress associated with the death of a father exacted a special toll on the developing fetus, causing a cascade of biological changes that eventuated in psychiatric problems later in life. Compared to those individuals whose fathers died after they were born (meaning that the fetuses were not subjected to stress hormones released by their pregnant mothers which, in turn, crossed the placenta), prenatally-exposed individuals had significantly higher incidences of schizophrenia and criminality. In contrast, those female babies whose fathers died after their birth had a higher frequency of birth complications when they later gave birth.

Further reading

Istvan, J. (1986). Stress, anxiety, and birth outcomes: a critical review of the evidence. *Psychological Bulletin, 100*, 331–48.

TWO

Prenatal Loss of Father and Psychiatric Disorders

Matti O. Huttunen and Pekka Niskanen

Children are known to be born with different modes of behavior and temperaments.[1,2] It has been suggested that certain temperament characteristics are associated with a high risk for psychiatric disorders during childhood.[1] The inborn temperament of the children has been considered to be mostly of genetic origin,[1,2] but the importance of various environmental events during the fetal development has not been studied.

There is considerable evidence that pregnancy and birth complications (PBC) have an important etiological role in a number of child and adult psychiatric disorders.[3-12] There is, however, no knowledge about the exact nature or the specificity of pregnancy and birth complications in the pathogenesis of mental disorders. It has been suggested that the mechanism of their action would be mediated by "minor" brain damages caused by anoxia during the delivery and perinatal period.

Animal research indisputably shows that various prenatal events can profoundly affect the behavior and neuronal functions of the offspring.[13-15] It has been proposed that during critical periods of brain differentation, physiological effectors, e.g., hormones or metabolites, may act as teratogens if present in unphysiological concentrations.[15] The pregnant mother represents the critical environment of the fetus just as the quality of early human relations represent the critical environment of the newborn.

Maternal stress has been shown to affect permanently the behavior as well as, for example, the turnover of brain noradrenaline in animals.[13,16]

Thus, there is a possibility that maternal stress during critical periods of fetal development permanently influences the mode of behavior and the temperament of the human child. In the present work we have tested the hypothesis of the etiological role of maternal stress during pregnancy in the psychiatric disorders by monitoring the number of psychiatric patients among a group of persons whose fathers had died before their children's births. The death of a spouse has been postulated to be the most stressful single life event in general.[17]

Subjects and Methods

The sample

Using the death registers of the city of Helsinki, we first collected the group of all men who had died in Helsinki between 1925 and 1957 before the age of 35 years – the idea being that this group would have been recent or expectant fathers at the time of their deaths. The birth dates of the children of these men were then gathered from the population registers of the Lutheran Church and of the city Helsinki. In this way we found a total number of 167 children whose fathers had died before their children's births (index group) and a group of 168 children whose fathers had died during their children's first year of life (control group). There were no differences in the age distribution of the cases in the two groups. The great majority of these fathers died during the years of the Second World War. The distribution of the social classes of the parents was similar in both of the groups. The numbers of males and females were 86 and 81, respectively, in the index group and 87 and 81, respectively, in the control group. The mean age of the pregnant mothers was 27.0 ± 4.4 years in the index group and 27.7 ± 4.7 years in the control group.

Follow-up

Using the population registers, we were able to follow the movements and marriages of the persons in both of the groups in the country. In the same way, the rate of emigration and the number of deaths could be monitored in the groups. Thirteen children of the index group died before the age of 15 years and three of them had moved out of the country before the age of 15 years; the corresponding numbers in the control group were eight and two, respectively.

Monitoring psychiatric patients

Finland is divided into districts for delivery of mental health care. Each district has a central psychiatric hospital and a central register of all the inpatients and outpatients within the district. Similarly, there are districts for outpatient care of alcoholics, with registers of their own. There is also a central criminal register of assaults leading to imprisonment. All three registers were checked to determine whether any of the persons in the index or control groups had been treated for psychiatric disorders or had committed a crime leading to imprisonment. The diagnoses were classified as recorded in the hospital records. In this report the diagnostic group "minor depressive or neurotic disorders" includes such hospital diagnoses as "neurasthenia," "reactive depression," "anxiety and phobic state," "neurosis neuroticodepressiva." The refined data of the individual patients are available from the authors.

Analysis of pregnancy and birth complications

The majority of the children born in Helsinki are delivered in two large central obstetricial clinics that keep detailed records of pregnancy and delivery. We were able to obtain delivery data on 93 persons in the index group and 91 persons in the control group. These obstetrical charts were then coded, using a four-point scale described by Mednick et al.[6] and Cohler et al.[10]

The child's birth weight and the duration of labor were separately recorded. Bleeding during labor was scored by one point, if it was reported to be less than 100ml, and by three points if there was more than 100ml of bleeding.

Statistical analyses

Statistical analysis of the results has been done using Student's t test and the χ^2 test.

Results

The total number of individuals who had been treated in psychiatric hospitals or committed crimes was quite high (35 cases out of a total of 335 persons), even if 26 children of the original group had either died or moved out of the country before reaching the age of 15 years (table 1) Consistent with the hypothesis of the study, there were significantly more persons with behavior disorders among the persons with prenatal loss of their fathers (24 cases) than among the control group with early postnatal loss of their fathers (11 cases). There were also two persons among the "well" cases of both groups who had possibly committed suicide. In addition, in the index group there was a woman who suffered from epilepsy.

The psychiatric cases in both groups were distributed quite evenly among the categories of psychiatric diagnoses. Both of the groups included a relatively high number of alcoholics and persons with personality disorders or asocial behavior (table 1). The number of patients with a hospital diagnosis of schizophrenia was considerably higher in the index group (six cases) than in the control group (one case). Even with the relatively small population studied, this difference reached statistical significance when the calculation was based on the number of patients who reached the age of 15 years.

We made an effort to obtain data on the deliveries of the persons in our sample. The means of the PBC rating scores, the birth weights, and the durations of labor were, however, not significantly different in the index and control groups. The psychiatric cases of the index group had a significantly lower mean PBC score, whereas the psychiatric cases in the control group showed a high frequency of pregnancy and birth complications (table 2). The mean age of the pregnant mothers of the psychiatric cases in the index and control groups did not differ significantly from that of the total sample.

We also analyzed the time of the fathers' deaths in relation to fetal development (figure 1). There does seem to be a tendency for the deaths of the fathers of the psychiatric cases in the index group to have occurred during the ninth to tenth months (11 cases) or the third to fifth months (9 cases) of fetal development. All the schizophrenics in the index group lost their fathers during these periods of their development. Had we originally hypothesized these months of pregnancy to be crucial

Fetal Influences on Later Development

Table 1 Psychiatric and behavior disorders among persons with prenatal (index) and early postnatal (control) loss of father

	Index group (N = 167)	Control group (N = 168)
Died before age of 15 yr	13	8
Moved abroad before age of 15 yr	3	2
Reached age of 15 yr in Finland	151	158
Schizophrenic psychoses	6*	1
Manic-depressive psychoses	0	2
Minor depressive and neurotic disorders	5	1
Alcoholism and/or personality disorders	7	4
Asocial behavior (criminal register)	5	3
Childhood behavior disorders	1	0
Total no. of cases with psychiatric or behavior disorders	24†	11
Possible suicides among the "well" cases	2	2
Epilepsia	1	0

The number of schizophrenic patients is significantly higher in the index group if the calculation is based on the number of the cases who reached the age of 15 years ($x^2 = 3.87$, P < 0.05). If the calculation is based on the total number of cases, the difference does not quite reach the statistical significance ($x^2 = 3.68$, P < 0.10).

† The number of psychiatric and behavior disorders among the index group is statistically significant if the calculation is based either on the total number of the cases or on the number of the cases who reached the age of 15 years ($x^2 = 5.47$, P < 0.025 or $x^2 = 6.13$, P < 0.025, respectively).

for psychiatric disorders, the observed difference in relation to the control group would have reached a high statistical significance.

Comment

The number in our total sample and the number of psychiatric cases in the two groups are so small that the present results cannot be considered as conclusive evidence for the proposed hypothesis of the etiological role of maternal stress during pregnancy in psychiatric and behavior disorders. Still, the results support the idea that prenatal loss of

Table 2   Birth and pregnancy complications (PBC) among the children with prenatal (index) or early postnatal (control) loss of their fathers*

	PBC ratingscore	Birth weight, gm	Duration of labor, hr
Index group	2.93 ± 2.62 (93)	3,421 ± 552 (93)	18.44 ± 12.4 (89)
Control group	3.21 ± 3.30 (91)	3,433 ± 499 (91)	15.00 ± 11.1 (88)
Psychiatric cases in index group	1.69 ± 0.87 (16)	3,514 ± 369 (16)	13.50 ± 6.96 (16)
Psychiatric cases in control group	4.50 ± 3.74 (7)	3,530 ± 522 (7)	13.92 ± 8.34 (7)

Mean ± SD. Numbers in parentheses represent number of cases.

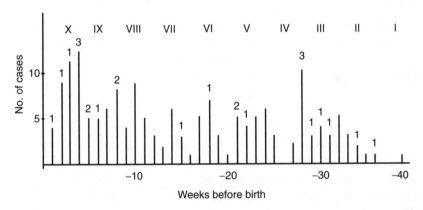

Figure 1   Fetal development and time of father's death among children with prenatal loss of father

the father could substantially increase the risk of the child for mental disorders.

The loss of the father during early childhood has been shown to increase the statistical risk of children for psychiatric disorders.[18,19] To study the possible specific effects of prenatal loss of the father, we used persons with early postnatal loss of their fathers as the control group. However, even the use of this relatively rigorous control group cannot exclude the possibility that the increased frequency of psychiatric disorders among children with prenatal loss of their fathers would stem from the disordered psychological interactions between the newly widowed mother and newborn child. Although we favor the hypothesis of the direct biological effects of maternal stress during pregnancy on the fetus, there does remain a possibility that the effects of prenatal loss of the father are at least partially mediated through the emotional insecurity of the widowed mother.

It is interesting that prenatal loss of the father with all of its psychic and social consequences did not increase the amount of pregnancy and birth complications. This lack of increased complications and the low PBC scores among the psychiatric patients of the index group suggest that the possible effects of maternal stress on the fetal brain were not mediated by "minor" brain damage induced by birth complications. On the other hand, it is noteworthy that the psychiatric cases of the control group showed a high amount of pregnancy and birth complications, which possibly could play some – as yet undefined – role in the pathogenesis of their disordered behavior.

It has been shown that the appearance of human hypothalamic nuclei occurs during the fourth month of fetal life.[14] In rats, the corresponding structural alterations of the hypothalamus are found to occur between the 16th and 18th day of fetal life.[14] Changes of sex hormone levels during this hypothalamic organization phase lead to persistent disturbances of gonadal function and/or sexual behavior in rats.[15] Maternal stress during this period of rat pregnancy has similarly been shown to lead to persistent alteration in the turnover of the brain noradrenaline and in the behavior of the offspring.[13,16] In view of these experimental findings, the observed high frequency of the deaths of the fathers of our psychiatric patients during the third to fifth months of pregnancy may not be a mere chance. Theoretically, maternal stress during this critical period of hypothalamic organization may well have permanent effects on the mode of behavior and temperament of the child. According to our results, a similar critical period of fetal brain development may be the ninth and tenth months of pregnancy. This finding could be another example of "functional" teratology,[15] in the same way as, for example, adult obesity has recently been proposed to be associated with prenatal starvation of the mother.[20] In any event, the actual possible mechanisms of action of maternal stress on the fetus require experimental research and can probably best be studied in detail in nonmammalian animal models, where fetuses develop outside the protective environment of the uterus.

We do not propose that maternal stress during pregnancy directly causes any psychiatric disorder. Rather, in our view the inborn temperament of the children is influenced by these prenatal environmental events, and some temperamental features could increase the risk of the growing child for behavior disorders.[1] The finer differentiation of the in utero environment, maternal stress, and subsequent development bears on the interpretations of current studies of the genetics of psychiatric disorders as well as ultimate concerns with prophylaxis.

Note

This investigation was supported in part by a grant from the Yrjö Jahnsson Foundation.

References

1 Thomas A., Chess S.: *Temperament and Development.* New York, Brunner/Mazel Inc, 1977.
2 Buss A. H., Plomin R.: *A Temperament Theory of Personality Development.* New York, John Wiley & Sons Inc, 1975.
3 Lillienfield A., Pasamanick B., Rogers M.: The relationship between pregnancy experience and the development of neuropsychiatric disorders in childhood. *Am J Public Health* 45:637, 1955.
4 Pollin W., Stabenau J.: Biological, psychological and historical differences in a series of monozygotic twins discordant for schizophrenia, in Rosenthal D., Kety S. S. (eds): *The Transmission of Schizophrenia.* New York, Pergamon Press Inc, 1968.
5 Mednick S.: Breakdown in individuals at high risk for schizophrenia: Possible predispositional perinatal factors. *Ment Hyg* 54:50–63, 1970.
6 Mednick S., Maura E., Schulsinger F., et al.: Perinatal conditions and infant development in children with schizophrenic parents. *Soc Biol* 18(suppl): S103–S113, 1971.
7 Pollack M., Woerner M.: Pre- and postnatal complications and "childhood schizophrenia": A comparison of five controlled studies. *J Child Psychol Psychiatry* 7:235–42, 1966.

8 Woerner M., Pollack M., Klein D.: Pregnancy and birth complications of schizophrenic patients: A comparison of schizophrenic and personality disorder patients with their siblings. *Acta Psychiatr Scand* 49:712–21, 1973.

9 Torrey E. F., Hersh S., McCabe K. D.: Early childhood psychosis and bleeding during pregnancy: A prospective study of gravid women and their offspring. *J Autism Child Schizo* 5:287–97, 1975.

10 Cohler B. J., Gallant D. H., Grunebaum H. U., et al.: Pregnancy and birth complications among mentally ill and well mothers and their children. *Soc Biol* 22:269–78, 1975.

11 Garmezy N.: Children at risk: The search for the antecedents of schizophrenia: I. Conceptual models and research methods. *Schizo Bull* Issue 8:14–90, 1974.

12 Garmezy N.: Children at risk: The search for the antecedents of schizophrenia: II. Ongoing research programs, issues, and intervention. *Schizo Bull* Issue 9:55–125, 1974.

13 Joffe J. M.: *Prenatal Determinents of Behavior*. London, Pergamon Press Ltd, 1969.

14 Dörner G., Staudt J.: Vergelichende morphologische Untersuchungen der Hypothalamusdifferenzierung bei Ratte und Mensch. *Endokrinologie* 59: 152–5, 1972.

15 Dörner G.: Environment-dependent brain differentation and fundamental processes of life. *Acta Biol Med Ger* 33:129–48, 1974.

16 Huttunen M. O.: Persistent alteration of turnover of brain noradrenaline in the offspring of rats subjected to stress during pregnancy. *Nature* 230:53–5, 1971.

17 Holmes T., Rahe R. H.: The social readjustment rating scale. *J Psychosom Res* 11:213–18, 1967.

18 Munro A.: Some psychiatric non-sequelae of childhood bereavement. *Br J Psychiatry* 115:305–11, 1969.

19 Trunell T. L.: The absent father's children's emotional disturbances. *Arch Gen Psychiatry* 19:180–8, 1968.

20 Ravelli G. P., Stein Z. A., Susser M. W.: Obesity in young men after famine exposure in utero and early infancy. *N Engl J Med* 295:349–53, 1976.

Prenatal Development of Monozygotic Twins and Concordance for Schizophrenia

Introduction

During the first weeks following conception, the embryo is surrounded by an amnion, a thin but durable membrane, holding fluid that serves as a shock absorber for the developing organism. Surrounding this amnion is another membrane that later will become the placenta. This membrane is called the *chorion*. In the following article, the authors take advantage of embryological knowledge about the chorion to make several very important points. Twinning for identical twins (MZs)[1] can occur at different points during early development. In approximately 40 percent of cases, the twinning occurs almost immediately following fertilization. In these cases, entirely separate chorions develop for each of the MZ co-twins, and later each will have its own placenta. In about 55–60 percent of cases, however, MZ twinning occurs somewhat later, after some cellular development of the first twin has already taken place. This means that the chorion has already been formed for the first twin, and therefore the co-twin will share this chorion (and later share the same placenta).

The reason this is important is that when twins share the same chorion/placenta, they are exposed to similar environmental toxins and diseases. If one of the twins is exposed to a virus, for example, the other is likely also to be exposed. However, when the twins have their own chorions/placentas, it is possible for one twin to escape a toxin that has infected its co-twin. As a result, *concordance*, or the degree to which the twins share characteristics such as IQ, personality, physical size, and, in the following article, psychopathology, is influenced by whether the twins had identical or separate chorions/placentas. If separate, then one twin could have brain damage due to exposure to a toxin that its co-twin escaped. So, even though MZ twins are genetically identical for most practical purposes, they can differ somewhat, and they can experience quite dissimilar intrauterine environments if they have separate chorions/placentas.

A moment's consideration will reveal why this is important for the nature–nurture controversy: if MZ twins that have a shared chorion/placenta are no more alike in the degree to which they are diagnosed as schizophrenic than are DZ twins or even ordinary siblings, this calls into question the extreme heritability stance of some, because much of what makes MZ twins so similar might be the result of shared *uterine* environments rather than shared *genes*. Such sources of similarity are more likely to come into play for adverse developmental consequences than for positive outcomes (Bronfenbrenner and Ceci, 1994). This is because adverse developmental outcomes (such as schizophrenia and mental retardation) are more dependent on characteristics of the intrauterine environment than are positive developmental outcomes, which usually are able to occur within a fairly wide range of environments. This point implies that although heritability estimates for *pathological* conditions such as schizophrenia might have been overestimated – because part of the twins' similarity was due to shared uterine environments (e.g., exposure to the same virus) – heritability estimates for *normal* functioning are probably not affected by whether the twins had separate chorions/placentas.

As you read the following article keep in mind that researchers have several tools to reveal retrospectively whether any pair of twins shared chorions/placentas, even if there is no hospital record regarding the number of placentas. Such tools include whether fingerprints, hair swirls, facial asymmetries, etc. are identical or are mirror images of each other. When the chorions are different for each twin, this means that twinning occurred very soon after fertilization; hence MZ twins' fingerprints, hair swirls, etc. would be identical because the two twins split at the moment of fertilization, and are genetically identical. On the other hand, when the twinning occurs only after the first organism has already started developing (and as a result, the co-twin ends up sharing the first twin's amnion but not the same early cellular developments), then some features of the twins will be mirror images. Additionally, there can be large differences in physical size and other characteristics when the twins share the same chorions/placentas. This may seem counterintuitive in that one might assume that MZs would be more similar when they shared the same chorions, but the opposite is usually the case, because it means that some development of the first twin occurred before the co-twin was formed. Of course, it is also the case that when MZs have separate chorions/placentas one of them could be exposed to a disease that the co-twin escaped, thus making them dissimilar. So, it is a complicated argument.

Note

1   MZ or monozygotic twins are gentically identical since they result from the division of the same zygote. Contrast with DZ, dizygotic twins (sometimes called fraternal twins), who result from the separate fertilization of two ova at around the same time. DZ twins are born at the same time, but are genetically no more similar than ordinary siblings who are born at different times.

Reference

Bronfenbrenner, U. and Ceci, S. J. (1994). Nature–nurture in developmental perspective: a bioecological theory. *Psychological Review, 101*, 568–86.

Further reading

Phillips, D. I. W. (1993). Twin studies in medical research: can they tell us whether diseases are genetically determined? *Lancet, 341*, 1005–9.

THREE

Prenatal Development of Monozygotic Twins and Concordance for Schizophrenia

James O. Davis, Jeanne A. Phelps, and H. Stefan Bracha

It is well established that monozygotic (MZ) twins are more likely to be concordant for schizophrenia than dizygotic (DZ) twins. Widely reported is Gottesman's (1991) summary, based on numerous twin studies, that the probandwise concordance for schizophrenia in MZ twins is approximately 48 percent, compared to only 17 percent for DZ twins. The MZ/DZ discrepancy is also found even with the more conservative pairwise estimation of concordance. In a meta-analysis of 21 studies, Walker et al. (1991) reported MZ/DZ pairwise concordances of 25 and 7 percent, respectively. There is high concordance for schizophrenia in MZ twins even when reared apart (Gottesman and Shields 1982). Bailey and Pillard (1993) credit these findings with helping to establish a "relative iron-clad fortress" (p. 241) for schizophrenia genetics research. The specific values for the concordance rates have been used to estimate heritability (Kendler and Diehl 1993) and to construct genetic models (Cromwell 1993).

Although the high MZ concordance and the MZ/DZ differences in concordance rates are generally attributed to genetic effects, it must be pointed out that MZ and DZ pairs do not have similar prenatal development (Phillips 1993). Furthermore, the prenatal environments can be different even for the two members of a twin pair (Melnick et al. 1978; Pridjian et al. 1991; Reed et al. 1991a, 1991b; Davis and Phelps 1995).

One of the main determinants of the prenatal environment and fetal development is the placenta. Davis and Phelps (1995) proposed that variations in twins' placentation could also account for differences in twin concordances. They discussed the protective function of the placenta and its relevance to the hypothesis proposed by others that prenatal infections may play a significant role in the etiology of schizophrenia (Torrey et al. 1988, 1994; Bracha et al. 1992; Pulver et al. 1992; Sham et al. 1992; Adams et al. 1993; Mednick et al. 1994).

In this article, we continue to explore placentation variation in twins as it relates to twin concordance for schizophrenia. First, we delineate the two major placentation or chorionic arrangements that occur in twinning and address how they may be relevant to a viral etiology of schizophrenia. Next, we present a strategy for estimating placentation retrospectively, followed by the results of applying this strategy to a sample of MZ twins with schizophrenia. Finally, we briefly discuss the implications of our findings.

Twin Placentation and its Relevance to the Viral Hypothesis

It has long been incorrectly held that all MZ twins share a single chorion, and according to Bryan (1992), this misinformation is still found in some medical textbooks. However, approximately one-third of MZ twins and all DZ twins are dichorionic (DC), developing separate placentas and chorions, as shown in figure 1a. In the case of MZ twins, DC placentation is the result of twinning before the fourth day following conception. The remaining two-thirds of MZ twins are monochorionic (MC), as shown in figure 1b, sharing one placenta and one chorion and, only rarely, one amnion (Bulmer 1970; Sadler 1990; Bryan 1992). Perinatal mortality is more common in MC–MZ than in DC–MZ twins (Bulmer 1970), so the percentage of adult MC–MZ twins may be reduced to 55 to 60 percent of all MZ pairs (Bulmer 1970; Reed et al. 1978).

Because the placenta exerts considerable influence on prenatal health and development there are some potentially important differences found between MC–MZ, DC–MZ and DZ twins (Reed et al. 1978, 1991a, 1991b; Phillips 1993). One conspicuous difference between MC and DC placentation involves fetal blood circulation. Most (85–100

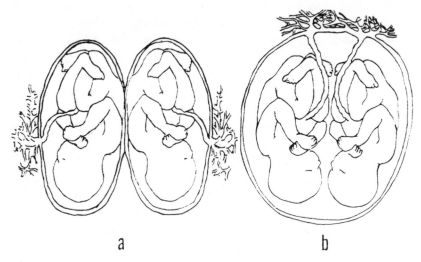

Figure 1   Dichorionic placentation (a) and monochorionic placentation (b)

percent) MC twins exchange blood through shared vascular communication, whereas DC twin pairs (whether MZ or DZ) very rarely exchange
blood (Strong and Corney 1967; Bulmer 1970; Pezzati et al. 1993). This
is relevant to the viral hypothesis because the shared vascular communication would encourage mutual infection when an infectious agent
crosses the shared placenta of an MC twin pair. On the other hand,
infections and other toxic insults could breach the placenta of only one
twin in a DC pair, leaving the cotwin unaffected (Scerbo et al. 1986;
Goedert et al. 1991). Thus MC twins are likely to be mutually affected
by such insults as bloodborne infections, while DC twins – with their
separate fetal circulations – cannot share infections through an
exchange of blood.

It is important to note that, in addition to creating similarities in MC
twins, shared circulation can lead to some obvious differences in a
subset (15–30 percent) of MC twins who develop "twin transfusion syndrome" (Strong and Corney 1967). This syndrome occurs when an arte-
riovenous shunt between the twins creates within-pair differences in
blood distribution and development. In severe cases, the donor twin may
be much smaller at birth as well as anemic (Bulmer 1970; Tan et al.
1979; Scerbo et al. 1986; Bryan 1992).

Retrospective Estimation of Placentation: A Strategy

Direct obstetrical information on placentation status in twins is not widely available. Therefore, researchers have used three retrospective markers: (1) analysis of birthweight differences (Munsinger 1977; Kamin 1978), which are suggestive of twin transfusion syndrome and therefore of MC placentation; (2) analysis of mirroring for hand preferences, which are suggestive of late twinning and therefore of MC placentation (Davis and Phelps, 1995); and (3) analysis of dermatoglyphic patterns (Reed et al. 1978, 1991a, 1991b), a technique that has been developed with samples of twins of known placentation. Each of these is discussed below.

Munsinger (1977) and Kamin (1978) used birthweight differences to investigate placentation effects on intelligence. Kamin's (1978) conclusion that MC twins were more alike on intelligence tests than were DC twins was supported by Melnick et al. (1978), who relied on a sample of twins of known placentation. Unfortunately, birthweight differences fail to correctly identify the majority of MC twins who do not suffer from chronic twin transfusion syndrome (Tan et al. 1979). Such differences provide a fairly valid but not very sensitive marker of MC placentation.

A subset of MC–MZ twins appear to mirror image for various features, including handedness, birthmarks, hair swirls, facial features, and fingerprints (Segal 1989; Lohr and Bracha 1992; Torrey et al. 1994). Mirroring is thought to occur when twinning takes place eight or more days after conception, when MC placentation is certain (Burn and Corney 1988). Davis and Phelps (1995) used hand-preference mirroring as a marker and found that MZ twin pairs with opposite-hand preferences were concordant for psychosis in 9 of 15 cases (60 percent), compared with only 18 of 56 MZ pairs (32 percent) with same-hand preferences. However, although mirroring for handedness may be a fairly valid marker of MC placentation, it is not a very sensitive marker because it occurs in only 20 to 25 percent of MZ twins.

Fingerprints offer a third solution to retrospective investigation of twin placentation effects. Fingertip dermatoglyphic patterns are formed during the early to mid second trimester, and although they are under strong genetic influence, they are also known to be influenced by in utero events; thus, even identical twins usually do not have identical prints (Reed et al. 1978; Bracha et al. 1992; Lohr and Bracha 1992; Godfrey et al. 1993). These skin patterns can also be influenced by fetal size, nutrition, infectious agents, maternal health, and fetal growth rates, all of which have been implicated in the etiology of schizophrenia (Bracha et al. 1991, 1992; Torrey et al. 1994). Dermatoglyphic measures are more promising as retrospective markers of placentation for several reasons. First, they do not rely on relatively rare traits (i.e., large birthweight differences or left-handedness). Obviously, all twins have fingerprints, whereas few have twin transfusion syndrome or left-hand preferences. Second, dermatoglyphic patterns, once formed in the early second trimester, do not change (as weight and perhaps handedness can), so they can provide indelible imprints of in utero events (Bracha et al. 1992). Third and most important, their effectiveness as a retrospective marker has been confirmed in twin samples of known placentation.

The usefulness of dermatoglyphic analysis for investigating placentation effects was first demonstrated by the work of Reed et al. (1978, 1991a, 1991b). Working with 107 twin pairs of known placentation, Reed et al. (1978) identified differences, sometimes subtle, in ridge counts and skin patterns associated with placentation status. These findings were later used in samples of twins of unknown placentation to investigate prenatal influences on type A behavior characteristics (Reed et al. 1991a) and high-density lipoprotein (Reed et al. 1991b).

Although Reed's work relied on standard matching of ridge counts and fingerprint patterns and did not consider mirroring in MZ twins, it is also possible to evaluate twins' fingerprints for signs of mirror imaging (Lohr and Bracha 1992). This is also an MC marker because mirroring is well established as an effect of late twinning (Springer and Deutsch 1981: Segal 1989; Bracha et al. 1992; Bryan 1992; Lohr and Bracha 1992; Torrey et al. 1994). Comparing fingerprints for mirroring relies on the same logic outlined for using hand-preference mirroring to estimate placentation (Davis and Phelps 1995).

The purpose of the present dermatoglyphic study was to combine standard matching and mirroring comparisons to determine if schizophrenia-concordant MZ twins have more retrospective markers of MC placentation than discordant pairs. We investigated two placentation markers reported by Reed et al. (1978): (1) total finger ridge count (TFRC), which should exhibit greater within-pair variability for MC twins; and (2) the four individual finger ridge counts (left middle finger total, the radial counts of the right and left index fingers, and the right middle radial counts), which varied significantly less for the MC than for the DC twins. We predicted that concordant twins would show greater within-pair variability for TFRC but less variability on the four individual finger ridge counts.

We also hypothesized that finger pattern and ridge count mirroring would occur more frequently in the concordant MZ twin pairs than in the discordant MZ pairs. This required comparing each finger to the cotwin's corresponding fingers on the same and the opposite hands. For example, the right index finger pattern and ridge counts of one twin would be compared with the patterns and ridge counts of the cotwin's right and left index fingers. If the fingers of the same hands matched better than the fingers of the opposing hands, it would indicate standard matching; better matches of the opposite hands would indicate mirroring. Ties indicate neither mirroring nor matching. Again, we expected more mirroring in concordant twins and more standard matching in discordant twins.

Method

Subjects

The twin panel employed for this work included 26 MZ pairs discordant for schizophrenia and 10 MZ pairs concordant for schizophrenia. Thirty-five pairs were originally recruited by the National Institute of Mental Health (NIMH) Twin Study Unit through questionnaires and literature distributed to the members of the National Alliance for the Mentally ill and the Canadian Friends of Schizophrenics (now the Schizophrenia Society of Canada). The original project was funded by NIMH and coordinated by the Twin Study Unit, then directed by Dr. E. Fuller Torrey. The description of the project and details regarding diagnoses and determination of zygosity have been reported by Torrey et al. (1994). The data from this twin panel have involved 55 investigators acknowledged by Torrey et al. (1994). We added one pair of discordant twins to the original panel, the only pair recruited in an effort to develop a larger registry. The protocol for all measurements of zygosity and fingerprinting of this pair was the same as that used for the 35 pairs from the NIMH twin panel.[1]

Fingerprint analysis

One of the authors (H.S.B.) was involved in the original collection and analysis of the fingerprints. The dermatoglyphic data have been described elsewhere when they were used to investigate prenatal development of the twins (Bracha et al. 1991, 1992; Torrey et al. 1994). This report is the first to rely on these fingerprints as markers of placentation.

Finger ridge counts, measures, and comparisons

Following conventional procedures (Slater 1963; Lykken 1978; Bracha et al. 1992; Godfrey et al. 1993), the absolute finger ridge count (AFRC) for each finger was determined by counting the number of ridges between the center of a loop and the single triradius of a loop, or by combining the ridge counts from the center of a whorl to its two triradii. Arch patterns have no triradii, so AFRCs for arch patterns are counted as zero. The AFRCs can be compared to measure similarity, as was done in early twin studies to help determine zygosity (Slater 1963; Lykken 1978; Markow and Gottesman 1989).

The TFRC of each individual was the sum of his other 10 AFRCs. Within-twin pair differences in TFRC were expressed as a percentage of the smaller count of the two twins (Bracha et al. 1992), which helps correct for the larger differences found in male twins and in larger twin pairs in general (Lykken 1978). The four ridge counts that were expected to vary less in concordant twins were combined and represented by the percentage they contributed to the total AFRC differences for each set of twins.

Mirroring and standard matching

We used two separate methods of determining mirroring; these were based on ridge patterns (whorls, radial loops, ulnar loops, plain and tented arches) and AFRCs. For both mirroring analyses, each finger was compared to the cotwin's same finger for standard matching and to the corresponding finger on the cotwin's opposite hand for mirroring. If more finger patterns matched to the opposite fingers, the pair was classified as "mirror imaged" for patterns. If there were more matches to the same-side fingers, the pair was categorized as "standard matched." Because it is possible for an equal number of matches to occur for both kinds of matching, some twin pairs cannot be judged as mirrored or matched on this variable.

To compare ridge counts for mirroring, the AFRC on each finger was also compared to that on the corresponding fingers on the same and opposing hands to determine the best match. The differences in a pair's AFRC scores were totaled for the 10 standard and 10 mirrored comparisons. An AFRC mirroring score was created for each pair by subtracting the AFRC mirroring differences from the standard matching differences.

Because our hypotheses were clearly in one direction, we chose the one-tailed probability values for all statistical analyses. When possible, point-biserial correlations were included to express the strength of the relationship between concordance status and the dermatoglyphic variables. Point biserial is a product-moment correlation calculated when one variable is continuous and the other is inherently dichotomous (Nunnally 1967). Planned chi-square tests were supplemented with Fisher's exact test when cell frequency dropped considerably below five, even though the chi-square distribution has been shown to render accurate conclusions even with sample sizes as small as eight (Spatz and Johnston 1989; Howell 1992).

Results

Table 1 presents the comparisons between concordant and discordant twin pairs for several dermatoglyphic variables.

Finger ridge count analyses

As seen in table 1, subset 1, TFRC varied more for the concordant than for the discordant twins. The mean within-pair differences in TFRC were 18.27 percent (SD = 19.43) for concordant twins and only 9.02 percent (SD = 7.80) for the discordant pairs ($t = 2.07$, $df = 34$, $p = 0.25$). The variance for within-pair differences was also greater for the concordant twins than for the discordant pairs ($F = 5.96$, $df = 9.25$, $p < 0.01$). The point-biserial correlation for the concordance group and the size of the within-pair differences was 0.34, $p = 0.25$.

Table 1 Summary of the major dermatoglyphic comparisons of monozygotic (MZ) twins concordant and discordant for schizophrenia

Dermatoglyphic variable	Concordant twins	Discordant twins	Test statistic	Estimated value
1 Differences in TFRC:				
Mean, %	18.27	9.02	t	2.07[a]
Sample SD	19.43	7.80	F	5.96[b]
2 AFRC totals for four DC–MZ markers:				
Mean, %	23.86	31.82	t	1.73[c]
Sample SD	10.64	16.05	F	2.28 NS
3 AFRC totals for twins:				
Mirroring, % (n)	60 (6)	23 (6)	x^2	4.43[a]
Matching, % (n)	40 (4)	77 (20)		
4 Twins with more patterns:				
Mirroring, % (n)	20 (2)	4 (1)	x^2	4.80[a]
Matching, % (n)	20 (2)	58 (15)		
5 Total number of MC markers:				
Mean, %	1.2	0.346	t	2.75[d]
Sample SD	0.919	0.562	F	2.28[c]

TFRC = total finger ridge count: SD = standard deviation; NS = not significant; AFRC = absolute finger ridge count: DC = dichorionic; MC = monochorionic.
[a]*p = 0.25*
[b]*p < 0.01*
[c]*p < 0.05*
[d]*p < 0.005*

In contrast, the four finger ridge counts that Reed et al. (1978) found to vary less for MC–MZ twins were found to vary less in the concordant twin pairs. As seen in table 1, subset 2, these four ridge counts accounted for 23.86 percent (SD = 10.64) of the total AFRC matching score differences in the concordant twins, and for 31.82 percent (SD = 16.05) of the differences in the discordant twins ($t = 1.73$, $df = 34$, $p < 0.05$).

Table 2 Number of concordant and discordant twin pairs with markers of monochorionic (MC) placentation

Total number of MC markers	Concordance for schizophrenia	
	Concordant pairs, $n = 10$	Discordant pairs, $n = 26$
	% (*n*)	% (*n*)
None	20 (2)	69.2 (18)
One	50 (5)	26.9 (7)
Two	20 (2)	3.9 (1)
Three	10 (1)	0 (0)

Mirror imaging and standard matching of finger ridge counts

Mirror imaging of finger ridge counts occurred more often in the concordant twins, while standard matching occurred more often in the discordant twins. As seen in table 2, subset 3, 6 (60 percent) of the 10 concordant pairs matched more fingers to the opposite hand (mirroring) than to the same hand (standard matching), whereas mirroring was found in only 6 (23 percent) of the 26 discordant pairs ($x^2 = 4.43$, $df = 1$, $p < 0.025$). The point-biserial correlation for the number of ill twins (one or two) and their mirroring score was 0.28 ($p < 0.05$).

Mirror imaging versus standard matching of fingerprint patterns

Six of the concordant and 10 of the discordant pairs had equal numbers of fingers that mirrored and matched for patterns, so these 16 pairs could not be included in this analysis. In table 1, subset 4, it can be seen that mirroring of finger ridge patterns was more prevalent in concordant twins, while discordant twins were inclined to match more of their patterns in the standard comparisons with the fingers of their cotwin's same hand. Two of the three twin pairs with more pattern mirroring were concordant for schizophrenia, while 15 of the 17 pairs with more standard matches were discordant ($x^2 = 4.80$, $df = 1$, $p = 0.025$). Fisher's exact test yielded probability equal to 0.08.

Combined dermatoglyphic signs of placentation

MC markers, including (1) within-pair TFRC differences greater than 20 percent, (2) mirroring of AFRCs, and (3) mirroring of finger ridge patterns, were totaled for each set of twins. As reported in table 1, subset 5, the mean number of MC markers for concordant twins was 1.2 per pair (SD = 0.919), compared to 0.346 per pair (SD = 0.562) for the discordant twins ($t = 2.75$, $p < 0.005$).

A summary of the results for combined MC markers by concordance status is shown in table 2. Of the 20 pairs with no MC markers, only 2 pairs (10 percent) were concordant. The concordance rates rose to 50 percent for pairs with one or more markers, and rose again to 75 percent for those twins with two or more MC markers. Table 2 also shows that 80 percent (8 of the 10) of the concordant pairs had at least one MC marker, compared to only 31 percent (8 of 26) of the discordant pairs ($x^2 = 7.089$, $df = 1$, $p < 0.005$). The point-biserial correlation for twin concordance and number of MC markers was 0.53 ($p < 0.001$).

Concordance estimates

Four methods were used to estimate DC–MZ concordance rates. First, based on standard matching, there were only 2 (11.8 percent) concordant pairs among the 17 pairs who showed this DC trait. Second, based upon a median split for AFRC mirroring, only 2 (11.1 percent) of 18 pairs below the median for mirroring were concordant for schizophrenia. Third, of the 20 pairs who had no MC markers, only 2 pairs (10 percent) were concordant (see table 2). Finally, we created a subgroup of 11 pairs that had a combination of indicators of DC placentation. Because they showed both standard matching of patterns as well as no evidence of MC markers, these 11 pairs were considered more likely to be DC; among these, only 1 concordant pair was found (9.1 percent).

Five methods were used to estimate MC–MZ concordance rates. The pairwise concordance for schizophrenia in the 18 MZ pairs with at least one MC placentation marker was 50 percent. The concordance for pairs with two or more markers rose to 75 percent (three or four pairs). Twelve pairs showed AFRC mirroring, and six (50 percent) of these were concordant. In the five pairs with TFRC differences above

20 percent, three (60 percent) were concordant. Of the three pairs that showed mirroring of finger ridge patterns, two (66 percent) were concordant.

Discussion

This report extends our earlier efforts to link concordance for schizophrenia in MZ twins with their placentation status (Davis and Phelps 1995) and prenatal development (Bracha et al. 1992). The results support the conclusion that concordance estimates in MZ twins can be refined by knowledge of placentation and that retrospective strategies for estimating placentation can be useful in twin research.

Dermatoglyphics appear to provide a fairly sensitive marker of placentation status. In general, we would expect approximately 55 to 60 percent of MZ twins to be MC (Bulmer 1970; Reed et al. 1978), and 44 percent of the MZ twins in this study were identified as having at least one MC marker. Estimates of concordance for schizophrenia averaged 60 percent in the twins displaying one or more MC markers. This estimate is consistent with our earlier study using mirrored hand preferences as a marker (Davis and Phelps 1995), in which we also reported 60 percent concordance in twins identified as MC. In contrast, concordance estimates for MZ twins with DC markers, either singly or in combination, averaged 10.7 percent. This figure is actually closer to previously reported pairwise rates of 7 and 6 percent for DZ twins than it is to reported pairwise MZ rates of 25 and 28 percent (Walker et al. 1991; Torrey 1992). Although these refined concordance estimates are based on small samples and retrospective estimations of placentation, the results are consistent and in the hypothesized direction. They are provocative because they emerged despite the low power of the statistical tests and the limitations of retrospectively determining placentation. As Reed et al. (1991a, p. 16) succinctly concluded in a reference to type A behavior: "It is the subset of monochorionic MZ twins . . . which inflates the MZ correlations." We believe the same may be true of schizophrenia.

There is some evidence that twins' concordance for infectious disease is similar to that found for schizophrenia. For example, Bracha (1986) and Torrey (1992) have reported that MZ/DZ pairwise concordance rates for multiple sclerosis and tuberculosis in twins are similar to the MZ/DZ rates for schizophrenia. We can add another comparison: in twins, schizophrenia concordances (based on dermatoglyphic markers) appear similar to concordances for congenital human immunodeficiency virus (HIV) infection (based on birthweight markers). Goedert et al. (1991) reported 56-percent concordance for HIV in twins with more than 10-percent birthweight differences (a possible sign of twin transfusion syndrome and MC placentation), while those with smaller birthweight differences were only 11-percent HIV concordant.

These findings seem particularly significant given the mounting evidence for the role of prenatal infections in the etiology of schizophrenia (e.g., Torrey et al. 1988, 1994; Bracha et al. 1992; Pulver et al. 1992; Sham et al. 1992; Adams et al. 1993; Mednick et al. 1994). Because of the shared fetal circulation in MC twins, the apparent higher concordance in these twins as compared to DC twins is certainly consistent with the viral hypothesis. It should be noted, however, that other interpretations are possible. Additional differences in prenatal environment due to variations in placentation, as well as additional risks associated with MC placentation itself, might contribute to brain pathology. Grafe (1993) has proposed that artery-to-artery or vein-to-vein anastomoses could create hemodynamic instability, and that these blood pressure fluctuations could lead to cerebral necrosis without requiring a blood-borne infection. Other possible confounds in MC–MZ twins could be created by fetal tissue pathology, such as rupture of the diamniotic membrane (Chen et al. 1994), placenta previa, and small placenta. Also, poorer fetal growth in general is expected in MC–MZ twins (Bulmer 1970; Phillips 1993).

Research on placentation effects in twins with schizophrenia will certainly be advanced when the best possible obstetric information regarding twins' placentas becomes available. (Several attempts to locate a panel of twins with schizophrenia and known placentation have not been successful.) Obtaining direct information on the placentation status of twin pairs with schizophrenia will require decades of patience. In the meantime, further refinement of dermatoglyphic markers of placental type would be beneficial, as would the continued exploration of other markers, such as handedness (Davis and Phelps 1995), birthweight differences (Munsinger 1977; Kamin 1978), and the mirroring of such ectodermal features as hair swirls (Torrey et al. 1994) and facial asymmetries (Lohr and Bracha 1992). As far as we know, this study and our earlier investigation of handedness were the first to use the phenomenon of mirroring to estimate placentation, and this seems a promising strategy. In addition, using combinations of all possible available markers is recommended in future research.

Twin research has been in the forefront of efforts to understand the etiology of schizophrenia and has often been used to investigate genetic effects. However, the shortfall from 100-percent concordance in MZ twins has stimulated the search for environmental influences, and twin studies can contribute to this effort as well. It appears likely that MC–MZ, DC–MZ, and possibly DZ twin pairs are affected very differently by prenatal events and can contribute to our knowledge about such influences.

Notes

1 The prints of one of the NIMH pairs were not included in this project because they were outliers on three of the measures. These prints were the only ones acquired through an outside agency, a local police department. The 109-percent difference in TFRC was more than 5 standard deviations (SDs) above the mean, and the pattern mirroring and standard pattern matching scores 4 and 3, respectively, were more than 3 SDs below the mean. In other words, the prints of this pair did not match well at all. In a previous report, these prints were treated as outliers because they did not alter the direction of statistical decisions (Bracha et al. 1992). Inasmuch as the prints were consistent with three of our predictions and inconsistent with only one prediction, it seemed prudent to omit these fingerprint data, which skew the results in the predicted direction more often than not but probably do not contribute to accuracy.

References

Adams, W.; Kendell, R.; Hare, E.; and Munk-Jorgensen, P. Epidemiological evidence that maternal influenza contributes to the aetiology of schizophrenia. *British Journal of Psychiatry*, 163:522–34, 1993.

Bailey, J. M., and Pillard, R. C. Reply to Theodore Lidz' reply to "A genetic study of male sexual orientation." *Archives of General Psychiatry*, 50:240–1, 1993.

Bracha, H. S. On concordance for tuberculosis and schizophrenia. [Letter] *American Journal of Psychiatry*, 143:1634, 1986.

Bracha, H. S.; Torrey, E. F.; Bigelow, L. B.; and Linington, B. B. Subtle signs of prenatal maldevelopment of the upper-limb ectoderm in schizophrenia: a monozygotic twin study of prenatal markers in psychosis. *Biological Psychiatry*, 30:719–25, 1991.

Bracha, H. S.; Torrey, E. F.; Gottesman, I. I.; Bigelow, L. B.; and Cuniff, C. Second trimester markers of fetal size in schizophrenia: a study of monozygotic twins. *American Journal of Psychiatry*, 149:1355–61, 1992.

Bryan, E. M. *Twins and Higher Multiple Births: A Guide to the Nature and Nurture*. London, England: Edward Arnold, 1992.

Bulmer, M. *The Biology of Twinning in Man*. Oxford, England: Clarendon, 1970.

Burn, J., and Corney, G. Zygosity determination and the types of twinning. In: MacGillivary, I., ed. *Twinning and Twins*. New York, NY: John Wiley & Sons, 1988, pp. 7–25.

Chen, S. E.; Trupin, L.; and Trupin, S. Antepartum rupture of diamniotic membranes separating monozygotic twins: a case report. *Journal of Reproductive Medicine*, 39:67–70, 1994.

Cromwell, R. L. Searching for the origins of schizophrenia. *Psychological Science*, 4:276–9, 1993.

Davis, J. O., and Phelps, J. A. Twins with schizophrenia: genes or germs? *Schizophrenia Bulletin*, 21(1):13–18, 1995.

Godfrey, K. M.; Barker, D. J. P.; Peace, J.; Cloke, J.; and Osmond, C. Relationship of fingerprints and shape of the palm to fetal growth and adult blood pressure. *British Medical Journal*, 307:405–9, 1993.

Goedert, J. J.; Duliege, A. M.; Amos, C. I.; Felton, S.; and Biggar, R. J. High-risk of HIV-1 infection for first-born twins. *Lancet*, 338:1471–5, 1991.

Gottesman, I. I. *Schizophrenia Genesis: The Origins of Madness*. New York, NY: W. H. Freeman & Company, 1991.

Gottesman, I. I., and Shields, J. *Schizophrenia: The Epigenetic Puzzle*. New York, NY: Cambridge University Press, 1982.

Grafe, M. R. Antenatal cerebral necrosis in monochorionic twins. *Pediatric Pathology*, 13:15–19, 1993.

Howell, D. C. *Statistical Methods for Psychology*. Boston, MA: PWS-KENT Publishing Company, 1992.

Kamin, L. J. Transfusion syndrome and the heritability of IQ. *Annals of Human Genetics*, 42:161–71, 1978.

Kendler, K. S., and Diehl, S. R. The genetics of schizophrenia: a current, genetic-epidemiologic perspective. *Schizophrenia Bulletin*, 19(2):261–85, 1993.

Lohr, J. B., and Bracha, H. S. A monozygotic mirror-image twin pair with discordant psychiatric illnesses: a neuropsychiatric and neurodevelopmental evaluation. *American Journal of Psychiatry*, 149:1091–5, 1992.

Lykken, D. T. The diagnosis of zygosity in twins. *Behavior Genetics*, 8:437–73, 1978.

Markow, A. M., and Gottesman, I. I. Fluctuating dermatoglyphic asymmetry in psychotic twins. *Psychiatry Research*, 29:37–43, 1989.

Mednick S. A.; Huttunen, M. O.; and Maction, R. A. Prenatal influenza infections and adult schizophrenia. *Schizophrenia Bulletin*, 20(2):263–7, 1994.

Melnick, M.; Myrianthopoulos, N. C.; and Christian, J. C. The effects of chorion type on variation in IQ in the NCPP twin population *American Journal of Human Genetics*, 30:425–33, 1978.

Munsinger, H. The identical-twin transfusion syndrome: a source of error in estimating IQ resemblance and heritability. *Annals of Human Genetics*, 40: 307–21, 1977.

Nunnally, J. C. *Psychometric Theory*. New York, NY: McGraw Hill Publishing Company, 1967.

Pezzati, M.; Gianciulli, D.; Carbone, C.; Mainardi, G.; Biadaioli, R.; Cosenza, E.; and Ruspantini, S. Acute fetofetal transfusion in dichorionic twins: a clinical case report. *Pediatria Medica e Chirurgica*, 15:305–6, 1993.

Phillips, D. I. W. Twin studies in medical research: can they tell us whether diseases are genetically determined? *Lancet*, 341:1008–9, 1993.

Pridjian, G.; Nugent, C.; and Barr, M., Jr. Twin gestation: influence of placentation on fetal growth. *American Journal of Obstetrics and Gynecology*, 165: 1394–1401, 1991.

Pulver, A. E.; Liang, K.; Brown, C. H.; Wolyniec, P.; McGrath, J.; Adler, L.; Tam, D.; Carpenter, W. T.; Jr.; and Childs, B. Risk factors in schizophrenia: season of birth, gender, and familial risk. *British Journal of Psychiatry*, 160:65–71, 1992.

Reed, T.; Carmelli, D.; and Rosenman, R. H. Effects of placentation on selected type A behaviors in adult males in the National Heart, Lung, and Blood Institute (NHLBI) twin study. *Behavior Genetics*, 21:9–19, 1991a.

Reed, T.; Christian, J. C.; Wood, P. D.; and Schaefer, E. J. Influence of placentation on high density lipoproteins in adult males: the National Heart, Lung, and Blood Institute (NHLBI) twin study. *Acta Geneticae Medicae et Gemellologiae*, 40:353–9, 1991b.

Reed, T.; Uchida, J. A.; Norton, J. A., Jr.; and Christian, J. C. Comparisons of dermatoglyphic patterns in monochorionic and dichorionic monozygotic twins. *American Journal of Human Genetics*, 30:383–91, 1978.

Sadler, T. W. *Langman's Medical Embryology*. Baltimore, MD: Williams & Wilkins Company, 1990.

Scerbo, J. C.; Rattan, P.; and Drukker, J. E. Twins and other multiple gestations. In: Knuppel, R. A., and Drukker, J. E., eds. *High-Risk Pregnancy: A Team Approach*. Philadelphia, PA: W. B. Saunders Company, 1986, pp. 335–61.

Segal, N. L. Origins and implications of handedness and relative birth weight for IQ in monozygotic twin pairs. *Neuropsychologia*, 27:549–61, 1989.

Sham, P. C.; O'Callaghan, E.; Takei, N.; Murray, G. K.; Hare, E. H.; and Murray, R. M. Schizophrenia following pre-natal exposure to influenza epidemics between 1939 and 1960. *British Journal of Psychiatry*, 160:461–6, 1992.

Slater, E. Diagnosis of zygosity by fingerprints. *Acta Psychiatrica Scandinavica*, 39:78–84, 1963.

Spatz, C., and Johnston, J. O. *Basic Statistics: Tales of Distributions.* Pacific Grove, CA: Brooks/Cole Publishing Company, 1989.

Springer, S. P., and Deutsch, G. *Left Brain, Right Brain.* San Francisco, CA: W. H. Freeman & Company, 1981.

Strong, S. J., and Corney, G. *The Placenta in Twin Pregnancy.* Oxford, England: Pergamon Press, 1967.

Tan, K. L.; Tan, R.; Tan, S. H.; and Tan, A. M. The twin transfusion syndrome. *Clinical Pediatrics,* 18:111–14, 1979.

Torrey, E. F. Are we overestimating the genetic contribution to schizophrenia? *Schizophrenia Bulletin,* 18(2):159–70, 1992.

Torrey, E. F., in collaboration with Bower, A. E.; Taylor, E. H.; and Gottesman, I. I. *Schizophrenia and Manic-Depressive Disorder: The Biological Roots of Mental Illness as Revealed by the Landmark Study of Identical Twins.* New York, NY: Basic Books, 1994.

Torrey, E. F.; Rawlings, R.; and Waldman, I. N. Schizophrenic births and viral diseases in two states. *Schizophrenia Research,* 1:73–7, 1988.

Walker, E.; Downey, G.; and Caspi, A. Twin studies of psychopathology: why do the concordance rates vary? *Schizophrenia Research,* 5:211–21, 1991.

Part II

Boy or Girl? Acquiring Gender Identity

Sex Reassignment at Birth and Gender Role Change with Puberty

Introduction

The next two articles deal with the critical role of biology in the formation of gender identity. We chose these articles to redress what we, as developmental psychologists, view to be a rather lopsided argument in favor of the supremacy of socialization in determining a child's gender identity. In most texts on child development, the reader learns that it is the way a child is reared that matters most in the formation of gender identity. We learn of Margaret Meade's observations in various cultures that led her to conclude that the environment was all-important, and we read about studies showing that genetic males who are misjudged at birth to be females, and subsequently reared as females, grow up to identify with that gender identity rather than the one coded by their genes. Missing from these descriptions, however, is the growing evidence that biology matters a great deal in the formation of a person's gender role.

Developmental scientists have known for a long time that hormones play a critical role in a number of behaviors, abilities, and traits. For instance, if a female monkey fetus is subjected to a bath of male hormones, she develops masculine behaviors (e.g., mounting during free play, dominance, and aggressiveness). Similarly, genetic males that are injected with female hormones acquire typical female characteristics. And yet, the situation for humans was often touted as more complex than that of other animals, and the critical role of socialization was considered all-important. We were told that no matter what a child's genetic endowment, the child would grow into the gender she or he was reared in. *Not so!*

New research, some of it like the article by Sigmundson and Diamond, rebuts the prior claims of socialization theorists by reinterviewing individuals who provided their critical support. We shall see that genetic males who were thought to be females and who were reared as females (dresses, long hair, etc.) often failed to acquire a female gender identity. They rebelled against it, refused to wear dresses, refused to urinate sitting down, and refused to be accepted as genetic females. Sadly, some of these cross-fostered individuals became depressed, even attempting suicide. Once their gender was surgically and/or hormonally corrected to match their genetic gender, they usually made immediate adaptations.

In the second of these two articles, Julianne Imperato-McGinley and her colleagues describe a man with a rare genetic disorder. At birth he was unambiguously declared to be a girl and was brought up as a girl, albeit displaying tomboyish behavior (likely caused by hormonal factors). At the onset of puberty "she" developed male sexual characteristics. On being given the opportunity to change gender "she" immediately had a male haircut, got male clothes, and adapted effortlessly to life as a man. This is not to say that it is better to be a boy than a girl, but simply that a girl with hairy arms and a beard may sometimes feel uncomfortable!

Perhaps the single most striking aspect of the following two articles is how quickly individuals who spent 10–20 years being reared as females were able to adopt a male sex-role identity. They often did this immediately. Thus, they were able to overcome many years of gender nurturing with little difficulty. Men who were raised as girls until adolescence and who were then suddenly treated with male hormones began to play more traditionally masculine sports, improved their spatial and mathematical abilities, dated females, and married.

To reiterate, we included these two articles not because we think socialization is unimportant in the formation of gender identity, but rather to redress the existing imbalance that suggests that biology is irrelevant. Clearly, after reading these articles you will agree that it is not.

Further reading

Imperato-McGinley, J., Peterson, R., Stoller, R., and Goodwin, W. (1979). Male pseudohermaphroditism secondary to 17β-hydroxysteroid dehydrogenase deficiency: gender role change with puberty. *Journal of Clinical Endocrinology and Metabolism*, 49, 391–5.

FOUR

Sex Reassignment at Birth

Milton Diamond and H. Keith Sigmundson

Among the more difficult decisions physicians have to make involve cases of ambiguous genitalia or markedly traumatized genitalia. The decision as to how to proceed typically follows this contemporary advice: "The decision to raise the child as a male centers around the potential for the phallus to function adequately in later sexual relations"[1(p. 580)] and "Because it is simpler to construct a vagina than a satisfactory penis, only the infant with a phallus of adequate size should be considered for a male gender assignment."[2(p. 1955)] These management proposals depend on a theory that says it is easier to make a good vagina than a good penis and because the identity of the child will reflect upbringing and the absence of an adequate penis would be psychosexually devastating, fashion the perineum into a normal looking vulva and vagina, and raise the individual as a girl. Such clinical advice, concerned primarily with surgical potentials, is relatively standard in medical texts[3–6] and reflects the current thinking of many physicians.[7]

This management philosophy is based on two beliefs held strongly enough by pediatricians and other physicians to be considered postulates: (1) individuals are psychosexually neutral at birth and (2) healthy psychosexual development is dependent on the appearance of the genitals. These ideas arise most strongly from the original work of Money and colleagues.[8–11(pp. 46–51),12] Typical pronouncements from that research include that "erotic outlook and orientation is an autonomous psychological phenomenon independent of genes and hormones and a permanent ineradicable one as well"[9(p. 1397)] and "[it] is more reasonable to suppose simply that, like hermaphrodites, all the human race follow the same pattern, namely, of psychological undifferentiation at birth."[10] The first postulate was derived not from normal individuals, but from hermaphrodites and pseudohermaphrodites. The second had only anecdotal support. Money[13] no longer holds such extreme views, but his involvement in this particular case and acceptance of the thesis was notable enough that it became a totem in the lay press and a classic for the academic and medical community. And, as already noted, the textbooks have not kept abreast of the new thinking.

Report of a Patient

The case involved a set of normal XY twins, one of whom, at 8 months of age, had his penis accidentally burned to ablation during phimosis repair by cautery.[11] After a great deal of debate, the child was seen for consultation at the Johns Hopkins Hospital, Baltimore, MD, and, following the beliefs mentioned earlier, the recommendation was made to raise the child as a girl. The pseudonym John will be used when referring to this individual when living as a male and the pseudonym Joan when living as a female. Orchiectomy and preliminary surgery followed within the year to facilitate feminization. Further surgery to fashion a full vagina was to wait until Joan was older. This management was monitored and reinforced with yearly visits to the Johns Hopkins Hospital. The treatment was described as developing successfully with John accepting life as Joan.[11]

> Although the girl is not yet a woman, her record to date offers convincing evidence that the gender identity gate is open at birth for a normal child no less than for one born with unfinished sex organs or one who was prenatally over or underexposed to androgen, and that it stays open at least for something over a year after birth.[12(p. 98)]

A follow-up stated: "The girl's subsequent history proves how well all three of them (parents and child) succeeded in adjusting to that decision."[12]

The effects of such reports were widespread. Sociology, psychology, and women's study texts were rewritten to argue that, as *Time* magazine (January 8, 1973) reported,

This dramatic case . . . provides strong support . . . that conventional patterns of masculine and feminine behavior can be altered. It also casts doubt on the theory that major sex differences, psychological as well as anatomical, are immutably set by the genes at conception.

Lay and social science writings still echo this case as do medical texts.[3–6,14] The following quote is typical:

The choice of gender should be based on the infant's anatomy, not the chromosomal karyotype. Often it is wiser to rear a genetic male as a female. It is relatively easy to create a vagina if one is absent, but it is not possible to create a really satisfactory penis if the phallus is absent or rudimentary. Only those males with a phallus of adequate size that will respond to testosterone at adolescence should be considered for male rearing. Otherwise, the baby should be reared as a female.[15(p. 396)]

Our current article challenges those reports and advice. It is based on a review of the medical clinical notes and impressions of therapists originally involved with the case and on contemporary interviews. One of us (H.K.S.) was head of the psychiatric management team to which the case was referred in the patient's home area. Although the patient was assigned to the immediate care of female psychiatrists to foster female identification and role modeling, H.K.S. maintained direct supervisory control of the case. The unique character of this case attracted the attention of the Britsh Broadcasting Co. and they invited M.D. as a consultant.[16] In 1994 and 1995, we collaboratively reinterviewed and recorded John, his mother, and his wife to provide updated accounts of his progress. Findings are listed in chronological order under the appropriate postulate for pediatric sexual assignment. John himself, while desiring to remain anonymous, strongly desires his case history be made available to the medical community to reduce the likelihood of others suffering his psychic trauma.

Postulate 1: Individuals are Psychosexually Neutral at Birth

Mother recalls:

As soon as he had the surgery, the doctor said I should now start treating him as a girl, doing girl things, and putting him in girl's clothes. But that was a disaster. I put this beautiful little dress on him . . . and he [immediately tried] to rip it off; I think he knew it was a dress and that it was for girls and he wasn't a girl.

On the other hand, Joan could act quite feminine when she wanted to and at approximately 6 years old was described as doing so, e.g., his mother was quoted as saying: "One thing that really amazes me is that she is so feminine. I've never seen a little girl so neat and tidy as she can be when she wants to be."[11(p. 119)] More often, however, Joan rejected such behavior. More commonly she, much more so than the twin brother, would mimic the father. One incident the mother related was typical. When the twins were 4 or 5 years old, they were watching their parents. Father was shaving and mother was applying makeup. Joan applied shaving cream and pretended to shave. When Joan was corrected and told to put on lipstick and makeup like mother, Joan said: "No, I don't want no makeup, I want to shave."

Girl's toys, clothes, and activities were repeatedly proffered to Joan and most often rejected. Throughout childhood Joan preferred boy's activities and games; she had little interest in dolls, sewing, or girl's activities. Ignoring the toys she was given, she would play with her brother's toys. She preferred to tinker with gadgets and tools, dress up in men's clothing, and take things apart to see what made them tick. She was regarded as a tomboy with an interest in playing soldier. Joan did not shun rough and tumble sports or avoid fights.

John recalls when the Joan of age 8 or 9 years wanted an umbrella:

I had a couple of bucks and went to the store to take a look at the umbrellas, and right beside the umbrellas was the toy section. I started to eyeball a machine gun. I said to myself, "Do I have enough money for that?" . . . I put the gun on the counter and asked the clerk if I had enough money. She had that look like "You don't have enough but we'll let you go anyway." I used it to play army with my brother.

Mother recalls Joan was in a dress at the time. The brother often refused to let Joan play with his toys, so she saved her allowance money and bought a truck of her own.

Joan's realization that she was not a girl jelled between ages 9 and 11 years. John relates:

> There were little things from early on. I began to see how different I felt and was, from what I was supposed to be. But I didn't know what it meant. I thought I was a freak or something. . . . I looked at myself and said I don't like this type of clothing, I don't like the types of toys I was always being given. I like hanging around with the guys and climbing trees and stuff like that and girls don't like any of that stuff. I looked in the mirror and [saw] my shoulders [were] so wide, I mean there [was] nothing feminine about me. I [was] skinny, but other than that, nothing. But that [was] how I figured it out. [I figured I was a guy] but I didn't want to admit it. I figured I didn't want to wind up opening a can of worms.

Joan knew she already had thoughts of suicide caused by this sort of cognitive dissonance and did not want additional stress.

Joan fought the boys and the girls who were always "razzing" her about her boy looks and her girl clothes. She had no friends; no one would play with her. "Every day I was picked on, every day I was teased, every day I was threatened. I said enough is enough." Mother relates that Joan was good looking as a girl. But, "When he started moving or talking, that gave him away, and the awkwardness and incongruities became apparent."

The other girls teased Joan so aggressively that she often retaliated forcefully. At age 14 years one girl sat behind Joan and continued to hit her. The adult John demonstrated: "I grabbed her like that, by the shirt, and rammed her round the wall like this, threw her on the ground . . . until the teacher grabbed me." This resulted in Joan being expelled from school.

Despite the absence of a penis, Joan often tried to stand to urinate. This made a mess as it was difficult to direct the urine stream. Although she learned to sit and void, she nevertheless continued to occasionally stand and urinate. Despite admonitions against the behavior and its untidiness, Joan persisted. At school, at age 14 years, she was caught standing to urinate in the girls' bathroom so often that the other girls refused to allow her entrance. Mother recalls the other girls threatening to "kill" her if she persisted. Joan would also sometimes go to the boy's lavatory to urinate.

Joan was put on an estrogen regimen at the age of 12 years but rebelled against taking the hormones. They made her "feel funny" and she did not want to feminize. She would often dispose of her daily dose. She was unhappy at developing breasts and would not wear a bra. Things came to a critical point at age 14 years. In discussing her breast development with her endocrinologist she confessed, "I suspected I was a boy since the second grade." The physician, who personally believed Joan should continue her medication and proceed as a girl, used that opening to explore the possible male and female paths available and what either one would mean. The local psychiatric team had noticed Joan's preference for boy's activities and refusal to accept female status so they already had discussed among themselves the possibility of accepting Joan's change back to a male. The endocrinologist explored Joan's options with her. Shortly thereafter, at age 14 years, Joan decided to switch to living as a male.

Joan was the daily butt of her peers' jibes and the local therapists, having knowledge of her previous suicidal thoughts, went along with the idea of sex re-assignment. In a tearful episode following John's prodding, his father told him of the history of what had transpired when he was an infant and why. John recalls: "All of a sudden everything clicked. For the first time things made sense and I understood who and what I was."

John requested male hormone shots and gladly took these. He also requested a mastectomy and phalloplasty. The mastectomy was completed at the age of 14 years; surgical procedures for phallus construction were at ages 15 and 16 years. After the surgical procedures, John adjusted well. As a boy he was relatively well accepted and popular with boys and girls. At 16 years, to attract girls, John obtained a windowless van with a bed and bar. Girls, who as a group had been teasing Joan, now began to have a crush on John. When occasions for sexual encounters arose, however, he was reluctant to move erotically. When he told one girlfriend why he was hesitant, that he was insecure about his penis, she gossiped at school and this hurt John very much. Nevertheless, his peers quickly rallied around him and he was accepted and the girl rejected.

John's life subsequently was not unlike that of other boys with an occult physical handicap. After his return to male living he felt his attitudes, behaviors, and body were in concert in a way they had not been when living as a girl. At age 25 years he married a women several years his senior and adopted her children.

Postulate 2: Healthy Psychosexual Development is Intimately Related to the Appearance of the Genitals

First in Baltimore and then with the local therapists prior to the sex re-reassignment, Joan's expressed feelings of not being a girl would draw ridicule. She would be told something such as: "All girls think such things when they're growing up." John recalls thinking: "You can't argue with a bunch of doctors in white coats; you're just a little kid and their minds are already made up. They didn't want to listen." To ease pressures to act as a girl, Joan would often not argue or fight the assignment and would "go along."

Beginning at age 7 years, Joan began to rebel against going for the consultations at the Johns Hopkins Hospital. Her reasons were discomfort and embarrassment with forced exposure of her genitals and constant attempts, particularly after the age of 8 years, to convince her to behave more like a girl and accept further vaginal repair. This was always strongly resisted and led to recurrent confrontations. To temper Joan's reluctance to travel to the consultants, her parents combined such visits with vacation trips.

In Baltimore the consultants enlisted male-to-female transsexuals to convince Joan of the advantages of being female and having a vagina constructed. She was so disturbed by this that in one instance Joan, at age 13 years, ran away from the hospital. She was found hiding on the roof of a nearby building. After age 14 years, Joan adamantly refused to return to the hospital. Joan then came fully under the care of local clinicians. This group consisted of several pediatricians, two pediatric surgeons, an endocrinologist, and a team of psychiatrists.

John recalls thinking, from preschool through elementary school, that physicians were more concerned with the appearance of Joan's genitals than was Joan. Her genitals were inspected at each visit to the Johns Hopkins Hospital. She thought they were making a big issue out of nothing and they gave her no reason to think otherwise. John recalls thinking: "Leave me be and then I'll be fine. . . . It's bizarre. My genitals are not bothering me; I don't know why it is bothering you guys so much."

When asked what Joan thought of her genitals as a youngster, John replied, "I didn't really have anything to compare myself against other than my brother when we were taking a bath." Mother confirmed that as a devout family in a very conservative religious community there would have been few opportunities for the twins to have seen anyone else's genitals. Nudity was never acceptable. At their yearly visit to the Johns Hopkins Hospital, the twins were made to stand naked for inspection by groups of clinicians and to inspect each other's genitalia. This experience, in itself, was recalled with strong negative emotions. John's brother, decades later, recalls the experience with tears.

John recalls frustration, which remains, at not having his feelings and desires recognized. Without consideration of genitals, despite the obvious absence of a penis, Joan nevertheless knew she was not a girl. When she tried to express such thoughts the physicians would change the subject. "[They] didn't want to hear what I had to say but wanted to tell me how I should feel." Clinical notes from the time report Joan saying she felt "like a trapped animal."

In middle school Joan had difficulty making friends. Her clothes and demeanor did not jibe. Because of her behavior, her peers teased her with names like "caveman" and "gorilla." Few children would play with her. None of Joan's peers knew anything of her genitals.

At first, as suggested by the consultants from the Johns Hopkins Hospital, the local physicians and her parents continued to treat Joan as a girl, preparing her for vaginal reconstructive surgery and life as a female. Psychotherapy, primarily by female therapists, was aimed at reinforcing her female identity and redirecting her male ideation. This course of action became increasingly difficult because of Joan's growing conviction that she was not right as a girl and anger at being treated like one. Joan's reactions were not unlike those in posttraumatic stress disorder, where the cause of the stress is not remembered. John recalls, "They kept making me feel as if I was a freak."

John knew what the clinicians wanted and recognized it was not what he wanted. Beginning at age 14 years, against the recommendations of the clinicians and family and without yet knowing of the original XY status, Joan refused to live as a girl. Jeans and shirts because of their gender-neutral status, became her preferred manner of dress; boy's games and pursuits her usual activities. Joan's daytime fantasies and night dreams during elementary school involved seeing herself "as this big guy, lots of muscles and a slick car and have[ing] all kinds of friends." She aspired to be a mechanic. She rejected requests to look at pictures of nude females, which she was supposed to emulate. Rorschach and Thematic Apperception Tests at the time elicited responses more typical of a boy than a girl. Her adamant rejection of female living and her improved demeanor and disposition when acting as a boy convinced the local therapists of the correctness of sexual re-reassignment.

Following the surgery for penile construction there was difficulty with urethral closure. Despite repeated attempts at repair, the problem was never rectified. John now urinates through a fistula at the base of his penis while sitting down. Much of the penis is without sensation, as are the areas of scarring from where the grafts were taken.

John's first sexual partner was a girl. He was 18 years old. While living as a girl and afterward as a boy, John was approached sexually by males. He claims never to have been attracted to them and his responses to such questions are matter-of-fact and not homophobic. John thinks his first recognizable sexual interest occurred at about age 16 or 17 years, although he did recall wanting to go see the "sexy" Rockettes in New York on one of his trips to see the consultants.

Coitus is occasional with his wife. This frequency, he claims, is sufficient for his needs but is less than his wife would desire. They mostly pleasure each other with a great deal of physical affection and mutual masturbation. John can have coital orgasm with ejaculation.

John recalls thinking it was small-minded of others to think all his personality was summed up in the presence or absence of a penis. He expressed it thus:

> Doctor . . . said, "it's gonna be tough, you're going to be picked on, you're gonna be very alone, you're not gonna find anybody [unless you have vaginal surgery and live as a female]." And I thought to myself, you know I wasn't very old at the time, but it dawned on me that these people gotta be pretty shallow if that's the only thing they think I've got going for me; that the only reason why people get married and have children and have a productive life is because of what they have between their legs. . . . If that's all they think of me, that they justify my worth by what I have between my legs, then I gotta be a complete loser.

General Comments

As an adult John was asked why he did not accept being a female rather than fighting it. His answer was simple. Doing so did not feel right. He wanted to please his parents and placate the physicians so he often went along with their decisions, but the conflict between his feelings and theirs was mentally devastating and would have led to suicide if he had been forced to continue.

The most often voiced and deeply felt emotion expressed by Joan was always feeling different from what was expected or desired by others. At first, as a toddler, the feeling of being different was relatively amorphous. Even as a preschooler, it shifted to clearly being different from girls. And later, in elementary school, she began to feel not only different from girls but similar to boys. Having a twin might have made this comparison much easier for Joan than it might have been for a singleton. Such a progression in thinking is common for atypical individuals such as homosexual males and females,[17] intersexed individuals, or those with ambiguous genitalia.[18]

The transition was gradual. When Joan thought she might really be a boy instead of the girl her parents and physicians told her she was, the psychic discord frightened her even though she had suspected since the second grade that it was true. When finally told the truth, she was relieved because her feelings now made sense. John's anger at not having been told the truth from the beginning persists.

Following John's sex re-reassignment, the family decided to disregard the clinical recommendation to move from their family home. Instead they stayed and were open about the change. Aside from the financial concerns, the parents judged that the word would get out anyway. This strategy seemed to work and John was accepted in a way that Joan never was.

John was given testosterone treatment following his return to male status. As is typical of many teenage boys, John began to work out with weights. He blossomed into an attractive muscular young man.

According to John's wife, "Before he came along I was a lot tougher on the kids because I had to be. [Now] John is the real hard one and I am the soft one. There is no doubt who wears the pants in this family."

John is a mature and forward-looking man with a keen sense of humor and balance. Although still bitter over his experience, he accepts what happened and is trying to make the most of his life with support from his wife, parents, and family. He has job satisfaction and is generally self-assured.

Comment

Long-term follow-up of case reports are unusual but often crucial. This update to a case originally accepted as a "classic" in fields ranging from medicine to the humanities completely reverses the conclusions and theory behind the original reports. Cases of infant sex reassignment require inspection and review after puberty; 5- and 10-year postsex reassignment follow-ups are still insufficient.

Possibly the initial impressions of the consultants[11,12] were appropriate at the time and Joan's behavior and thinking shifted with development. However, clinical notes and the impressions of the local physicians at the time, as well as John's contemporary recollections, indicate that he was at no time fully accepting of sex reassignment. The local physicians expressed their reservations early on.[16] Only when it became obvious to the local team that the original management program of maintaining this child as a girl proved no longer tenable and psychologically damaging, even life threatening, did they revise their thinking.

It is also possible that interpretations from the early years were mistaken. Results contrary to one's hypotheses and management plans are often difficult to see. Manifestations of typical boy behaviors would thus repeatedly be interpreted as tomboyish. This seems to have been the case for preferred activities, games, toys, and clothing. The conclusions that hermaphrodites and pseudohermaphrodites offer a model for normal development had been challenged before.[19-24] The implications of such challenges, however, do not seem to have been accepted or integrated by most pediatricians or surgeons.[7]

Joan was repeatedly admonished for behaving like a boy. Such management is in keeping with the belief that any agreement with doubt expressed by the patient will decrease the likelihood of a successful outcome.[25-8] To contend that Joan did not accept her imposed sex because of ambiguity in treatments, though, is circular reasoning. No evidence of such ambiguity exists and the initial reports held that the rearing was appropriate.[11,12] It is known, particularly from transsexuals, that casting doubt on an individual's sexual identity usually forces that person to introspection and eventual security regarding a preferred life direction, even if it is contrary to upbringing, parent's wishes, and social and cultural norms, and if it results in less than adequate genitalia.[29,30]

In the case under consideration, the initial management protocol was predicated on postulates that considered a male's self-image dependent on a functional penis. Although such adequacy is important, there is no body of data establishing its centrality.

Other considerations are in order. Gender reassignment as proposed for John, and the postulates on which it is based, assume the individual will learn to accept rearing-appropriate, sex-typical behaviors, particularly when the genitals are at issue. These situations range from the urinary to erotic to narcissistic. Such behaviors, however important, are only one aspect of an individual's total sexuality. An individual's sexual profile comprises at least five levels: gender patterns, reproduction, sexual identity, arousal and physiological mechanisms, and sexual orientation, recalled by the acronym PRIMO.[31,32]

The sex reassignment of John to Joan addressed only the gender patterns and gender roles to which he would be subject. Expectations were that adjustments in his identity and other levels would follow. Joan did indeed become aware of the social expectations consistent with the female gender, but these were not in keeping with those with which he felt comfortable. Standing to urinate, despite its housekeeping and social consequences, is a dramatic display of preference. The sex reassignment obviously failed in the area in which it was designed most to succeed.

But it failed at the other four levels as well. The contrast between the female gender-typical behaviors the child was being asked to accept and her inner-directed behavior preferences presented a discordance that demanded resolution. Joan's analysis of the situation was that she best fit in not as a girl but as a boy. Despite her upbringing, Joan's sexual identity developed as a male. Sex reassignment also obviously went against Joan's or John's reproductive character. Castration removed any reproductive capacity. Certainly John was unaware of this as a child. He resents this now and decries the loss. Castration also removed the androgen source for sex-typical mechanisms of sexual arousal and other physiological processes. His ability to ejaculate returned with androgen treatment. The castration and surgical scarring, however, have reduced erotic sensitivity to the perineum and, consequently, reduced this pleasure. And notably, as many studies strongly indicate, sexual orientation is prenatally organized or at least predisposed.[33–40] The sex reassignment did nothing to affect sexual orientation. Joan remained totally gynecophilic despite being reared as a girl.

Comments from John's parents reveal another important consideration. With a sex reassignment they were asked to make a dramatic psychological adjustment in rearing an otherwise normal child. Mother herself required psychiatric treatment to help manage her feelings. The penile ablation aside, the parents were more comfortable dealing with their child's original sex and the accident than with the reassigned sex. Although they had tried to make a success of the sex reassignment, they were supportive, while guilt ridden, when Joan decided to become John.

The last decade has offered much support for a biological substrate for sexual behavior. In addition to the genetic research mentioned, there are many neurological and other reports that point in this direction.[31,32,41–56] The evidence seems overwhelming that normal humans are not psychosexually neutral at birth but are, in keeping with their mammalian heritage, predisposed and biased to interact with environmental, familial, and social forces in either a male or female mode. This classic case demonstrates this. And the fact that this predisposition was particularly expressed at puberty, a critical period, is logical and has been predicted.[20,44]

Although this article deals with a classic case of sex reassignment often cited in the literature, follow-ups to related cases are available. Reilly and Woodhouse[57] described 20 patients with micropenises who were reared as boys. None of them had any doubt as to the correctness of the assignment as males. Other reports describe males originally reassigned as females who switched back and successfully lived as males, despite the absence of a normal penis.[19,32,58–62] Several of these cases offer findings similar to ours, including the ages at which various milestones were passed, feelings developed, and the reassignment challenged.[59,60] Another more recent case illustrates this.

Reiner[63] described an adolescent Hmong immigrant who precipitously dropped out of school at age 14. On subsequent interview she declared, though she was unequivocally raised as a girl from birth, "I am not a girl, I am a boy." Findings from a physical examination revealed a 46-chromosome, XY male with mixed gonadal dysgenesis with a female-appearing pelvis with clitoral hypertrophy. Her school friends had all been boys. She enjoyed rough and tumble play, avoided dolls and girl's activities, and dressed in a gender-neutral or boy's way. Her feelings of being different, being a boy, developed from the age of 8 years and came to a head at 14 years. Treatment involved surgery and endocrine therapy. This individual, after a period of some depression, progressively developed into a gynecophilic, sexually active male.

These cases of successful gender change, as well as the present one, also challenge the belief that such a switch after the age of 2 years will be devastating. Indeed, in these cases it was salutary.

It must be acknowledged that cases of males accepting life as females after the destruction of their penises have been reported.[64] These reports, however, do not detail the individuals' sexual or personal lives.

Conclusions

Considering this case follow-up, and as far as an extensive literature review can attest, there is no known case where a 46-chromosome, XY male, unequivocally so at birth, has ever easily and fully accepted an imposed life as an androphilic female regardless of physical and medical intervention. True, surgical reconstruction of traumatized male or ambiguous genitalia to those of a female is mechanically easier than constructing a penis. But the attendant sex reassignment might be an unacceptable psychic price to pay. Concomitantly, no support exists for the postulates that individuals are psychosexually neutral at birth or that healthy psychosexual development is dependent on the appearance of the genitals. Certainly long-term follow-up on other cases is needed.

In the interim, however, we offer new guidelines. We believe that any 46-chromosome, XY individual born normal and with a normal nervous system, in keeping with the psychosexual bias thus prenatally imposed, should be raised as a male. Surgery to repair any genital problem, although difficult, should be conducted in keeping with this paradigm. This decision is not a simple one to make[7,13,18,63,65–7] and analysis should continue.

As parents will still want their children to be and look normal as soon after birth or injury as possible, physicians will have to provide the best advice and care consistent with current knowledge. We suggest referring the parents and child to appropriate and periodic long-term counseling rather than to immediate surgery and sex reassignment, which seems a simple and immediate solution to a complicated problem. With this management, a male's predisposition to act as a boy and his actual behavior will be reinforced in daily interactions and on all sexual levels and his fertility will be preserved. Social difficulties may reveal themselves as puberty is experienced. However, there is no evidence that with proper counseling and surgical repair when best indicated, adjustment will not be managed as well as teenagers manage other severe handicaps. Future reports will determine if we are correct.

References

1 Duckett J. W., Baskin L. S. Genitoplasty for intersex anomalies. *Eur J Pediatr.* 1993;152(suppl 2):580–4.

2 Perimutter A. D., Reitelman C. Surgical management of intersexuality. In: Walsh P. C., Retik A. B., Stamey T. A., Vaughan J. R., eds. *Campbell's Urology.* 6th edn. Philadelphia. PA: W. B. Saunders Co.; 1992:1951–66.

3 Behrman R. E., Kliegman R. M. *Nelson Essentials of Pediatrics.* 2nd edn. Philadelphia, PA: W. B. Saunders Co.; 1994:636–7.

4 Blethen S. L., Weldon W. Disorders of external genitalia differentiation. In: Kelly V. C., ed. *Practice of Pediatrics.* Philadelphia, PA: Harper & Row Publication Inc.; 1985:1–23.

5 Catlin E. A., Crawford J. D. Neonatal endocrinology. In: Oski F. A., ed. *Principles and Practices of Pediatrics.* Philadelphia, PA: J. B. Lippincott; 1990:420–9.

6 Ratzan S. K. Endocrine and metabolic disorders. In: Dworkin P. H., ed. *Pediatrics.* 3rd edn. Baltimore, MD: Williams & Wilkins; 1996:523–65.

7 Kessler S. J. The medical construction of gender: case management of intersexed infants. *Signs: J Women Culture Soc.* 1990;16:3–26.

8 Money J., Hampson J. G., Hampson J. L. An examination of some basic sexual concepts: the evidence of human hermaphroditism. *Bull Johns Hopkins Hosp.* 1955;97:301–19.

9 Money J. Sex hormones and other variables in human eroticism. In: Young W. C., ed. *Sex and Internal Secretions.* 3rd edn. Baltimore, MD: Williams & Wilkins; 1961:1383–1400.

10 Money J. Cytogenetic and psychosexual incongruities with a note on space-form blindness. *Am J Psychiatry.* 1963;119:820–7.

11 Money J., Ehrhardt A. A. *Man and Woman/Boy and Girl.* Baltimore, MD: Johns Hopkins University Press; 1972.

12 Money J., Tucker P. *Sexual Signatures: On Being a Man or Woman.* Boston, MA: Little Brown & Co. Inc.; 1975:95–8.

13 Money J. *Sex Errors of the Body and Related Syndromes: A Guide to Counseling Children, Adolescents, and Their Families.* 2nd edn. Baltimore, MD: Paul H. Brookes Publishing Co.; 1994:132.

14 Burg F. D., Merrill R. E., Winter R. J., Schaible D. H. *Treatment of Infants, Children and Adolescents*. Philadelphia, PA: W. B. Saunders Co.; 1990:8–9.

15 Donahoe P. K., Hendren W. H. I. Evaluation of the newborn with ambiguous genitalia. *Pediatr Clin North Am*. 1976;23:361–70.

16 Diamond M. Sexual identity, monozygotic twins reared in discordant sex roles and a BBC follow-up. *Arch Sex Behav*. 1982;11:181–5.

17 Savin-Williams R. C. Self-labeling and disclosure among gay, lesbian and bisexual youths. In: Green R. J., Laird J., eds. *Lesbians and Gays in Couples and Families*. San Francisco. CA: Jossey-Bass Inc. Pubs; 1996: 153–82.

18 Diamond M. Sexual identity and sexual orientation in children with traumatized or ambiguous genitalia. *J Sex Res*. In press.

19 Cappon D., Ezrin C., Lynes P. Psychosexual identification (psychogender) in the intersexed. *Can Psychiatry J*. 1959;4:90–106.

20 Diamond M. A critical evaluation of the ontogeny of human sexual behavior. *Q Rev Biol*. 1965;40:147–75.

21 Roth M., Ball J. R. B. Psychiatric aspects of intersexuality. In: Armstrong O. N., Marshall A. J., eds. *Intersexuality: In Vertebrates Including Man*. London, England: Academic Press Inc. Ltd; 1964:395–443.

22 Money J., Zuger B. Critique and rebuttal. *Psychosom Med*. 1970;3:463–7.

23 Zuger B. Gender role determination: a critical review of the evidence from hermaphroditism. *Psychosom Med*. 1970;32:449–63.

24 Zuger B. Comments on "gender role differentiation in hermaphrodites." *Arch Sex Behav*. 1975;4:579–81.

25 Lev-Ran A. Gender role differentiation in hermaphrodites. *Arch Sex Behav*. 1974;3:391.

26 Money J. Hormones, hormonal anomalies, and psychological health-care. In: Kappy M. S., Blizzard R. M., Migeon C. J., eds. *Wilkin's Diagnosis and Treatment of Endocrine Disorders in Childhood and Adolescence*. 4th edn. Springfield II: Charles C. Thomas Publishers; 1994:1141–78.

27 Stoller R. J. The Intersexed patient – counsel and management. In: Wahl C. W., ed. *Sexual Problems: Diagnosis and Treatment in Medical Practice*. New York, NY: Free Press; 1967:149–62.

28 Stoller R. J. *Sex and Gender: On the Development of Masculinity and Femininity*. New York, NY: Science House; 1968:231–40.

29 Diamond M. Self-testing: a check on sexual levels. In: Builough B., Bullough V. L., eds. *Cross Dressing and Transgenderism*. Buffalo, NY: Prometheus Books. In press.

30 Diamond M. Self-testing among transsexuals: a check on sexual identity. *J Psychol Hum Sex*. 1996;8:61–82.

31 Diamond M. Some genetic considerations in the development of sexual orientation. In: Haug M., Whalen R. E., Aron C., Olsen K. L., eds. *The*

Development of Sex Differences and Similarities in Behavior. Dordrecht, the Netherlands: Kluwer Academic Publishers; 1993:291–309.

32 Diamond M. Biological aspects of sexual orientation and identity. In: Diamant L., McAnulty R., eds. *The Psychology of Sexual Orientation, Behavior and Identity: A Handbook*. Westport, CT: Greenwood Press Inc.; 1995:45–80.

33 Bailey J. M., Pillard R. C. A genetic study of male sexual orientation. *Arch Gen Psychiatry*. 1991;48:1089–96.

34 Bailey J. M., Pillard R. C., Neale M. C., Agyei Y. Heritable factors influence sexual orientation in women. *Arch Gen Psychiatry*. 1993;50:217–23.

35 Bailey J. M., Bell A. P. Familial aggregation of female sexual orientation. *Behav Genet*. 1993;23:312–22.

36 Hamer D. H., Hu S., Magnuson V. L., Hu N., Pattatucci A. M. L. A linkage between DNA markers on the X chromosome and male sexual orientation. *Science*. 1993;261:321–7.

37 Pillard R., Poumadere J., Carretta R. A family study of sexual orientation. *Arch Sex Behav*. 1982;11:511–20.

38 Pillard R., Weinnch J. Evidence of familial nature of male homosexuality. *Arch Gen Psychiatry*. 1986;43:808–12.

39 Turner W. J. Homosexuality, type 1: an Xq28 phenomenon. *Arch Sex Behav*. 1995;24:109–34.

40 Whitam F., Diamond M., Martin J. Homosexual orientation in twins: a report on 61 pairs and 3 triplet sets. *Arch Sex Behav*. 1993;22:187–206.

41 Allen L. S., Hines M., Shryne J. E., Gorski R. A. Two sexually dimorphic cell groups in the human brain. *J Neurosci*. 1989;9:497–506.

42 Allen L. S., Gorski R. A. Sexual orientation and the size of the anterior commissure in the human brain. *Proc Natl Acad Sci USA*. 1992;89: 7199–202.

43 Diamond M. Genetic-endocrine interactions and human psychosexuality. In: Diamond M., ed. *Perspectives in Reproduction and Sexual Behavior*. Bloomington, In: University of Indiana Press; 1968:417–43.

44 Diamond M. Sexual identity and sex roles. In: Bullough V., ed. *The Frontiers of Sex Research*. Buffalo, NY: Prometheus Books; 1979:33–56.

45 Diamond M. Bisexualität aus biologischer sicht. In: Haeberle E. J., Gindorf R., eds. *Bisexualitäten: Ideologie und Praxis des Sexualkontaktes mit beiden Geschlechtern*. Stuttgart, Germany: Gustav/Fischer Verlag; 1994:41–8.

46 Gorski R. A., Gordon J. H., Shrayne J. E., Southam A. M. Evidence for a morphological sex difference within the medial preoptic area for the rat brain. *Brain Res*. 1978;148:333–46.

47 Gorski R. A. Hormone-induced sex differences in hypothalamic structure. *Bull Tokyo Metrop Inst Neurosci*. 1988;16:67–90.

48 Hines M. Gonadal hormones and human cognitive development. In:

Balthazart J., ed. *Hormones, Brain and Behaviour in Vertabrates: 1. Sexual Differentiation. Neuroanatomical Aspects. Neurotransmitters and Neuropeptides.* Farmington, CT: S. Karger AG; 1990:51–63.

49 Hines M. Hormonal and neural correlates of sex-typed behavioral in human beings. In: Haug M., Whalen R. E., Aron C., Olsen K. L., eds. *The Development of Sex Differences and Similarities in Behavior.* Dordrecht, the Netherlands: Kluwer Academic Publishers; 1993:131–49.

50 LeVay S. A difference in hypothalamic structure between heterosexual and homosexual men. *Science.* 1991;253:1034–7.

51 LeVay S. *The Sexual Brain.* Cambridge, MA: MIT Press; 1993.

52 LeVay S., Hamer D. H. Evidence for a biological influence in male homosexuality. *Sci Am.* 1994;May:44–9.

53 Swaab D. F., Fliers E. A sexually dimorphic nucleus in the human brain. *Science.* 1985;228:1112–15.

54 Swaab D. F., Hofman M. A. Sexual differentiation of the human hypothalamus: ontogeny of the sexually dimorphic nucleus of the preoptic area. *Dev Brain Res.* 1988;44:314–18.

55 Swaab D. F., Hofman M. A. An enlarged suprachiasmatic nucleus in homosexual men. *Brain Res.* 1990;537:141–8.

56 Swaab D. F., Gooren L. J. G., Hofman M. A. Brain research, gender and sexual orientation. *J Homosex.* 1995;28:283–301.

57 Reilly J. M., Woodhouse C. R. J. Small penis and the male sexual role. *J Urol.* 1989;142:569–72.

58 Burns E., Segaloff A., Carrera G. M. Reassignment of sex: report of 3 cases. *J Urol.* 1960;84:126.

59 Dicks G. H., Childers A. T. The social transformation of a boy who had lived his first fourteen years as a girl: a case history. *Am J Orthopsychaitry.* 1934;4:508–17.

60 Ghabrial F., Girgis S. M. Reorientation of sex: report of two cases. *Int J Fertil.* 1962;7:249–58.

61 Hoenig J. The origins of gender identity. In: Steiner W. B., ed. *Gender Dysphoria: Development, Research, Management.* New York, NY: Plenum Press; 1985:11–32.

62 Khupisco V. The tragic boy who refused to be turned into a girl. In: *Sunday Times Johannesburg.* May 21, 1995.

63 Reiner W. G. Case study: sex reassignment in a teenage girl. *J Am Acad Child Adolesc Psychiatry.* 1996;35:799–803.

64 Gearhart J. P. Total ablation of the penis after circumcision with electrocautery: a method of management and long-term followup. *J Urol.* 1989;142:799–801.

65 Fausto-Sterling A. The five sexes: why male and female are not enough. *Science.* 1993;1993:20–5.

66 Meyer-Bahlburg H. F. L. Gender identity development in intersex patients. *Child Adolesc Psychiatry Clin North Am.* 1993;2:501–11.

67 Zucker K. J., Bradley S. J. *Gender Identity Disorder and Psychosexual Problems in Children and Adolescents.* New York, NY: Guilford Press; 1995:265–82.

FIVE

Gender Role Change with Puberty

Julianne Imperato-McGinley, Ralph E. Peterson, Robert Stoller, and Willard E. Goodwin

The first case of male pseudohermaphroditism secondary to 17β-hydroxysteroid dehydrogenase deficiency was reported in 1965 by Neher and Khant.[1] Presently, there are 8 reports of 11 individuals, including 2 siblings, with this condition.[1-14] With one exception, all subjects were thought to be girls at birth because of female-appearing genitalia. Only one child was born with ambiguous genitalia and changed to a male sex of rearing at 1 year of age.[6]

With two exceptions, all subjects raised as girls were castrated before puberty or during their teenage years. One subject, who was not diagnosed and not castrated until age 46 years, has maintained a female gender identity. The other noncastrated subject was diagnosed at age 28 years but began living as a male at age 17 years. The subject of this report is a 31-year-old male pseudohermaphrodite with 17β-hydroxysteroid dehydrogenase deficiency who was unambiguously raised as a female from birth through childhood. Despite this, at puberty he adopted a male gender role with ease.[15] The detailed psychosexual aspects of the case were previously reported.[15] [. . .]

Case Report

The patient is a 31-year-old male pseudohermaphrodite raised as a girl from birth to 14 years of age.[15]

The child, the first of four siblings, was born in a hospital in California and incontrovertibly declared to be a girl. The newborn hospital record describes a female phenotype.

From an early age, however, the child showed preference for boys' activities and her fantasy life was similar to that of boys her age. Yet before puberty, neither the child nor her parents thought that she was anything other than a girl.

At age 12 years she developed hair on her arms and legs and her clitoris (phallus) began to grow. At age 13 years, her voice deepened, and by age 14 years, she was without breast development and menses. She became increasingly unhappy at home, barely obtained passing grades in school, and had few friends. Embarrassment over her physical appearance finally caused her to drop out of school. The persistently "hoarse" voice prompted a visit to the family physician who noted the ambiguous genitalia and referred her to UCLA for further evaluation.

Evaluation at UCLA in 1961 revealed a 5'10" tall adolescent with a deep voice, strong muscular build, [. . .] ample axillary and pubic hair, and a male escutcheon. The phallus was approximately 4 cm long. [. . .] A diagnosis of male pseudohermaphroditism was made.

The adolescent was sent for psychiatric evaluation and the initial impression was that her appearance and manner were totally masculine; she appeared awkward in female clothes. After evaluation, it was decided to allow a gender role change if the patient desired. She immediately went home, changed to boys' clothing, obtained a boy's haircut, and thereafter looked and behaved like a normal boy. This was confirmed when the adolescent was seen a few days later, and in the 17 years that followed, he has been a well adjusted masculine man.

After the gender role change, the family moved to a neighborhood where they were unknown. The subject was accepted at the new high school and no doubts were raised about his masculinity. He became an athlete, began dating girls, excelled as a student, and was among the first in his class in mathematics, a subject in which he did very poorly when he thought he was a girl. He finished high school, college, and his postgraduate education. He married at the age of 25 years, and the couple has been able to engage in mutually satisfactory sexual intercourse. [. . .]

There is no family history of pseudohermaphroditism and the parents are not known to be related.

A recent physical examination revealed a 6′ tall handsome male with masculine build, deep voice, and heavy heard. He had marked hair on his chest, abdomen, arms, and legs. [. . .] The phallus was 5 cm in length. [. . .]

Psychosexual evaluation

During childhood and early adolescence, although this subject never thought that he was anything but female, he exhibited tomboyish behavior. With the events of a masculine puberty, embarrassment over a muscular android appearance and masculine mannerisms caused withdrawal from her peers and a poor academic performance. When told that she was male, she was able to switch to a male gender role with ease, as if finally understanding why she looked and behaved the way she did. This was a remarkable occurrence, since interview data with the subject and parents never revealed any ambiguity in the female sex of rearing.

As soon as this subject was permitted to change to a masculine role, what appeared to be a character disorder, as manifested by depression, poor peer relations, inadequate work at school, and a low level of performance in all areas immediately disappeared. It was replaced by an open, natural masculinity leading to an unbroken series of successful encounters with life, including a happy marriage and a successful professional career.

His strength of character was again powerfully tested when suddenly confronted with cancer and painful and debilitating surgical treatment and chemotherapy. He has never succumbed either to unwarranted denial of his problems or to hopelessness.

Discussion

The subject of this study [. . .] has been followed by a psychiatrist since age 14 years. The patient was unambiguously raised as female; yet despite this, he was easily able to change to a male gender role at age 14 years. Interestingly, even in early childhood when he thought he was female, he exhibited tomboyish behavior and resisted all maternal efforts to encourage femininity. The data suggest that some hormonal factor or biological force, as previously postulated by Stoller,[15] was strong enough in this subject to override the female sex of rearing. [. . .]

Thus, it can be theorized that masculinization of the brain in this subject occurred *in utero* [, . . .] and with the events of a male puberty, this subject was able to change to a male gender role with ease.

We have previously reported 18 male pseudohermaphrodites [. . .] who were unambiguously raised as females.[16,17,18] Yet despite the female sex of rearing, in 17 of the 18 subjects, a male gender identity evolved during the events of puberty, and 16 of the subjects changed to a male gender role. Interviews with these subjects reveal that the change in gender identity occurred over a period of years, with the affected subjects passing through stages of not "feeling like girls" to "feeling like men" to the final conviction that they were indeed men. [. . .] The psychosexual data from these subjects suggest that androgen (T) exposure of the brain *in utero*, during the neonatal period, and at puberty has an impact in the determination of a male gender identity and, under certain circumstances, can override the female sex of rearing. [. . .]

References

1 Neher, R., and F. W. Kahnt, Gonadal steroid biosynthesis *in vitro* in four cases of testicular feminization, androgens in normal and pathological conditions, International Congress Series no. 101, Excerpta Medica, Amsterdam, 1965, p. 130.

2 De Peretti, E., J. M. Saez, and J. Bertrand, Familial male pseudohermaphroditism (MPH) due to 17-ketosteroid reductase defect: *in vitro* study and testicular incubation, Proceedings of the Third International Congress on Hormonal Steroids, Excerpta Medica International Congress Series no. 210, 1970, p. 205.

3 Saez, J. M., E. De Peretti, A. M. Morera, M. David, and J. Bertrand, Familial male pseudohermaphroditism with gynecomastia due to a testicular 17-ketosteroid reductase defect. I. Studies *in vivo*, *J Clin Endocrinol Metab* **32:** 604, 1971.

4 Saez, J. M., A. M. Morera, and E. De Peretti, Further *in vivo* studies in male pseudohermaphroditism with gynecomastia due to a testicular 17-ketosteroid reductase defect (compared to a case of testicular feminization), *J Clin Endocrinol Metab* **34:** 598, 1972.

5 Goebelsmann, U., R. Horton, J. H. Mestman, J. J. Arce, Y. Nagata, R. M. Nakamura, I. H. Thorneycroft, and D. R. Mishell, Jr., Male pseudohermaph-

roditism due to testicular 17β hydroxysteroid dehydrogenase deficiency, *J Clin Endocrinol Metab* **36:** 867, 1973.

6 Knorr, D., F. Bidlingmaier, and D. Engelhardt, Reifenstein's syndrome, a 17β-hydroxysteroid-oxydoreductase deficiency, *Acta Endocrinol [Suppl] (Kbh)* **173:** 37, 1973.

7 Tourniaire, J., B. Laubie, J. Saez, T. K. Leung, J. Perrin, N. Dutrieux, and P. Guinet, Pseudohermaphrodisme male familial par deficit testiculaire en 17-ketosteroids-reductase, *Ann Endocrinol (Paris)* **34:** 461, 1973.

8 Knorr, D., R. Bidlingmaier, O. Butenandt, and D. Engelhardt, 17β Hydroxy-steroid-Oxydoreduktase-Mangel bei Pseudohermaphroditismus maskulinus vom Type des Reifenstein-Syndrome, *Klin Wochenschr* **52:** 537, 1974.

9 Givens, J. R., W. J. Wiser, R. L. Summitt, I. H. Kerber, R. N. Anderson, E. E. Pittway, and S. A. Fish, Familial male pseudohermaphroditism without gynecomastia due to deficient testicular 17-ketosteroid reductase activity, *N Engl J Med* **291:** 938, 1974.

10 Goebelsmann, U., T. D. Hall, W. I. Paul, and F. Z. Stanczyk, *In vitro* steroid metabolic studies in testicular 17β-reduction deficiency, *J Clin Endocrinol Metab* **41:** 1136, 1975.

11 Shaison, G., and L. R. Sitruk, Male pseudohermaphroditism due to testicular 17-ketosteroid reductase deficiency, *Horm Metab Res* **8:** 307, 1976.

12 Akesode, F. A., W. J. Meyer III, and C. J. Migeon, Male pseudohermaphroditism with gynecomastia due to testicular 17-ketosteroid reductase deficiency, *Clin Endocrinol (Oxf)* **7:** 443, 1977.

13 Virdis, R., R. Saenger, B. Senior, and M. I. New, Endocrine studies in a pubertal male pseudohermaphrodite with 17-ketosteroid reductase deficiency, *Acta Endocrinol (Kbh)* **87:** 212, 1978.

14 Stanczyk, F. Z., U. Goebelsmann, and R. M. Nakamura, Further *in vitro* steroid metabolic studies of testicular 17β-reduction deficiency, *J Steroid Biochem* **9:** 153, 1978.

15 Stoller, R., A contribution to the study of gender identity, *Int J Psychoanal* **45:** 220, 1964.

16 Peterson, R. E., J. Imperato-McGinley, T. Gautier, and E. Sturla, Male pseudohermaphroditism due to steroid 5α-reductase deficiency, *Am J Med* **62:** 170, 1977.

17 Imperato-McGinley, J., L. Guerro, R. Gautier, and R. E. Peterson, Steroid 5α-reductase deficiency in man. An inherited form of male pseudohermaphroditism, *Science* **186:** 1213, 1974.

18 Imperato-McGinley, J., R. E. Peterson, T. Gautier, and E. Sturla, Androgens and the evolution of male gender identity in male pseudohermaphrodites with 5α-reductase deficiency, *N Engl J Med* **300:** 1233, 1979.

Part III

Social and Personality Development

How to Succeed in Childhood

Introduction

Perhaps no thesis has engendered more attention and controversy in recent years than that of Judith Rich Harris'. In an award-winning article in the *Psychological Review*, she reviewed research from developmental psychology, developmental biology, personality, cognitive psychology, learning theory, psycholinguistics, and social psychology to argue that peers matter more than parents.

In the following article, Harris points out that she does not claim that genes are unimportant in social development – indeed, she argues that developmental psychologists have overestimated the power of the social environment, and have overlooked the relative ineffectiveness of advice given to parents. She asserts that the peer group, perhaps for reasons having to do with its survival value over the millennia, is a far stronger force in children's lives than are parents. Granted, parental values and dicta have an influence on how children behave while in the parental home; however, once children venture into the larger social world it is their peer group that determines how they will behave, which language or accent they will adopt, and whether they will endorse certain values.

Harris reserves her ire most for those who assume, with few convincing data, that children grow into responsible adults by modeling what they observe at home. As you will see from her article, she claims the effectiveness of parents ends at the family doorstep; when children go outside, it is their peers' values and aspirations that count most. Some scholars have disagreed with Harris's position, but to her credit she has advanced the debate enormously by forcing those who espouse traditional views about the potency of parents to "put up or shut up," as it were. Harris has correctly noted that the implicit assumptions researchers make have not always been supported by rigorous empirical studies.

Further reading

Harris, J. R. (1995). Where is the child's environment?: a group socialization theory of development. *Psychological Review, 102*, 458–89.

LeDoux, J. E. (1998). Nature vs. nurture: the pendulum still swings with plenty of momentum. *Chronicle of Higher Education*, December 11, 87–8.

Williams, W. M. (1998). Do parents matter? Scholars need to explain what research really shows. "Point of View" Invited Editorial, *Chronicle of Higher Education*, December 11, B6–B7.

SIX

How to Succeed in Childhood

Judith Rich Harris

Every day, tell your children that you love them. Hug them at least once every 24 hours. Never hit them. If they do something wrong, don't say, "You're bad!" Say, "What you did was bad." No, wait – even that might be too harsh. Say, instead, "What you did made me unhappy."

The people who are in the business of giving out this sort of advice are very angry at me, and with good reason. I'm the author of *The Nurture Assumption* – the book that allegedly claims that "parents don't matter." Though that's not what the book actually says, the advice givers are nonetheless justified in their anger. I don't pull punches, and I'm not impressed by their air of benevolent omniscience. Their advice is based not on scientific evidence but on prevailing cultural myths.

The advice isn't wrong; it's just ineffective. Whether parents do or don't follow it has no measurable effect on how their children turn out. There is a great deal of evidence that the differences in how parents rear their children are not responsible for the differences among the children. I've reviewed this evidence in my book; I will not do it again here.

Let me, however, bring one thing to your attention: the advice given to parents in the early part of this century was almost the mirror image of the advice that is given today. In the early part of this century, parents were not warned against damaging their children's self-esteem; they were warned against "spoiling" them. Too much attention and affection were thought to be bad for kids. In those days, spanking was considered not just the parents' right but their duty.

Partly as a result of the major retoolings in the advice industry, child-rearing styles have changed drastically over the course of this century. Although abusive parents have always existed, run-of-the-mill parents – the large majority of the population – administer more hugs and fewer spankings than they used to.

Now ask yourself this: Are children turning out better? Are they happier and better adjusted than they were in the earlier part of the century? Less aggressive? Less anxious? Nicer?

It was Sigmund Freud who gave us the idea that parents are the be-all and end-all of the child's world. According to Freudian theory, children learn right from wrong – that is, they learn to behave in ways their parents and their society deem acceptable – by identifying with their parents. In the calm after the storm of the oedipal crisis, or the reduced-for-quick-sale female version of the oedipal crisis, the child supposedly identifies with the parent of the same sex.

Freud's name is no longer heard much in academic departments of psychology, but the theory that children learn how to behave by identifying with their parents is still accepted. Every textbook in developmental psychology (including, I confess, the one I co-authored) has its obligatory photo of a father shaving and a little boy pretending to shave. Little boys imitate their fathers, little girls imitate their mothers, and, according to the theory, that's how children learn to be grownups. It takes them a while, of course, to perfect the act.

It's a theory that could have been thought up only by a grownup. From the child's point of view, it makes no sense at all. What happens when children try to behave like grownups is that, more often than not, it gets them into trouble. Consider this story, told by Selma Fraiberg, a child psychologist whose book *The Magic Years* was popular in the 1960s:

> Thirty-month-old Julia finds herself alone in the kitchen while her mother is on the telephone. A bowl of eggs is on the table. An urge is experienced by Julia to make scrambled eggs. . . . When Julia's mother returns to the kitchen, she finds her daughter cheerfully plopping eggs on the linoleum and scolding herself sharply for each plop, "NoNoNo. Mustn't dood it! NoNoNo. *Mustn't* dood it!"

Fraiberg attributed Julia's lapse to the fact that she had not yet acquired a superego, presumably because she had not yet identified with her mother. But look at what was Julia doing when her mother came back and caught her egg-handed: she was imitating her mother! And yet Mother was not pleased.

Children cannot learn how to behave appropriately by imitating their parents. Parents do all sorts of things that children are not allowed to do – I don't have to list them, do I? – and many of them look like fun to people who are not allowed to do them. Such prohibitions are found not only in our own society but everywhere, and involve not only activities such as making scrambled eggs but patterns of social behavior as well. Around the world, children who behave too much like grownups are considered impertinent.

Sure, children sometimes pretend to be adults. They also pretend to be horses and monsters and babies, but that doesn't mean they aspire to be horses or monsters or babies. Freud jumped to the wrong conclusions, and so did several generations of developmental psychologists. A child's goal is not to become an adult; a child's goal is to be a successful child.

What does it take to be a successful child? The child's first job is to learn how to get along with her parents and siblings and to do the things that are expected of her at home. This is a very important job – no question about it. But it is only the first of the child's jobs, and in the long run it is overshadowed in importance by the child's second job: to learn how to get along with the members of her own generation and to do the things that are expected of her outside the home.

Almost every psychologist, Freudian or not, believes that what the child learns (or doesn't learn) in job 1 helps her to succeed (or fail) in job 2. But this belief is based on an obsolete idea of how the child's mind works, and there is good evidence that it is wrong.

Consider the experiments of developmental psychologist Carolyn Rovee-Collier. A young baby lies on its back in a crib. A mobile with dangling doodads hangs overhead. A ribbon runs from the baby's right ankle to the mobile in such a way that whenever the baby kicks its right leg, the doodads jiggle. Babies are delighted to discover that they can make something happen; they quickly learn how to make the mobile move. Two weeks later, if you show them the mobile again, they will immediately start kicking that right leg.

But only if you haven't changed anything. If the doodads hanging from the mobile are blue instead of red, or if the liner surrounding the crib has a pattern of squares instead of circles, or if the crib is placed in a different room, they will gape at the mobile cluelessly, as if they've never seen such a thing in their lives.

It's not that they're stupid. Babies enter the world with a mind designed for learning and they start using it right away. But the learning device comes with a warning label: what you learn in one situation might not work in another. Babies do not assume that what they learned about the mobile with the red doodads will work for the mobile with the blue doodads. They do not assume that what worked in the bedroom will work in the den. And they do not assume that what worked with their mother will work with their father or the babysitter or their jealous big sister or the kids at the daycare center.

Fortunately, the child's mind is equipped with plenty of storage capacity. As the cognitive scientist Steven Pinker put it in his foreword to my book, "Relationships with parents, with siblings, with peers, and with strangers could not be more different, and the trillion-synapse human brain is hardly short of the computational power it would take to keep each one in a separate mental account."

That's exactly what the child does: keeps each one in a separate mental account. Studies have shown that a baby with a depressed mother behaves in a subdued fashion in the presence of its mother, but behaves normally with a caregiver who is not depressed. A toddler taught by his mother to play elaborate fantasy games does not play these games when he's with his playmates – he and his playmates devise their own games. A preschooler who has perfected the delicate art of getting along with a bossy older sibling is no more likely than a first-born to allow her peers in nursery school to dominate her. A school-age child who says she hates her younger brother – they fight like cats and dogs, their mother complains – is as likely as any other child to have warm and serene peer relationships. Most telling, the child who follows the rules at home, even when no one is watching, may lie or cheat in the schoolroom or on the playground, and vice versa.

Children learn separately how to behave at home and how to behave outside the home, and parents can influence only the way they behave at home. Children behave differently in different social settings because different behaviors are required. Displays of emotion that are acceptable at home are not acceptable outside the home. A clever remark that would be rewarded with a laugh at home will land a child in the principal's office at school. Parents are often surprised to discover that the child they see at home is not the child the teacher sees. I imagine teachers get tired of hearing parents exclaim, "Really! Are you sure you're talking about *my* child?"

The compartmentalized world of childhood is vividly illustrated by the child of immigrant parents. When immigrants settle in a neighborhood of native-born Americans, their children become bicultural, at least for a while. At home they practice their parents' culture and language, outside the home they adopt the culture and language of their peers. But though their two worlds are separate, they are not equal. Little by little, the outside world takes precedence: the children adopt the language and culture of their peers and bring that language and culture home. Their parents go on addressing them in Russian or Korean or Portuguese, but the children reply in English. What the children of immigrants end up with is not a compromise, not a blend. They end up, pure and simple, with the language and culture of their peers. The only aspects of their parents' culture they retain are things that are carried out at home, such as cooking.

Late-twentieth-century native-born Americans of European descent are as ethnocentric as the members of any other culture. They think there is only one way to raise children – the way they do it. But that is not the way children are reared in the kinds of cultures studied by anthropologists and ethologists. The German ethologist Irenäus Eibl-Eibesfeldt has described what childhood is like in the hunter-gatherer and tribal societies he spent many years observing.

In traditional cultures, the baby is coddled for two or three years – carried about by its mother and nursed whenever it whimpers. Then, when the next baby comes along, the child is sent off to play in the local play group, usually in the care of an older sibling. In his 1989 book *Human Ethology*, Eibl-Eibesfeldt describes how children are socialized in these societies:

> Three-year-old children are able to join in a play group, and it is in such play groups that children are truly raised. The older ones explain the rules of play and will admonish those who do not adhere to them, such as by taking something away from another or otherwise being aggressive. Thus

the child's socialization occurs mainly within the play group. . . . By playing together in the children's group the members learn what aggravates others and which rules they must obey. This occurs in most cultures in which people live in small communities.

Once their tenure in their mothers' arms has ended, children in traditional cultures become members of a group. This is the way human children were designed to be reared. They were designed by evolution to become members of a group, because that's the way our ancestors lived for millions of years. Throughout the evolution of our species, the individual's survival depended upon the survival of his or her group, and the one who became a valued member of that group had an edge over the one who was merely tolerated.

Human groups started out small: in a hunter-gatherer band, everyone knows everyone else and most are blood relatives. But once agriculture began to provide our ancestors with a more or less dependable supply of food, groups got bigger. Eventually they became large enough that not everyone in them knew everyone else. As long ago as 1500 bc they were sometimes that large. There is a story in the Old Testament about a conversation Joshua had with a stranger, shortly before the Battle of Jericho. They met outside the walls of the beleaguered town, and Joshua's first question to the stranger was, "Are you for us or for our adversaries?"

Are you one of *us* or one of *them?* The group had become an idea, a concept, and the concept was defined as much by what you weren't as by what you were. And the answer to the question could be a matter of life or death. When the walls came tumbling down, Joshua and his troops killed every man, woman, and child in Jericho. Even in Joshua's time, genocide was not a novelty: fighting between groups, and wholesale slaughter of the losers, had been going on for ages. According to the evolutionary biologist Jared Diamond, it is "part of our human and prehuman heritage."

Are you one of *us* or one of *them?* It was the question African Americans asked of Colin Powell. It was the question deaf people asked of a Miss America who couldn't hear very well but who preferred to communicate in a spoken language. I once saw a six-year-old go up to a 14-year-old and ask him, "Are you a kid or a grownup?"

The human mind likes to categorize. It is not deterred by the fact that nature often fails to arrange things in convenient clumps but instead provides a continuum. We have no difficulty splitting up continua. Night and day are as different as, well, night and day, even though you can't tell where one leaves off and the other begins. The mind constructs categories for people – male or female, kid or grownup, white or black, deaf or hearing – and does not hesitate to draw the lines, even if it's sometimes hard to decide whether a particular individual goes on one side or the other.

Babies only a few months old can categorize. By the time they reach their first birthday, they are capable of dividing up the members of their social world into categories based on age and sex: they distinguish between men and women, between adults and children. A preference for the members of their own social category also shows up early. One-year-olds are wary of strange adults but are attracted to other children, even ones they've never met before. By the age of two, children are beginning to show a preference for members of their own sex. This preference grows steadily stronger over the next few years. School-age girls and boys will play together in places where there aren't many children, but when they have a choice of playmates, they tend to form all-girl and all-boy groups. This is true the world around.

The brain we won in the evolutionary lottery gave us the ability to categorize, and we use that skill on people as well as things. Our long evolutionary history of fighting with other groups predisposes us to identify with one social category, to like our own category best, and to feel wary of (or hostile toward) members of other categories. The emotions and motivations that were originally applied to real physical groups are now applied to groups that are only concepts: "Americans" or "Democrats" or "the class of 2001." You don't have to like the other members of your group in order to consider yourself one of them; you don't even have to know who they are. The British social psychologist Henri Tajfel asked his subjects – a bunch of Bristol schoolboys – to estimate the number of dots flashed on a screen. Then half the boys were privately told that they were "overestimators," the others that they were "underestimators." That was all it took to make them favor their own group. They didn't even know which of their schoolmates were in their group and which were in the other.

The most famous experiment in social psychology is the Robber's Cave study. Muzafer Sherif and his colleagues started with 22 11-year-old boys, carefully selected to be as alike as possible, and divided them into two equal groups. The groups – the "Rattlers" and the "Eagles" – were separately transported to the Robber's Cave summer camp in a wilderness area of Oklahoma. For a while, neither group knew of the other's existence. But the first time the Rattlers heard the Eagles playing in the distance, they reacted with hostility. They wanted to "run them off." When the boys were brought together in games arranged by researchers disguised as camp counselors, push quickly came to shove. Before long, the two groups were raiding each other's cabins and filling socks with stones in preparation for retaliatory raids.

When people are divided (or divide themselves) into two groups, hostility is one common result. The other, which happens more reliably though it is less well known, is called the "group contrast effect." The mere division into two groups tends to make each group see the other as different from itself in an unfavorable way, and that makes its members *want* to be different from the other group. The result is that any pre-existing differences between the groups tend to widen, and if there aren't any differences to begin with, the members create them. Groups develop contrasting norms, contrasting images of themselves.

In the Robber's Cave study, it happened very quickly. Within a few days of their first encounter, the Eagles had decided that the Rattlers used too many "cuss-words" and resolved to give up cussing; they began to say a prayer before every game. The Rattlers, who saw themselves as tough and manly, continued to favor scatology over eschatology. If an Eagle turned an ankle or skinned a knee, it was all right for him to cry. A Rattler who sustained a similar injury might cuss a bit, but he would bear up stoically.

The idea for group socialization theory came to me while I was reading an article on juvenile delinquency. The article reported that breaking the law is highly common among adolescents, even among those who were well behaved as children and who are destined to turn into law-abiding adults. This unendearing foible was attributed to the frustration teenagers experience at not being adults: they are longing for the power and privilege of adulthood.

"Wait a minute," I thought. "That's not right. If teenagers really wanted to be adults, they wouldn't be spraying graffiti on overpasses or swiping nail polish from drugstores. If they really wanted to emulate adults they would be doing boring adult things, like sorting the laundry or figuring out their taxes. Teenagers aren't trying to be like adults; they are trying to *contrast* themselves with adults! They are showing their loyalty to their own group and their disdain for adult's rules!"

I don't know what put the idea into my head; at the time, I didn't know beans about social psychology. It took eight months of reading to fill the gaps in my education. What I learned in those eight months was that there is a lot of good evidence to back up my hunch, and that it applies not only to teenagers but to young children as well.

Sociologist William Corsaro has spent many years observing nursery school children in the United States and Italy. Here is his description of four-year-olds in an Italian *scuola materna*, a government-sponsored nursery school:

> In the process of resisting adult rules, the children develop a sense of community and a group identity. [I would have put it the other way around: I think group identity leads to the resistance.] The children's resistance to adult rules can be seen as a routine because it is a daily occurrence in the nursery school and is produced in a style that is easily recognizable to members of the peer culture. Such activity is often highly exaggerated (for instance, making faces behind the teacher's back or running around) or is prefaced by "calls for the attention" of other children (such as, "look what I got" in reference to possession of a forbidden object, or "look what I'm doing" to call attention to a restricted activity.

Group contrast effects show up most clearly when "groupness" – Henri Tajfel's term – is salient. Children see adults as serious and sedentary, so when the social categories *kids* and *grownups* are salient – as they might be, for instance, when the teacher is being particularly bossy – the children become sillier and more active. They demonstrate their fealty to their own age group by making faces and running around.

This has nothing to do with whether they like their teachers personally. You can like people even if they're members of a different group and even if you don't much like that group – a conflict of interests summed up in the saying, "Some of my best friends are Jews." When groupness is salient, even young children contrast themselves with adults and collude with each other in defying them. And yet some of their best friends are grownups.

Learning how to behave properly is complicated, because proper behavior depends on which social category you're in. In every society, the rules of behavior depend on whether you're a grownup or a kid, a female or a male, a prince or a peon. Children first have to figure out the social categories that are relevant in their society, and then decide which category they belong in, then tailor their behavior to the other members of their category.

That brief description seems to imply that socialization makes children more alike, and so it does, in some ways. But groups also work to create or exaggerate differences among their members – differences in personality. Even identical twins reared in the same home do not have identical personalities. When groupness is not salient – when there is no other group around to serve as a foil – a group tends to fall apart into individuals, and differences among them emerge or increase. In boy's groups, for example, there is usually a dominance hierarchy, or "pecking order." I have found evidence that dominant boys develop different personalities from those at the bottom of the ladder.

Groups also typecast their members, pinning labels on them – joker, nerd, brain – that can have lifelong repercussions. And children find out about themselves by comparing themselves with their group mates. They come to think well or poorly of themselves by judging how they compare with the other members of their own group. It doesn't matter if they don't measure up to the standards of another group. A third-grade boy can think of himself as smart if he knows more than most of his fellow third-graders. He doesn't have to know more than a fourth-grader.

According to my theory, the culture acts upon children not through their parents but through the peer group. Children's groups have their own cultures, loosely based on the adult culture. They can pick and choose from the adult culture, and it's impossible to predict what they'll include. Anything that's common to the majority of the kids in the group may be incorporated into the children's culture, whether they learned it from their parents or from the television set. If most of the children learned to say "please" and "thank you" at home, they will probably continue to do so when they're with their peers. The child whose parents failed to teach her that custom will pick it up from the other children: it will be transmitted to her, via the peer group, from the parents of her peers. Similarly, if most of the children watch a particular TV show, the behaviors and attitudes depicted in the show may be incorporated into the norms of their group. The child whose parents do not permit him to watch that show will nonetheless be exposed to those behaviors and attitudes. They are transmitted to him via the peer group.

Thus, even though individual parents may have no lasting effects on their children's behavior, the larger culture does have an effect. Child-rearing practices common to most of the people in a culture, such as teaching children to say "please" and "thank you," can have an effect. And the media can have an effect.

In the hunter-gatherer or tribal society, there was no privacy: everybody knew what everybody else was doing. Nowadays children can't ordinarily watch their neighbors making love, having babies, fighting, and dying, but they can watch these things happening on the television screen. Television has become their window on society, their village square. They take what they see on the screen to be an indication of what life is like – what life is supposed to be – and they incorporate it into their children's cultures.

One of my goals in writing *The Nurture Assumption* was to lighten some of the burdens of modern parenthood. Back in the 1940s, when I was young, the parents of a troublesome child – my parents, for instance – got sympathy, not blame. Nowadays parents are likely to be held culpable for anything that goes wrong with their child, even if they've done their best. The evidence I've assembled in my book indicates that there is a limit to what parents can do: how their child turns out is largely out of their hands. Their major contribution occurs at the moment of conception. This doesn't mean it's mostly genetic; it means that the environment that shapes the child's personality and social behavior is outside the home.

I am not advocating irresponsibility. Parents are in charge of how their children behave at home. They can decide where their children will grow up and, at least in the early years, who their peers will be. They are the chief determiners of whether their children's life at home will be happy or miserable, and they have a moral obligation to keep it from being miserable. My theory does not grant people the license to treat children in a cruel or negligent way.

Although individual parents have little power to influence the culture of children's peer groups, larger numbers of parents acting together have a great deal of power, and so does the society as a whole. Through the prevailing methods of child rearing it fosters, and through influences – especially the media – that act directly on peer-group norms and values, a society shapes the adults of the future. Are we shaping them the way we ought to?

Genes, Environment, and Personality

Introduction

In the next article, Bouchard briefly reviews the nature–nurture evidence from three large twin registries. He shows that approximately 40 percent of the variance in personality characteristics is genetically influenced. This value is slightly lower than the heritability estimates endorsed a generation ago, a result of more sophisticated mathematical models and complex thinking on the part of current behavior geneticists. It is also somewhat lower than the 0.5 heritability for general intelligence which is noted in reading 12 by Plomin and DeFries. Bouchard notes that the genes one inherits drive the selection of environments, prodding people to approach certain activities and avoid others.

Perhaps the most important message in Bouchard's article is that most of the similarity among members of the same family is the result of genes. He argues that if we want to identify environmental factors that shape personality, we should "look for influences that operate differentially among children in the same family" (p. 1701).

Further reading

Bouchard, T. J., Jr., and McGue, M. (1990). Genetic and environmental influences on adult personality: an analysis of adopted twins reared apart. *Journal of Personality*, 58, 263–92.

SEVEN

Genes, Environment, and Personality
Thomas J. Bouchard Jr.

The idea that genetic factors influence behavior, including personality, is very old. The most compelling evidence has always been, as Darwin[1] noted, the successful domestication of animals.

> So in regard to mental qualities, their transmission is manifest in our dogs, horses and other domestic animals. Besides special tastes and habits, general intelligence, courage, bad and good tempers, etc., are certainly transmitted.

Unlike genetic influences on the intelligence quotient, which have been studied continuously since the time of Galton a century ago, the study of genetic influences on personality has had a much briefer history. Although Galton discussed genetic influence on personality, the lack of reliable and valid measures of personality qualities hampered progress. In addition, until recently, psychologists could not agree on which were the important traits of personality. Currently there is a modest consensus that five broad traits or "super factors" are necessary to describe personality – extraversion, neuroticism, conscientiousness, agreeableness, and openness[2] (see table 1).

Until the early 1980s, the evidence for genetic influence on personality derived almost exclusively from twin studies that utilized very modest sample sizes and measured different variables. Heritability was estimated as twice the difference between the correlation for identical or

Table 1 Five main determinants of personality

Extraversion: Surgency, Introversion-Extraversion (–), Dominance, *Positive Emotionality*

Is outgoing, decisive, persuasive, and enjoys leadership roles	Is retiring, reserved, withdrawn, and does not enjoy being the center of attention

Neuroticism: Anxiety, Emotional Stability (–), Stress Reactivity, *Negative Emotionality*

Is emotionally unstable, nervous, irritable, and prone to worry	Quickly gets over upsetting experiences, stable, and not prone to worries and fears

Conscientiousness: Conformity, Dependability, Authoritarianism (–), *Constraint*

Is planful, organized, responsible, practical, and dependable	Is impulsive, careless, irresponsible, and cannot be depended upon

Agreeableness: Likability, Friendliness, Pleasant, *Aggression (–)*

Is sympathetic, warm, kind, good-natured, and will not take advantage of others	Is quarrelsome, aggressive, unfriendly, cold, and vindictive

Openness: Culture, Intellect, Sophistication, Imagination, *Absorption*

Is insightful, curious, original, imaginative, and open to novel experiences and stimuli	Has narrow interests, is unintelligent, unreflective, and shallow

---

Negative signs indicate trait names that characterized to opposite end of the dimension. The italic trait terms indicate the Multidimensional Personality Questionnaire factors or scales used to measure these five characteristics in the Minnesota study of twins reared apart.

monozygotic (MZ) twins and that for fraternal or dizygotic (DZ) twins. The typical conclusion was that about 50 percent of the observed variance in personality is due to genetic factors.[3] The influence on personality of the shared home environment (estimated as twice the DZ correlation minus the MZ value) was concluded to be small or even negligible. These simple equations make a number of assumptions, including (1) on average DZ twins share half as many genes in common by descent as MZ twins, (2) the genes act additively, and (3) MZ and DZ twins experience the same shared environmental influences. If the assumptions are correct, the difference between the two types of twins reflects one-half the genetic influence on the trait being studied.

The conclusion that 50 percent of the variation in personality is genetic was not universally embraced. Many psychologists questioned that MZ and DZ twins experience the same home environment and ascribed much of the greater similarity of MZ twins over DZ twins to more similar environmental treatment of the MZ than the DZ twins. It also seemed implausible to psychologists that being reared in the same home would have so little influence on sibling similarity. Consequently these findings were not generally accepted outside of behavioral genetics.

In recent years, three trends have converged to transform our understanding of genetic and environmental influences on personality traits. First, studies of twins reared together with very large sample sizes, in some instances over 2,000 pairs of each sex and zygosity, have been carried out. Second, data have been gathered from monozygotic and dizygotic twins reared apart (MZA and DZA), as well as from both biological and adoptive families. Third, powerful methods of model fitting have been introduced that allow full utilization of the available information and statistical testing of competing hypotheses.[4,5]

Figure 1 compares the results of the early twin studies, an analysis of an extremely large data set assembled by Loehlin,[6] and our own analysis of MZA ($n = 59$) and DZA ($n = 47$) data from the Minnesota study of twins reared apart (MISTRA) and MZT ($n = 522$) and DZT ($n = 408$) twins from the Minnesota Twin Registry.[7] The Loehlin analysis yields an estimated genetic influence of 42 percent (with a sizable contribution from nonadditive genetic factors – influences that are configural and not inherited in a simple additive manner) and a very modest contribution of the shared environment. The most parsimonious fit to the Minnesota data is a simple additive genetic model for all five traits with an estimate of genetic influence of 46 percent. Addition of nonadditive genetic and shared environmental parameters does not, however, significantly change the fit of the model, and those data are shown in the figure for comparison with the Loehlin analysis. Both approaches yield estimates of genetic influence of just over 40 percent and modest estimates of shared environmental influence (7 percent). Of the remaining variance, about half is due to nonshared environmental influences and half to error of measurement. Thus, about two-thirds of

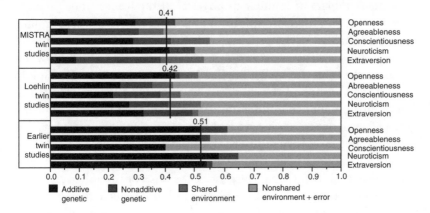

Figure 1   Sources of variation in personality in three sets of data

the reliable variance in measured personality traits is due to genetic influence.

The early studies of twins appear to have only slightly overestimated the degree of genetic influence on personality variation, and the main contribution of the more sophisticated recent analyses is that some of the genetic influence seems to be due to nonadditive genetic variance for all five traits. All three analyses yield quite small estimates of shared environmental influence. This is now a well-replicated finding in behavior genetics, and its implications are straightforward. The similarity we see in personality between biological relatives is almost entirely genetic in origin. If we wish to study environmental influences on personality development in families, we must look for influences that operate differentially among children in the same family.[8]

However, simply demonstrating that systematic differences in treatment within the family exist does not suffice to prove that such treatments explain personality differences. First, the treatment may have no effect. For example, differences in socialization due to birth order exist, but contrary to widespread belief,[9] they do not influence personality.[10] Second, as Lytton[11] has demonstrated, the differential behavior of children is often the cause of differential parental behavior rather than a consequence. Third, arguments as to the purported importance of environmental factors in shaping personality, though superficially plausible, often fail to stand up to scrutiny when subjected to quantitative analysis. Consider physical attractiveness. It is often argued that because twins reared apart are similar in physical attractiveness they must be treated alike, and therefore this is an important source of their similarity in personality.[9,12] The problem with this argument is that physical attractiveness is so poorly correlated with personality traits that, when numbers are fit to the model implied by the argument, it can explain only a trivial portion of the similarity between MZA twins.[8,10] In truth, how nontraumatic environmental determinants influence the normal range of variance in adult personality remains largely a mystery. This variation may even turn out to be the equivalent of noise.[13]

Current thinking holds that each individual picks and chooses from a range of stimuli and events largely on the basis of his or her genotype and creates a unique set of experiences – that is, people help to create their own environments.[14] This view of human development does not deny the existence of inadequate and debilitating environments nor does it minimize the role of learning. Rather, it views humans as dynamic creative organisms for whom the opportunity to learn and to experience new environments amplifies the effects of the genotype on the phenotype. It also reminds us of our links to the biological world and our evolutionary history. This brings us to the core problem of the genetics of personality – the function of the variation in personality traits. The purpose of this variation is undoubtedly rooted in the fact that humans have adapted to life in face-to-face groups (sociality). Unraveling the role human individual differences play in evolution is the next big hurdle,[15] and its solution will turn the behavior genetics of human personality from a descriptive discipline to an explanatory one.

References

1 C. Darwin, *The Descent of Man and Selection in Relation to Sex* (Murray, London, 1871; reprinted by Modern Library, New York, 1967).
2 L. R. Goldberg, *Am. Psychol.* **48**, 26 (1993).
3 R. C. Nichols, *Homo* **29**, 158 (1978).
4 L. J. Eaves, H. J. Eysenck, N. G. Martin, *Genes, Culture and Personality: An Empirical Approach* (Academic Press, New York, 1989).
5 M. C. Neale and L. R. Cardon, eds, *Methodology for Genetic Studies of Twins and Families* (Kluwer Academic, Dordrecht, 1992).
6 J. C. Loehlin, *Genes and Environment in Personality Development* (Sage, Newbury Park, CA, 1992).
7 T. J. Bouchard Jr., D. T. Lykken, M. McGue, N. L. Segal, A. Tellegen, *Science* **250**, 223 (1990).

8 D. Rowe, *The Limits of Family Influence: Genes, Experience, and Behavior* (Guilford, New York, 1994).

9 L. W. Hoffman, *Psychol. Bull.* **110**, 187 (1991).

10 T. J. Bouchard Jr., in *Basic Issues in Personality*, I. Deary and J. Hettema, eds (Kluwer Academic, Dordrecht, 1993).

11 H. Lytton, *Dev. Psychol.* **26**, 705 (1990).

12 B. D. Ford, *Am. Psychol.* **48**, 1294 (1993).

13 P. C. M. Molenar, D. I. Boomsma, C. V. Dolan, *Behav. Genet.* **6**, 519 (1993).

14 S. Scarr, *Child Dev.* **63**, 1 (1992).

15 D. M. Buss, in *Twins as a Tool of Behavioral Genetics*, T. J. Bouchard Jr. and P. Propping, eds (Wiley, Chichester, 1993).

Part IV

Infancy and Early Childhood Influences on IQ Development

Developmental Catch-up, and Deficit, Following Adoption After Severe Global Early Privation

Introduction

Rutter and his colleagues provide data that argue convincingly for the plasticity of human development, at least within certain limits. Over a hundred Romanian babies came to the UK following early experiences that were characterized by severe neglect. Half of these children were below the third percentile in body size, head circumference, and developmental level. Yet, if they entered the UK by six months of age, they made remarkable recoveries, becoming almost indistinguishable from English babies that were adopted. Children who were not adopted until they were older did not fare as well, however. In fact, age of entry to the UK was the single biggest factor in predicting cognitive status at age four. Clearly, nurture matters; notwithstanding the possibility of large genetic influences operating among these adoptees, Rutter et al.'s data show that the environment, particularly when it is seriously deprived, can exact a significant toll on children's physical and intellectual functioning.

Rutter et al.'s findings are chock full of fascinating results. One particularly intriguing result is that although there was a modest correlation between head circumference and IQ at age four (0.25), there was not the expected correlation between head circumference at the time these children entered the UK and their later IQ at age four. Romanian children who entered the UK late and whose IQs were sub-average (91.7–96.7) were no smaller than their peers who were adopted earlier but whose IQs were between 105.9 and 115.7. Even having a head circumference below the third percentile – usually taken as an index of severe malnutrition – was not predictive of the later IQ being low. An important, but only suggested, finding was that Romanian adoptees who came late to the UK (but who prior to coming were not in institutional care) fared much like the Romanian babies who had entered the UK prior to six months.

Rutter et al.'s findings provide strong support for the power of the environment to shape cognitive outcomes. Future research will be needed to determine the specific factors that actually *cause* good versus poor cognitive outcomes in various developmental contexts.

Further reading

Skuse, D. (1984). Extreme deprivation in early childhood. *Journal of Child Psychology and Psychiatry*, 25, 543–72. (This article provides a theoretical review of the issues involved in recovery from extreme deprivation, while reading 9 provides a fascinating glimpse into the recovery of a specific form of abuse that is so severe as to lead to physical stunting.)

EIGHT

Developmental Catch-up, and Deficit, Following Adoption after Severe Global Early Privation

Michael Rutter and the English and Romanian Adoptees (ERA) study team†

Introduction

Over the years, sharply divergent opinions have been expressed about the long-term importance for psychological development of experiences in the first two years of life. Some have viewed them as having a critical and lasting impact that is difficult to alter (Pilling and Pringle, 1978). Others have doubted their effects because of infants' limited ability to process their experiences cognitively (Kagan, 1984). Some have emphasized the high potential for radical change after the early years (Clarke and Clarke, 1976), and yet others have seen the long-term consequences as dependent on the cumulative impact of experiences beginning in infancy (Lipsitt, 1983). Determination of the specific effects of early experiences, as distinct from those of later experiences, has been difficult because of the strong associations between the two in most ordinary circumstances (Rutter, 1981). There has had to be reliance on the rare cases of individual children rescued after rearing in extremely

† Lucie Andersen-Wood, Celia Beckett, Diana Bredenkamp, Jenny Castle, Judy Dunn, Kathryn Ehrich, Christine Groothues, Alexandra Harborne, Dale Hay, Jessica Jewett, Lisa Keaveney, Jana Kreppner, Julie Messer, Thomas O'Connor, David Quinton, and Adele White.

abnormal circumstances such as being isolated in cellars (Skuse, 1984), follow-up studies of severely abused/neglected children showing growth failure (Money, Annecillo, and Kelley, 1983a, 1983b), or the few follow-up studies of children adopted after early privation (Colombo, De la Parra, and Lopez, 1992; Lien, Meyer, and Winick, 1977; Winick, Meyer, and Harris, 1975). The findings have given rise to the view that it is usual for there to be rapid recovery following "rescue" and provision of a normal rearing environment (Skuse, 1984). However some of the samples were very small (e.g. only 16 adoptees in the Colombo et al. study, 1992); the relevant data were sparse; and outcome has often had to be evaluated only in relation to outdated general population norms. The follow-up was often incomplete (for example, a third of the children were not traced in Winick et al.'s study of Korean orphans; and IQ data were available on only just over half of those followed into school). The assessments have also been limited in scope. With the exception of two recent studies of Canadian adoptees from Romania (Ames, 1997; Chisholm, Carter, Ames, and Morison, 1995; Fisher, Ames, Chisholm, and Savoie, 1997; Marcovitch et al., 1997), there are virtually no published data on children's social functioning following severe early privation.

There is a much larger literature on the physical catch-up of children severely malnourished in infancy (see review by Martorell, Kettel Khan, and Schroeder, 1994). The evidence is clear that children who remain in the setting in which they experienced malnutrition and exhibited physical stunting show little or no catch-up in growth later in life. By contrast, major improvements in living conditions (whether by food supplementation or adoption) trigger catch-up growth. This effect is most marked and may be complete if the later life circumstances are really good (as would usually be the case with adoption) and if the change occurs in the first couple of years of life. One study, however, found a reduction in the age of puberty, which may limit ultimate height by curtailing the period of physical growth (Proos, Hofvander, and Tuvemo, 1991a, 1991b).

The opportunity to examine the psychological effects of early global deprivation more systematically arose from the adoption into English families, following the fall of the Ceaucescu regime, of a large number of children reared in the extremely poor conditions of Romanian institutions; a high proportion of such children are known to show severe developmental retardation as well as growth failure and widespread infections, including intestinal parasites (Johnson et al., 1992; Kaler and Freeman, 1994). Compared with previous studies of institution-reared children, there were two major advantages; (1) that the great majority of the children entered institutional care in early infancy, and (2) that the children's age at placement in UK families was largely a function of their age at the time of the fall of the regime. Few children returned from institutions to their biological families in Romania and there were no UK adoptions before the regime fell. Accordingly, it was possible to examine whether the degree of recovery was affected by the length of privation experienced. The study involved a dual strategy: first an examination of recovery following the move to the UK, and consequent radical change in circumstances, allowed an assessment of the degree to which the initial deficits or retardation at the time of entry to the UK were a result of a prior depriving environment; and second, the extent to which the continuation of a deficit could be related to some plausible mediating variable (such as duration of privation or degree of malnutrition) provided a means of inferring causal influences on longer-term outcome (Rutter, 1994).

Sample and Methods

The study was drawn from the 324 children adopted from Romania into families resident in England between February 1990 and September 1992, aged below 42 months at the time of entry to the UK, and dealt with through the legal channels of the UK and/or therefore processed by the UK Department of Health and Home Office. An unknown number of children entered the UK illegally and these were not included in our sampling frame. We also excluded, for practical reasons, those in Scotland, Wales, Ireland, the Isle of Man, and the Channel Isles. Stratified sampling was employed with the aim of obtaining a target number of 13 boys and 13 girls placed between the ages of 0 and 3 months, and 13 placed between 3 and 6 months, and therefore 10 boys and 10 girls in each of the 6-month age bands up to 42 months. Random selection was employed within age bands. In the older age bands, the available numbers fell below target and in these circumstances we took all children into the sample. Eighty-one percent of the parents approached agreed to participate in the study. Half of the children had received an entirely institutional upbringing, four-fifths had been reared in institutions for most of their life, and only 9 percent had been reared throughout in a family setting. The great majority had entered an institution in the neonatal period (the mean age at entry was 0.34 months; $SD = 1.26$).

A comparison group of within-country adoptees, placed before the age of 6 months, was selected through a range of local authority and voluntary adoption agencies. Because the adoption agencies provided us with names of within-country adoptions only after they had contacted parents themselves and obtained their agreement, we do not have exactly comparable figures on the participation rate in that sample. However, from the information available to us, it appears that about half of the parents who were approached agreed to take part.

Ideally, several comparison groups would have been useful. Thus, examination of the effects of adoption would have been facilitated by a study of children who remained in Romanian orphanages and who were not adopted. This seemed redundant in view of the extensive evidence that such children fare very badly (Johnson et al., 1992; Kaler and Freeman, 1994). The choice of early-adopted within-UK adoptees was made on the basis of wanting a "best scenario" group, controlling for the experience of adoption and of rearing in above-average homes, but differing with respect to an absence of severe early nutritional and psychological privation.

Inevitably, such a group differed ethnically but most of the Romanian adoptees did not physically appear racially different and, although ethnic issues may be important later (Tizard and Phoenix, 1993), it did not seem likely that they would be so in early childhood. Anthropometrically, ethnic variations seem unlikely to be relevant for our samples (Ulijaszek, 1994) and there is no evidence that they will be relevant for cognitive development. Contrasts according to age of adoption are important but it is essential that they control for prior experiences. Accordingly they are best undertaken within the sample of Romanian adoptees, rather than between groups.

The final sample comprised 111 children whose records indicated that they entered England before the age of 2 years; 54 children who entered between 24 and 42 months; and 52 within-country adoptees. The present report is based solely on the first and third groups, both of whom were assessed at age 4 years (and who are currently being reassessed at age 6 years); the second group were assessed only at age 6 years as they were too old at the start of the study for assessment at age 4.

Both groups of adopting parents had educational attainments and an occupational level above general population norms but there were no statistically significant differences between them in these respects. The main difference between the adopting parents of Romanian children and the adopting parents of UK children was that the former were somewhat older at the time of placement (a mean age of fathers of 39.0 years vs. 36.0 and of mothers of 36.6 vs. 34.2) and included a considerably higher proportion who already had biological children of their own (34 percent vs. 2 percent) and a much lower proportion who had adopted previously (4 percent vs. 40 percent). However, the families adopting from Romania were more likely to have adopted more than one child either at the same time or within a year of the first placement (25 percent vs. 1 percent). Only a quarter of these pairs of adoptions within a year involved biological siblings. Within the group of families adopting children from Romania, there were no significant differences in family characteristics in relation to the children's age at the time of entering the UK.

The children's height, weight, and head circumference were assessed on the basis of both the Romanian records and the physical examinations undertaken at the time the children entered the UK. The Romanian records were rather skimpy and often lacking in detail on the date of the examination but so far as these anthropometric measurements were concerned they agreed reasonably well with those undertaken in the UK. (Pearson product–moment correlations of 0.60 for weight and 0.53 for head circumference) apart from those on height ($r = 0.12$). The intercorrelations between height and weight were nevertheless reasonably comparable for the two sets of assessments (0.45 in UK vs. 0.50 in Romania), as were those between weight and head circumference (0.62 vs. 0.67) and between height and head circumference (0.26 vs. 0.51). There were 14 children for whom we had no measured weight at entry and for 11 of these cases we used the Romanian measurements.

The norms used to derive standard scores for height, weight, and head circumference were based on Buckler (1990). All physical measurements are reported in standard deviation units (Boyce and Cole, 1993). This metric provides a continuous measure of physical development that is not confounded by age. For example, a score of −2.32 for weight indicates that the child's weight is 2.32 standard deviations *below* the UK general population norm for a given age.

Because extremely low anthropometric measures are likely to index nutritional privation, whereas variations within the normal range may not do so, the data were also dealt with in terms of the proportions below the third percentile on UK norms.

Unfortunately, neither the Romanian records nor the assessments at UK entry included systematic quantified developmental assessments. Accordingly, it was necessary to rely on parental reporting. The great majority of parents had baby books giving contemporaneous details of developmental milestones and many also had video recordings. The recall task was also much easier than most both because it referred to an especially memorable time period and because parents were being asked to remember the children's actual behaviour at that time and *not* the dates when particular skills were acquired. In order to derive a quantified dimensional score, the parents were asked to complete Denver Developmental Scales (Frankenburg, van Doorninck, Liddell, and Dick, 1986) retrospectively on the children's performance and attainments at the time of entry to the UK, using whichever contemporaneous records they had available. The Denver Scales are designed to be used by parents to focus on attainments (such as lifting the head, standing whilst holding on, and making meaningful "da-da" sounds) that are readily observable. The scores were transformed into developmental quotients by allocating developmental age according to the age of the item immediately preceding the second failed item, dividing this by the child's chronological age, and multiplying by 100. Especially with retarded babies, such scores can give either a zero quotient because the child is not able to do anything or an unrealistically high quotient because of the effect of one or two passes when dealing with a very small number of items. Accordingly, actual scores were used within the plus and minus 3 SD range but, to reduce the effect of extreme outliners, scores above or below these cut-offs were allocated a random score in the 3 to 4 SD range. The number of scores that had to be dealt with in this way was substantial, mainly because of the large number ($N = 47$) with scores in the severely retarded range but also the few ($N = 10$) with unusually high scores.

The children's developmental level at age 4 years was assessed using the Denver Scales in the same way plus individual testing of the children on the McCarthy Scales (McCarthy, 1972). The General Cognitive Index (GCI) of the McCarthy Scales has been found to correlate highly (0.70s to 0.80s) with Binet and Wechsler IQs (Keith,

1985; McCarthy, 1972). In the case of the few children ($N = 4$) who were untestable on the complete McCarthy Scales of Children's Abilities, the Merrill Palmer Scale or subtests of the McCarthy were used. Based on findings on those scores, it was decided to allocate each of them a randomly generated McCarthy score between 40 and 50 when dealing with the findings dimensionally. In this paper, the general cognitive index of the McCarthy Scales is used throughout. Details of the patterns of cognitive functioning will be presented separately, as will the findings from other language and cognitive measures. In addition, there were detailed measures of socioemotional and behavioural functioning, also reported elsewhere.

Conditions in Romania

Some of the residential institutions were officially labelled "hospitals" and some "orphanages", but in practice there were few major differences between them in that both provided long-term care for children whose parents had given up looking after them for one reason or another. The conditions in these institutions varied from poor to appalling. In most instances the children were mainly confined to cots; there were few, if any, toys or playthings; there was very little talk from caregivers; no personalized caregiving; feeding of gruel by bottles with large teats, often left propped up; and variable, but sometimes harsh, physical environments. Thus, washing often consisted of being hosed down with cold water. These descriptions closely match those provided by other investigators (Groze and Ileana, 1996; Johnson et al., 1992; Kaler and Freeman, 1994). The home conditions of the few children not in institutions were also usually very poor.

Most of the children who entered institutions in the neonatal period remained there (but with some moves between institutions) until they came to the UK. Early family experiences were dealt with by subdividing the sample of adoptees from Romania according to their pattern of family or institutionalized rearing in Romania. Out of the sample of 111, only 18 had been reared in a family setting throughout (with less than two weeks in an institution), another 5 had had family rearing for up to half of their life in Romania, 36 had been reared in institutions for at least half (but not all) of their life (in almost most cases this amounted to nearly all their life), and the largest group (52) had been reared in institutions throughout. Perhaps surprisingly, the pattern of rearing did not differ significantly between those who entered the UK in early infancy (operationally defined as under 6 months) and those who entered the country later. Because there were so few children who experienced small periods of institutional care, the main analyses treated care in terms of a dichotomy according to the presence or absence of institutional rearing for at least two weeks. This variable was used as a predictor, in addition to the child's age at the time of entry to the UK. Of the 58 children who entered the UK under the age of 6 months, 12 had not received institutional care compared with 6 out of 53 for those who entered the UK when aged 6 months or older, a difference that fell well short of statistical significance.

The children's age at the time of entry to the UK was dealt with as a dimensional measure in the first instance because there was no strong a priori reason to expect a nonlinear relationship with outcome. However, because the UK adoptees comparison group had all been placed before the age of 6 months, the outcome findings for the Romanian adoptees was also considered separately according to whether or not entry to the UK was before the age of 6 months.

Adoption breakdown

The rate of adoption breakdown in the Romanian sample was extremely low: 1.8 percent in the group as a whole (i.e. including those who entered the UK at up to 42 months of age). This figure is below that found among within-UK adoptees of comparable age at adoption (Thoburn, 1993).

Results

Results are presented in three segments. First, the developmental status of Romanian adoptees when they entered the UK is discussed. Second, physical growth and cognitive development differences between UK and Romanian adoptees and between subgroups of Romanian adoptees are reported. Third, the predictors of cognitive development at the year 4 assessment are described. Where possible, predictor variables were examined both as dimensional and as categorical variables. This analytic strategy contrasts the prediction of individual differences within the normal range to prediction from extreme group membership (see weight, below). Means analyses are based on analysis of variance

Table 1 Circumstances and conditions of Romanian adoptees before and at the time of entry to UK

	(N)	Mean	SD
Age at first entry to institutional care	(93)	0.34 mths	1.26
Age at leaving institutional care	(93)	8.38 mths	6.34
Age at entering UK	(111)	6.59 mths	5.87
Age-standardized weight as measured in Romania	(98)	−2.44 SD	1.59
Age-standardized weight as measured at UK entry	(97)	−2.37 SD	1.79
Age-standardized weight as measured at UK entry (including subset of cases with weight measured in Romania)	(108)	−2.21 SD	1.66
Age-standardized height as measured in Romania	(94)	−1.96 SD	1.80
Age-standardized height as measured at UK entry	(58)	−1.95 SD	1.96
Age-standardized head circumference as measured in Romania	(91)	−2.27 SD	1.65
Age-standardized head circumference as measured at UK entry	(61)	−2.14 SD	1.80

	(N)	DQ	SD
Retrospective Denver quotient at entry	(98)	62.89	41.24

methods; post hoc comparisons were based on Student–Newman–Keuls test. Regression analyses presented in the third section are based on a simultaneous entry procedure.

Most of the children were in a poor physical state at the time of entry to the UK. Severe malnutrition was the rule; chronic and recurrent respiratory infections were rife; chronic intestinal infections (including giardia) were common; and many of the children had skin disorders of one kind or another.

As table 1 indicates, at the time of entry to the UK the children were severely developmentally impaired on all measures. On both the Romanian and UK assessments, the mean head circumference and weight were more than 2 *SD* below UK norms and the mean height was approximately at the minus 2 *SD* point. Moreover, overall, about half were below the third percentile: 51 percent ($N = 108$) on weight; 34 percent ($N = 58$) on height; and 38 percent ($N = 61$) on head circumference on the UK measures.

The findings on the Denver Scale were closely comparable, with the mean of 63 being in the mildly retarded range. Fifty-nine percent of the children had a developmental quotient below 50 and a further 15 percent had a developmental quotient in the mildly impaired (50–69) range.

Because any assessment of cognitive catch-up is necessarily crucially dependent on the validity of the retrospective Denver scores, it is necessary to examine this matter in some detail. It was tackled in several different ways. First, reference was made to data on children studied in Romanian institutions. Kaler and Freeman (1994) found a mean Bayley mental age of 9.5 months (*SD* 7.0) in their sample at a mean chrono logical age of 35 months; of the 25 children studied, 20 were functioning at levels less than half their chronological age. Second, the Johnson et al. (1992) findings on children from Romania adopted into US families were used as a guide. Only 10 percent of the 31 children aged over 12 months at the time of evaluation shortly after entry into the US were judged to be developmentally normal. Both sets of data are closely in line with our own. Third, in the minority of cases where they were available, we obtained the medical records taken in the UK as soon as possible after entry to the country. Systematic developmental assessments were rarely undertaken but the general descriptions (and specific findings where recorded) were generally in good accord with the parental descriptions. Finally, we used the pattern of correlations (see table 2).

In essence, the main findings are that the Denver score for the child's functioning at the time of UK entry showed a moderate positive correlation with the anthropometric measurements at that time (which would be expected if the score constituted a valid estimate), but weak and statistically nonsignificant correlations with the anthropometric measures at age 4 (the opposite of what would be expected on the basis of a hypothesis that retrospective recall was biased by current status). Similarly, the Denver score at 4 years showed a substantial correlation (0.52) with the McCarthy GCI score at the same age, suggesting moderate contemporaneous validity, a level that is as high as could be expected with a screening measure. The comparable correlation

Table 2 Correlations with Denver quotient (DQ) at entry and at age 4 years

	DQ at entry		DQ at 4 years	
	Score	(N)	Score	(N)
Head circumference (at entry)	0.32*	(58)	0.18	(57)
Head circumference (4 years)	0.17	(89)	0.20	(83)
Height (at entry)	0.29*	(55)	0.22	(54)
Height (4 years)	0.00	(94)	0.23*	(90)
Weight (at entry)[a]	0.34**	(95)	0.11	(90)
Weight (4 years)	0.04	(97)	0.04	(93)
Denver (4 years)	0.45**	(91)	–	–
McCarthy score (4 years)	0.34**	(97)	0.52**	(93)
Whether reared in institution	−0.35**	(98)	−0.19	(93)

[a] *Weight at entry includes weight as measured at entry into UK and subset of cases for which weight in Romania was used.*
*$p < 0.05$; **$p < 0.01$.

for the Denver at UK entry was lower (0.34), again arguing against retrospective bias.

In view of the fact that the Denver is a screening questionnaire, it would not be justifiable to place too much reliance on precise scores. Nevertheless, considered as a whole, the evidence is entirely consistent in indicating that the Romanian adoptees as a group showed major developmental retardation at the time of entry to the UK, that over half were functioning in the retarded range, and that the Denver scores provide a reasonable, albeit rough and ready, rank ordering of the children's level of developmental functioning.

Differences among Romanian adoptees according to experience of institutional rearing

The small subsample of 18 children from Romania who had experienced less than two weeks of institutional care differed markedly from the remainder in being less impaired at the time of UK entry. Thus, their mean initial Denver score was 96.7 ($N = 15$) compared with 56.8 ($N = 83$), and their weight 1.28 SD ($N = 17$) below the UK mean compared with 2.38 SD ($N = 91$) below the UK mean – both differences being statistically significant; $p = 0.0004$ and 0.012 respectively. These differences held within both the group admitted to the UK below the age of 6 months and those admitted when older. The contrasts on the Denver score were 110.4 ($N = 10$) vs. 68.3 ($N = 41$), $p < 0.05$ for the former subgroup and 69.3 ($N = 5$) vs. 45.5 ($N = 42$), $p < 0.05$ for the latter. The comparable figures on weight at entry were $-1.9\,SD$ ($N = 11$) vs. -2.2 ($N = 45$) (not statistically significant) and -0.15 ($N = 6$) vs. -2.6 ($N = 46$), $p < 0.001$. It is evident that these family-reared subgroups constitute a useful internal control of children from Romania who were much less developmentally impaired and, hence, who presumably experienced a much milder set of depriving experiences.

Differences among Romanian adoptees according to age at UK entry

Our research design is dependent on the validity of two key comparisons. The first involves comparability with respect to age of entry to the adopting family of the within-UK adoptees and the Romanian children entering the UK before 6 months of age. The two groups were closely similar in that respect (2.5 months vs. 3.5 months). The main control therefore resides in the very deprived early circumstances of the Romanian children.

The second involves comparability within the Romanian sample, according to age of entry to the UK, with respect to the prior circumstances in Romania and to their anthropometric measurements at the time of entry (see table 3). Good comparability was evident. As already noted, the children admitted to the UK before the age of 6 months did not differ from later admitted children in their experience of rearing in a family setting.

The early admitted children, however, had had a significantly shorter period of family care before entering an institution (0.07 months vs. 0.62 months, $p = 0.03$), but even in the group entering the UK when older, the period of family care was very brief. None of the anthropometric measures differed significantly according to age at entry, although there was a very weak tendency for those admitted when older to be slightly more impaired (e.g. weight at entry was $-2.3\,SD$ as compared with $-2.1\,SD$). The children admitted after 6 months of age, however, had a significantly lower initial Denver score (mean of 48.1 vs. 76.5; $p < 0.001$). In view of the lack of differences on the anthropo-

Table 3   Age and circumstances at entry to UK

	Under 6 months at entry Mean (*SD*)	6 months or older at entry Mean (*SD*)
Weight	−2.1 (1.7)	−2.3 (1.7)
Height	−1.8 (1.6)	−2.2 (2.4)
Head circumference	−2.1 (2.1)	−2.2 (1.3)
Denver quotient	76.5 (48.1)	48.1 (25.4)
Age first in institution[a]	0.07 (0.25)	0.62 (1.7)

[a] Age in months.

metric measures, this probably reflects the limitations of the Denver for assessing developmental level in early infancy.

Developmental catch-up

Physical catch-up by age 4 years was very substantial (see table 4). Compared with the 51 percent below the third percentile in weight at entry to the UK, there were only 2 percent of the Romanian adoptees below the third percentile at 4 years. Similarly, at 4 years, only 1 percent were below the third percentile on height and only 13 percent on head circumference. Nevertheless, the Romanian adoptees as a group were slightly lighter, slightly shorter, and had a slightly smaller head circumference than the within-UK adoptees. By contrast, however, there were no anthropometric differences within the Romanian group according to the age when they entered the UK.

The developmental catch-up was equally impressive, but not quite complete in those placed after the age of 6 months. Both the Denver and McCarthy scores of the Romanian children placed before the age of 6 months were closely comparable with those of the within-UK adoptees, despite the severe physical and developmental retardation evident at the time of entry to the UK (see earlier). The catch-up in cognitive functioning was not a function of family rearing. The mean McCarthy GCI score was 100 for the children who had not experienced institutional rearing and 107 for those who had. The trend

Table 4 Anthropometric and cognitive measures at 4 years

| | Within-UK adoptees | | Romanian adoptees[a] | | | |
| | | | Entry before <6 mths | | Entry at/after ≥6 mths | |
	Mean	(*SD*)	Mean	(*SD*)	Mean	(*SD*)
Anthropometric measurements (standard scores)						
Weight $F(2,154) = 4.21$*[b]	0.45	(0.79)	−0.02	(0.92)	0.04	(0.94)
Height $F(2,151) = 6.57$*[b]	0.25	(0.91)	−0.29	(0.89)	−0.36	(1.02)
Head circumference $F(2,144) = 15.59$**[c]	−0.46	(0.84)	−1.10	(0.96)	−1.50	(0.97)
Cognitive level						
Denver quotient $F(2,128) = 12.03$***[d]	117.7	(24.3)	115.7	(23.4)	96.7	(21.3)
McCarthy GCI $F(2,156) = 15.78$***[d]	109.4	(14.8)	105.9	(17.9)	91.7	(18.00)

[a] *Age at entry <6 months or ≥6 months.*
[b] *UK > 0–6, 6–24;* [c] *UK > 0–6 > 6–24;* [d] *UK 0–6 > 6–24.*
*$p < 0.05$; **$p < 0.01$; ***$p < 0.001$.*

within the institution-reared group for those who experienced some family care to score more highly (113 vs. 104) fell well short of statistical significance.

The mean scores of the Romanian children adopted between the ages of 6 and 24 months were only slightly below 100 but, on both the Denver and McCarthy Scales, they were more than a dozen points below those of the within-UK adoptee group. The fact that the latter had a mean well above 100 emphasizes both the general finding that IQ scores have risen over time (Flynn, 1980) and also that the general population mean is no longer 100 on tests standardized some years ago. If we had relied on test norms instead of having a comparison group, the catch-up would have appeared misleadingly complete.

It is necessary to consider whether the slightly depressed mean cognitive score in the Romanian children adopted after the age of 6 months reflects a general slight shift downwards, or a subgroup of intellectually impaired children, or both. The findings showed that there was both a slight shift downwards in the group as a whole and a small subgroup (*N*

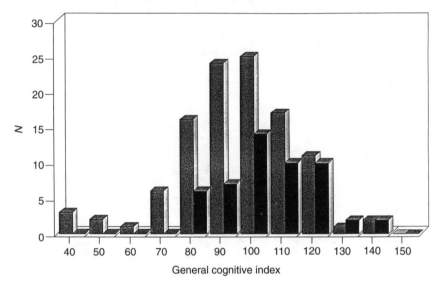

Figure 1   McCarthy scores at 4 years in Romanian adoptees and within-UK
adoptees

= 7) of intellectually impaired children not found in the within-UK
sample (see figure 1).

Factors associated with cognitive level at age 4 years

The analyses on factors associated with cognitive level at age 4 years
were first undertaken with the variables treated as dimensions (see
table 5). So far as age at entry to the UK was concerned, there was
no good a priori reason not to do so. The scattergram shown in figure 2
indicates little age effect within the first 6 months (a group already
found *not* to differ from the within-UK adoptees), but an apparently
linear effect thereafter. A simultaneous entry multiple-regression
analysis (in which the effect of each variable is net of the effect of
the other variables) showed that age at entry to the UK was much
the most powerful predictor of the general cognitive index at 4 years

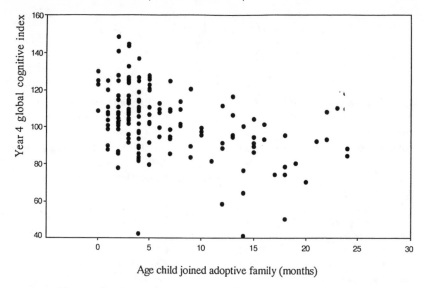

Figure 2   Age at entry to UK and cognitive level at 4 years

Table 5   Prediction of global cognitive index at 4 years from age of entry and early developmental indicators

	Beta	R^2
Simultaneous entry predictors ($N = 94$)		
Age at entry	−0.41***	
Ever in institution (yes/no)[a]	0.07	
Denver score at entry	0.27*	
Weight at entry	0.14	
R^2		0.34***

[a]*"Ever in institution" is a dichotomous variable ($0 = no$, $1 = yes$); the other variables are dimensional variables.*
*$p < 0.05$; ***$p < 0.001$.*

(a beta weight of −0.41; $p < 0.001$). There was also a significant, but weaker effect of Denver score at entry (beta weight of 0.27; $p < 0.05$) but no effect of weight at entry (beta weight = 0.14; $p = 0.2$). Because head circumference at entry showed no association ($r = 0.11$) with cognitive outcome it was not entered into the regression; the same applied to height at entry ($r = 0.18$). Neither family rearing nor the duration of family care prior to institutional admission showed an association with the cognitive score at 4 years in the group as a whole.

Table 6   At entry predictors of McCarthy scores at 4 years

Situation at entry	(N)	McCarthy score Mean	(SD)	Statistical significance
Age				
0 < 6 mths	(56)	105.9	(17.9)	$p < 0.001$ (0–6 mths vs. 6–24 mths)
6 < 12 mths	(23)	98.0	(14.5)	$F(2,105) = 11.48$
12 < 24 mths	(29)	86.7	(19.2)	Contrasts 0–6, 6–12 > 12–24
Weight				
Below 3rd percentile	(54)	97.9	(15.9)	n.s.
Above 3rd percentile	(51)	101.6	(21.3)	$F(1,105) = 2.34$
Head circumference				
Below 3rd percentile	(20)	104.0	(16.7)	n.s.
Above 3rd percentile	(41)	99.6	(20.3)	$F(1,59) = 0.72$
Denver quotient				
Below 50	(56)	95.5	(16.9)	$p = 0.055$
Above 50	(41)	103.2	(22.0)	$F(1,95) = 3.77$

However, the mean GCI for the tiny subgroup ($N = 6$) of children entering the UK after 6 months who had not experienced institutional rearing was 102 (as compared with 90 for those reared in institutions), and therefore closely comparable both with that for the children entering the UK before 6 months (106) and for the within-UK adoptees group (109). The inference is that the remaining cognitive deficit was likely to be a consequence of some aspect of institutional rearing.

Because it could be argued that a weight, or head circumference, below the third percentile has a different meaning from variations within the normal range (with only the former reflecting a degree of malnu-trition likely to compromise brain growth or impair long-term cognitive functioning), the data were reanalysed in categorical terms (see table 6). The findings for age at entry were essentially the same as those in the dimensional analysis. Again this was the "initial" variable with the strongest effect. The mean score for those entering before 6 months was 8 points above those entering between the ages of 6 and 12 months, and 19 points above those entering after 12 months (but before 24 months). A weight below the third percentile had only a nonsignificant effect, with just a 6-point difference. A Denver quotient

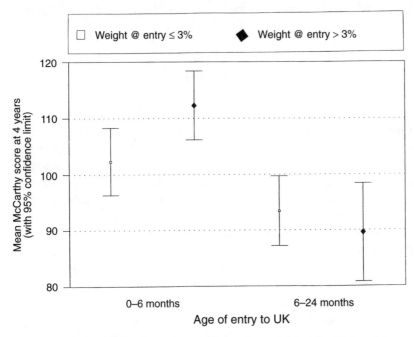

Figure 3   McCarthy scores at 4 years by weight and age at entry

below 50 was associated with a difference of nearly 8 points, an effect that fell just short of statistical significance. There was no appreciable effect of head circumference at entry. There was, however, a weak but statistically significant effect of head circumference at 4 years ($r = 0.25$) on the cognitive score at the same age. This association applied only in those whose weight at entry to the UK was above the third percentile ($r = 0.31$), being near zero ($r = 0.08$) in those with a weight below that cut-off.

As figure 3 shows, the effect of age at entry was greater among the children with a weight above the third percentile (a difference of 22 points) than in those with an initial weight below the third percentile (a difference of 9 points). This strongly suggests that the effect is not simply a consequence of level of malnutrition. Conversely, however, the fact that weight at entry was only weakly (but significantly; $p < 0.05$) associated with cognitive level at 4 years within a group whose members entered the UK before 6 months (a 10-point difference and not at all associated in those admitted later) suggests that variations in degree of malnutrition are not a major determinant of cognitive outcome.

Discussion

Like other studies capitalizing on "natural experiments" created by an unusual set of circumstances, this follow-up study of children adopted into well-functioning families after severe global early privation had several unavoidable limitations. First, there were no satisfactory systematic data on the characteristics of the biological parents and, hence, no information on possible genetic influences. Doubtless these played a role in individual differences within the groups of adoptees. On the other hand, it is completely implausible that they could account for the developmental catch-up found. It is equally unlikely that they could play a role in the effects of the children's age at leaving institutional care on outcome. That is because, unlike in previous studies, there is no evidence that children had been placed for adoption or returned to the biological parents before the fall of the Ceaucescu regime. Second, few data were available on the reasons for the children being admitted to institutions. Again, it is implausible that such reasons played any substantial role in our findings; this is because almost all of the children entered the institutions as very young infants. Accordingly, there was no scope for the children to have been placed as a result of their own handicaps. Third, we had no systematic contemporaneous measurements of the children's developmental level at the time of entering the UK, and hence had to rely on parents' retrospective accounts. Because of this, precise quantification of the degree of cognitive catch-up was not possible. On the other hand, other studies of children in Romania and the parents' own written records (and video tapes in many instances) made clear the very substantial retardation in most cases. Also, as described, we undertook several different types of analyses to detect bias and found no evidence of its presence. The finding that there had been major cognitive catch-up is secure, even if its exact extent remains uncertain. For the reasons given, the effects of the children's age at UK entry on cognitive level at 4 years cannot plausibly be attributed to variations in the recall of the children's initial developmental level.

The children adopted from Romanian orphanages were more severely deprived, physically and psychologically, than almost any other sizeable group of children previously studied. At the time of entry to the UK just over half had a weight below the third percentile and a similar proportion had a developmental quotient in the retarded range. The conditions in Romanian institutions, in all aspects, were incomparably worse than those in the UK or indeed in almost all other industrialized countries. Nevertheless, despite this profoundly unpromising start, the degree of cognitive catch-up by the age of 4 years was spectacular. Thus, in the group as a whole the developmental quotient on the Denver Scales rose from a mean of 63 to a mean of 107, and in the subgroup who experienced institutional rearing and who were admitted to the UK after the age of 6 months the mean rose from 45 to 90. This dramatic catch-up following a major change in the circumstances of rearing provides clear evidence that the initial developmental retardation was caused by the profoundly depriving circumstances of their early institutional rearing.

The cognitive catch-up in the Romanian children who entered this country under the age of 6 months following institutional rearing appears to have been virtually complete by the age of 4 years in that no differences from the within-UK adoptees, or from the subgroup of children from Romania who did not experience institutional rearing, were found. The respective GCI means on the McCarthy Scales at 4 years were 107, 109, and 100. It is, of course, too early to be sure that there will be no long-term sequelae (and it should be noted that they were still slightly below UK norms for physical growth) but the indications so far are very positive.

The situation with respect to those who came to the UK after the age of 6 months following institutional rearing was also very positive; their mean McCarthy score of 90 was well within the normal range and a few of the children had scores that were above average. Nevertheless, their mean was a standard deviation below that (109) of the group of within-UK adoptees and also below that (102) of the small subgroup of children from Romania entering the UK after the age of 6 months but who had not experienced an institutional upbringing. The second follow-up at age 6 years will be important in showing the extent to which there is further catch-up over the age period from 4 to 6, and the 4-year-old findings cannot be seen as providing a picture of the ultimate outcome.

The Canadian study findings are similar. Of the 46 children reared in Romanian institutions and adopted between the ages of 8 and 68 months (median of 19 months), 31 were tested on the Stanford-Binet at $4\frac{1}{2}$ years (Ames, 1997). Their mean IQ was 90 compared with 98 for the 27 Romanian children adopted before 4 months of age, and 109 for a comparison group of 30 non-adopted Canadian children.

The meaning of both the cognitive catch-up in the group as a whole, and the relative cognitive deficit in those entering the UK after the age of 6 months, can be inferred from the findings on predictor variables. Much the strongest predictor was the child's age at the time of entry to the UK. This inevitably reflected both the duration of severe privation in Romania and the span of time in the UK adoptive families, the two being colinear and inseparable. Because the minimum period in the UK was two years, for duration in the adoptive home to be the main causal variable there would have to be a further catch-up of some 19 points during the time after 4 years of age. This seems implausible, and the findings on the children seen so far at age 6 years do not suggest further catch-up of anything approaching that magnitude.

The weakness of the weight at entry as a predictor stands out in contrast. It had no significant predictive power in multivariate analyses when dealt with either as a dimension or categorically in terms of a weight below the third percentile. Also, the finding that head circumference at age 4 years was not associated with the GCI at the same age in those with an initial weight below the third percentile implies a lack of a lasting effect of early subnutrition on brain growth. The implication is that severe malnutrition per se or variations in the degree of undernutrition (in a group most of whom were markedly underweight) had no major continuing effect on cognitive performance after a period of at least two years rearing in an adoptive home with dedicated parents of mostly above-average educational background. An important caveat, however, needs to be attached to that inference. It may be that the *duration* of serious malnutrition rather than its degree at any one point in time is what matters with respect to long-term sequelae.

The only sizeable study in the literature that is at all comparable is that by Winick et al. (1975) and Lien et al. (1977). In Winick et al.'s report of US-adopted Korean children renourished before age 2 years and adopted by age 3 years, they found a mean IQ at follow-up of 102 for children initially below the 3rd percentile of weight and height, compared with 106 for those between the 3rd and 24th percentiles (Johnson et al., 1992), and 112 for those at or above the 25th percentile. Lien et al.'s later study of children from the same sample adopted *after* age 2 years showed differences of the same order: 95, 101, and 105, but with appreciably lower means compared with the Winick et al. sample.

There was *no* effect of nutritional status for children renourished after age 3 years (in most cases there was a long time period between renourishment in Korea and adoption into a US family). Moreover, in the group as a whole, the age on arrival in the US had an effect on scholastic achievement as great as the effect from nutrition; there was no interaction between the two effects.

The marked difference in level of functioning at age 4 years in our sample as compared with that reported for the Romanian adoptees at the time they joined their adoptive families, together with the dose-response relationship between age at entry and cognitive score at 4 years, strongly suggests that the initial developmental deficit was a function of the children's prolonged experience of grossly depriving conditions, and that the subsequent catch-up was a function of the radical improvement in rearing conditions. Although the Denver developmental quotients cannot be taken as more than a rather crude indicator of level of functioning, all the evidence clearly indicates that most of the children were substantially delayed in their development at the time of coming to the UK, many severely so. Although, unavoidably, the initial scores were bases on retrospective recall, the available evidence supports a substantial degree of validity and provides no indication of bias.

The data available so far do not allow a clear differentiation between the effects of nutritional privation and psychological privation because the great majority of children experienced both. Nevertheless, the findings are striking in showing no independent effect of weight at the time of entry to the UK on the cognitive scores at age 4 years. By contrast, there was a major effect of the children's age at entry. It may be concluded that the total duration of privation during the first two years of life is more important as a predictor of cognitive outcome than is the extent to which the privation involved subnutrition. The inference, therefore, is that psychological privation constituted an important part of the risk experiences prior to coming to the UK. Two qualifications, however, need to be added. First, in almost all cases, psychological privation was accompanied by a degree of malnutrition. Accordingly, it may be that the effects of psychological privation are increased by the co-occurrence of malnutrition. Second, the non-nutritional aspects of privation included not only a marked lack of play and communicative experiences but also, in some cases, possible physical and sexual abuse and the use of heavy medication as a means of behavioural control.

The Romanian sample studied does seem to differ from the Korean orphans previously investigated by Winick and Lien in the extreme degree of psychological privation suffered (unfortunately neither of the published reports by Winick et al., 1975, and by Lien et al., 1977, gives satisfactory detail on the conditions of rearing). The degree of psychological privation was also, almost certainly, much more extreme than that in the socially disadvantaged, malnourished children in developing countries who have been studied. Accordingly, the much greater effect found in the Romanian sample for age at leaving institutional care, among children all of whom had left by age 2 years, implies a role for psychological privation. This is also indicated by the major effect of age at entry even in those children whose weight was at or above the third percentile. Currently, we are combining multiple data to derive a summary measure of the degree of psychological privation and its use may clarify the situation. However, the data on the conditions in the institutions as experienced by individual children are extremely sparse, and the range is narrow (all being poor).

Two findings with respect to variations in outcome within the Romanian adoptees appear particularly important. First, we found no measurable deficit in those who came to the UK before the age of 6 months. Not only were their cognitive levels well up to UK norms, they did not differ from those of the within-UK adoptees. This applied to those reared in institutions throughout; also their cognitive resilience was not a function of any lesser degree of malnutrition as judged by height, weight, and head circumference. It is too early to be sure there will be no sequelae but the evidence to date shows a high degree of recovery in a group exposed to an extreme degree of nutritional and psychological privation.

The relative cognitive deficit of about one standard deviation in the group who came to the UK after the age of 6 months stands out in contrast. It is too early to know whether the deficit will reduce with an increasing time in the adoptive home but, especially as the deficit was greater than 10 points in those who came to the UK after the age of 12 months than it was in those entering between 6 and 12 months, it seems likely that some degree of persisting deficit will remain. Nevertheless, it should not necessarily be assumed that the relative deficit on the McCarthy Scales GCI at age 4 years is measuring a lasting intellectual impairment. Test performance, perhaps especially in the preschool years, is influenced by attentional, motivational, and behavioural features. As described elsewhere, the overall group of adoptees from Romania showed some increase in problems in these domains. The follow-up at age 6 years will be helpful in sorting out how far they influenced cognitive performance.

Possible artefacts need to be considered, but our study has several major advantages over previous research that help rule them out. First, the deficit could be a consequence of handicapped children being placed in institutional care. That seems most unlikely both because the great majority of the children entered institutions as young infants and because no children with diagnosable handicaps were included. Second, as pointed out by Clarke and Clarke (1976), most previous findings on the worse outcome of late-adopted children suffer from the limitation that the children may not have been adopted when younger because they were developing less well. That is not likely to apply to this sample because adoption was not an option prior to the fall of the Ceaucescu regime and the children's age on leaving the institution, therefore, was not a function of their having been rejected earlier for adoption. Third, the deficit could be a consequence of the later-adopted children having a lesser cognitive potential as a result of their genetic background. No usable data on the latter are obtainable but there is no reason to suppose that the children's genetic potential should, or even could, vary according to their age at the time of entry to the UK. We may conclude that the cognitive deficit is likely to be a valid consequence of gross early privation. The implication is that the sequelae are a consequence of both psychological and nutritional privation, with the former likely to be of greater importance.

Acknowledgements

The study was supported by the Medical Research Council and by a grant from the Department of Health. We are very grateful to the families for their great cooperation during all phases of the study, and to the many other people who have provided us with information. We are also very indebted to Karen Langridge, the study administrator, for help in ways too numerous to detail.

References

Ames, E. W. (1997). *The Development of Romanian Orphanage Children Adopted to Canada*. Final report to Human Resources Development, Canada.

Boyce, L., and Cole, T. (1993). *Growth Programme. Version 1 & 2*. Ware, UK: Castlemead Publications.

Buckler, J. (1990). *A Longitudinal Study of Adolescent Growth*. London: Springer-Verlag.

Chisholm, K., Carter, M. C., Ames, E. W., and Morison, S. J. (1995). Attachment security and indiscriminately friendly behavior in children adopted from Romanian orphanages. *Development and Psychopathology, 7,* 283–94.

Clarke, A. M., and Clarke, A. D. B. (eds) (1976). *Early Experience: Myth and Evidence*. London: Open Books.

Colombo, M., De la Parra, A., and Lopez, I. (1992). Intellectual and physical outcome of children undernourished in early life is influenced by later environmental conditions. *Developmental Medicine and Child Neurology, 34,* 611–22.

Fisher, L., Ames, E. W., Chisholm, K., and Savoie, L. (1997). Problems reported by parents of Romanian orphans adopted to British Columbia. *International Journal of Behavioural Development, 20,* 67–82.

Flynn, J. R. (1980). *Race, IQ and Jensen*. London: Routledge and Kegan Paul.

Frankenburg, W. K., van Doorninck, W. J., Liddell, T. N., and Dick, N. P. (1986). *Revised Denver Prescreening Developmental Questionnaire (R-PDQ)*. High Wycombe, UK: DDM Incorporated/The Test Agency.

Groze, V., and Ileana, D. (1996). Follow-up study of adopted children from Romania. *Child and Adolescent Social Work Journal, 13,* 541–65.

Johnson, D. E., Miller, L. C., Iverson, S., Thomas, W., Franchino, B., Dole, K., Kiernan, M. T., Georgieff, M. K., and Hostetter, M. K. (1992). The health of children adopted from Romania. *Journal of the American Medical Association, 268,* 3446–51.

Kagan, J. (1984). *The Nature of the Child*. New York: Basic Books.

Kaler, S. R., and Freeman, B. J. (1994). Analysis of environmental deprivation: cognitive and social development in Romanian orphans. *Journal of Child Psychology and Psychiatry, 35,* 769–81.

Keith, T. Z. (1985). McCarthy Scales of Children's Abilities. In D. J. Keyser and R. C. Sweetland (eds), *Test Critiques (Vol. 4)* (pp. 394–9). Kansas City, MO: Test Corporation of America.

Lien, N. M., Meyer, K. K., and Winick, M. (1977). Early malnutrition and "late" adoption: a study of their effects on development of Korean orphans adopted into American families. *American Journal of Clinical Nutrition, 30,* 1734–9.

Lipsitt, L. P. (1983). Stress in infancy: toward understanding the origins of coping behavior. In N. Garmezy and M. Rutter (eds), *Stress, Coping and Development in Children* (pp. 161–90). New York: McGraw-Hill.

Marcovitch, S., Goldberg, S., Gold, A., Washington, L., Wasson, C., Krekewich, K., and Handley-Derry, M. (1997). Determinants of behavioural problems in Romanian children adopted in Ontario. *International Journal of Behavioural Development, 20,* 17–32.

Martorell, R., Kettel Khan, L., and Schroeder, D. G. (1994). Reversibility of stunting: epidemiological findings in children from developing countries. *European Journal of Clinical Nutrition, 48,* S45–S57.

McCarthy, D. (1972). *The McCarthy Scales of Children's Abilities.* New York: The Psychological Corporation/Harcourt Brace Jovanovich.

Money, J., Annecillo, C., and Kelley, J. F. (1983a). Growth of intelligence: failure and catch-up associated respectively with abuse and rescue in the syndrome on abuse dwarfism. *Psychoneuroendocrinology, 8,* 309–19.

Money, J., Annecillo, C., and Kelley, J. F. (1983b). Abuse-dwarfism syndrome: after rescue, statural and intellectual catch-up growth correlate. *Journal of Clinical Child Psychology, 12,* 279–83.

Pilling, D., and Pringle, M. K. (1978). *Controversial Issues in Child Development.* London: Elek.

Proos, L. A., Hofvander, Y., and Tuvemo, T. (1991a). Menarcheal age and growth pattern of Indian girls adopted in Sweden. I. Menarcheal age. *Acta Paediatrica Scandinavia, 80,* 852–8.

Proos, L. A., Hofvander, Y., and Tuvemo, T. (1991b). Menarcheal age and growth pattern of Indian girls adopted in Sweden. II. Catch-up growth and final height. *Indian Journal of Pediatrics, 58,* 105–14.

Rutter, M. (1981). *Maternal Deprivation Reassessed* (2nd edn). Harmondsworth, UK: Penguin.

Rutter, M. (1994). Beyond longitudinal data: causes, consequences, changes and continuity. *Journal of Consulting and Clinical Psychology, 62,* 928–40.

Skuse, D. (1984). Extreme deprivation in early childhood – II. Theoretical issues and a comparative review. *Journal of Child Psychology and Psychiatry, 25,* 543–72.

Thoburn, J. (1993). *Success and Failure in Permanent Family Placement.* Aldershot, UK: Avebury.

Tizard, B., and Phoenix, A. (1993). *Black, White or Mixed Race? Race and Racism in the Lives of Young People of Mixed Parentage.* London: Routledge.

Ulijaszek, S. J. (1994). Between-population variation in pre-adolescent growth. *European Journal of Clinical Nutrition, 48,* S5–S14.

Winick, M., Meyer, K. K., and Harris, R. C. (1975). Malnutrition and environmental enrichment by early adoption: development of adopted Korean children differing greatly in early nutritional status is examined. *Science, 190,* 1173–5.

Early Experience and the Life Path

Introduction

The next article has much in common with reading 8. As Rutter et al. discussed the severely malnourished and developmentally delayed Romanian babies who came to the UK and were adopted at a fairly young age, and who then went on to make good recoveries by age four, Clarke and Clarke describe the fate of infants who were seriously neglected but who went on to recover effectively after adoption. And like Rutter et al., Clarke and Clarke point out that recovery was often incomplete for those children who were adopted very late and/or who suffered congenital or later organic deficits. The importance of Clarke and Clarke's research has been to point out the erroneous reasoning behind the traditional, static developmental view that early life experiences predetermine later outcomes. Clearly, Clarke and Clarke's findings show that it does not: babies born into adverse circumstances can be remediated by adoption into nurturant homes; and alternatively, babies born into good homes who, through life's vicissitudes, find themselves reared by neglectful foster parents can regress. Neither outcome is consistent with the traditional view that early life experience sets the child on an immutable path.

Further reading

Money, J., Annecillo, C., and Kelley, J. F. (1983). Growth of intelligence: failure and catch-up associated respectively with abuse and rescue in the syndrome on abuse dwarfism. *Psychoeuroendocrinology*, *8*, 309–19.

NINE

Early Experience and the Life Path

Ann Clarke and Alan Clarke

Perhaps the most pervasive view concerning long-term development has been that early experiences predetermine the individual's future. For Freud, the first five years were regarded as critical; for J. B. Watson it was the experience of the first two years which would make or mar the life path. In contrast to this super-environmentalism, yet with the same predeterministic implications, was the extreme genetic notion of personal constancy espoused by Spearman.

These early twentieth-century theories, reviving philosophical notions over many centuries, were reinforced by Bowlby's (1951) highly influential monograph. For him good mothering was almost useless if delayed beyond two and a half years; the prolonged deprivation of maternal care might have grave and far-reaching effects on the child's character and thus the whole of his or her future life. Bowlby et al.'s (1956) part recantation and courageous indication of having "overstated" his case went virtually unnoticed.

In 1951, the same year as Bowlby's publication, we inherited a psychology department in a hospital for what are now termed persons with learning disabilities. They were held legally under the Mental Deficiency Act 1913, and the majority were adolescent or young adult people with mild disabilities. Almost all had been drawn from either very adverse conditions characterized by cruelty or neglect, or at best from 'ordinary' bad homes. To our very great surprise, in the course of routine assessment, we noted IQ increments, sometimes substantial.

A pilot study indicated that such changes were common, and we advanced five alternative hypotheses to account for the findings. Only one was supported: a record of early *severe* adversity predicted later improvement, and this was ultimately found to extend to social adaptation. There followed four controlled studies of this adolescent and young adult population, involving some 200 persons (Clarke and Clarke, 1954; Clarke et al., 1958). The hypothesis was again confirmed. At the time of the first study (1954), we raised the question of whether these results might generalize to other deprived populations, and if so, whether Bowlby's theory might require modification. Our surprising rule seemed to be that, in our *unusual* groups of people, the worse the background the better the prognosis following minimal intervention. Our data forced us to hypothesize that early psychological damage could scarcely become any worse; it might remain the same, or there might be recovery. It had proved to be the latter. Such processes were later aptly termed "the self-righting tendency" (Waddington, 1966).

Our initial search for generalization of these findings was at once rewarded by Lewis's (1954) study of the improving status of early deprived children removed from unsatisfactory conditions. From time to time, therefore, we monitored and reviewed the field (e.g. 1968, 1976, 1984, 1992) confirming the generality of our original hypothesis and highlighting the range of individual differences, depending on both personal and social factors, in the extent of recovery processes. Yet, as Kagan (1992) indicates, there remains an ascendant assumption in developmental work that there is an indefinite preservation of a young child's salient qualities, whether intellectual ability or secure attachment: "There is an inconsistency between the contemporary commitment to the importance of the local context which changes, and the capacity of early encounters to create immutable structures which will be preserved" (p. 993).

Research Problems – and Solutions

There are problems in establishing the predictive roles of particular periods of development when the individual remains within a somewhat unchanging context. Hence studies which show some modest link between early and later characteristics can be bedevilled by environmental continuities. Nevertheless, many such longitudinal studies show that, if early experiences were powerfully predictive, some individuals escape their apparent destiny. Thus Kolvin et al. (1990) showed that a population of previously deprived children included 13 percent who were living entirely normally as adults. Tonge et al.'s (1983) follow-up of children from multi-problem families indicated that in adulthood, about one third lived normally, one third were marginal and another third remained seriously deprived like their parents. Ferguson et al. (1994) believe that with the passage of time young people, having left their original family environments, may be exposed to further life and socialization experiences which can override their earlier social learning. There are other important studies (e.g. Rutter et al., 1990) which indicate the role of individual personal factors, as well as of social supportive ones, in promoting escape from early adversity.

A more crucial research paradigm is desirable, one which, as we have from time to time indicated, involves a *marked* change in the individual's life circumstances. In these cases one asks whether the effects of early experiences are maintained or overcome. Here are two possibilities: "good" early experiences followed by adverse conditions – do the former protect against the latter? "Bad" early experiences followed by fortunate changes – do the latter overcome the former? In practice, the second example is far more often reflected in the literature, hence a brief review of some of this evidence will be offered.

Children Rescued from Severe Adversity

The most stringent test of our thesis is to consider the outcome for children removed from conditions which must almost have threatened their survival. Studies by Davis (1947) were important, but lacked long-term follow-up; the child Anna, a six-year-old rescued from terrible conditions, received no specialist help, made limited progress and died at age 10 and a half. Isabelle, however, the child of a deaf mute mother, both imprisoned in an attic, had severe disabilities on discovery at age six – lacking speech, suffering rickets and seemingly unaware of relationships of any kind. With specialist help she made rapid progress cognitively, scholastically and emotionally. On final follow-up at age 14 she had already passed the educational grades for age 12 and was continuing to improve.

The best-known, most detailed and lengthiest study is by Koluchova (1972, 1976, 1991), and since we had the privilege of bringing these findings to the notice of the English-speaking world, we have had the advantage of further information from the author. In its barest outline the facts are as follows.

Identical twin boys, born in 1960, lost their mother shortly after birth, were cared for by a social agency for a year and then fostered by a maternal aunt for a further six months. Their development was normal. Their father, who may have had intellectual limitations, remarried, but his new wife proved to be excessively cruel to the twins, banishing them to the cellar for the next five and a half years and beating them from time to time. Neighbours were frightened of this woman, and were aware that all was not well. On discovery at the age of seven the twins were dwarfed in stature, lacking speech, suffering from rickets and failing to understand the meaning of pictures. The doctors who examined them confidently predicted permanent physical and mental handicap. Legally removed from their parents, they first underwent a programme of physical remediation, and initially entered a school for children with severe learning disabilities. After some time, the boys were legally adopted by exceptionally dedicated women. Scholastically, from a state of profound disability they caught up with age peers and achieved emotional and intellectual normality. After basic education they went on to technical school, training as typewriter mechanics, but later undertook further education, specializing in electronics. Both were drafted for national service, and later married and had children. They are said to be entirely stable, lacking abnormalities and enjoying warm relationships. One is a computer technician and the other a technical training instructor.

Skuse (1984) has reviewed cases like these, concluding that "in the absence of genetic or congenital anomalies . . . victims of such deprivation have an excellent prognosis", provided of course that appropriate and long-term remedial action is undertaken. Note that Skuse's firm prediction is precisely the opposite of that of the original Bowlby model. As implied, where there is the likelihood of an organic problem super-added to gross deprivation, as in the sad case of Genie (Curtiss, 1977), the prognosis is poor. Later studies of psychologically damaged and also malnourished children confirm Skuse's view (e.g. Thompson, 1986). However, long-term, enduring gains are often obtained at heavy cost to those undertaking initial intervention during the period while earlier damage fades. The view that congenital and later organic problems diminish the child's potential responsiveness to change cannot be overemphasized, as many researchers indicate (e.g. Skuse et al., 1994). Hence, although sometimes correlated, one must distinguish between the effects of biological as opposed to social early experience.

Of course, one should never rely solely on a few case histories. Those children who made startling recoveries might be exceptionally resilient. To check the generality of recovery processes one needs to see what happens when less severely deprived children are removed to better conditions. If the "rule" is correct, then one would expect to find less dramatic changes but of similar direction. This is, in fact, what researchers have shown.

Children Rescued from Less Severe Adversity

In earlier publications we have reviewed studies of groups of children removed from various depriving circumstances. Here, for reasons of space, we will consider just one research area, late adopted children, for whom the prognosis should have been poor if early experience were prepotent. This is another demanding test of our thesis. Before adoption such children have mostly lived sad lives, and in decades when there has been a shortage of young adoptable babies, one is bound to ask why adoption was delayed. Apart from mother's consent withheld, there are also reports of adverse family histories, developmental retardation and difficult behaviour.

The Skeels (1966) prospective study is a classic, originating in an accidental discovery that two infants with learning disabilities, transferred from a very inadequate orphanage to a "colony" for people with learning disabilities, made rapid gains. As the only youngsters there, they received immense interest and stimulation so that at age three and a half they were adopted. As a repetition of this discovery, 11 further children were transferred and nine were ultimately adopted. Twenty-five years after the last contact they were followed up and found to be very ordinary citizens, unmarked by their early austere experiences (see also Clarke and Clarke, 1976, pp. 214–23).

The Kadushin (1970) study of children adopted late (average seven years), having been legally removed from adversity at an average of three and a half, followed by placement in an average of more than two foster homes, made a considerable impact on adoption practices. Followed up at an average of almost 14 years, between 82 and 87 percent of adoptive parents expressed satisfaction about the outcome. This large group showed a greater degree of mental health and stability than might have been expected from their background and early developmental histories (cf. Lewis, 1954).

A well-known adoption study by Barbara Tizard (1977) concerned children taken into care early in life and remaining in the institution for between two and seven years, until some were restored to their natural mothers and some were adopted. They were followed up at ages four and a half and eight, after a baseline assessment at age two. Data are presented on the adoptees' intellectual and social progress; at age four and a half they were doing well, with the majority of parents indicating their children's deep attachment to them. They were, however, overfriendly with strangers. An even better picture emerged at age eight, but the children's concentration was reported by teachers to be poor; they were restless and inclined to be unpopular with other children. They remained strongly attached to their parents.

A further follow-up of this group was carried out by Hodges and Tizard (1989) by which time the children had reached the age of 16. In general terms, things had gone well for 23 out of 25 adoptees; family relations for most were satisfactory, differing only a little from a carefully selected comparison group of adolescents who had never been in care. But their relationships with those outside the family, especially with peers, were less satisfactory than in the comparison group, this finding being concordant with all other adoption studies.

The most striking finding lay in the differences between adopted and restored children; on all measures, intellectual, scholastic and emotional, the latter were disadvantaged compared with the adoptees. They and their parents were less often attached to each other, and where there were siblings, these were preferred to the restored child. It seems clear that the adoptive families strongly encouraged the development of attachments while those of the restored children hindered them. The children as adolescents reflected in both groups their long-term family ecological settings.

A further example has been provided by Triseliotis and Russell (1984) in a retrospective study of 44 adults who had been adopted late. They had at first experienced several placements and had been considered as dubious candidates for adoption because of adverse family backgrounds and emotional disturbance. The book contains a wealth of detail about their lives, including educational histories and personal and social status. The authors comment on their good adult adjustment, and their escape from the effects of severe deprivation in the context of a new, caring environment.

Discussion

It is difficult to assess the long-term effects of early experience within ordinary, ongoing contexts, but when sharp and continuing environmental change occurs one can be more certain whether or not early effects persist. Longitudinal studies of children rescued from adversity meet this criterion. See also Sroufe et al. (1990).

Some researchers, including ourselves, have suggested that different processes may show different degrees of vulnerability to adversity, with cognitive the best buffered and emotional the least. However, in some of the studies reviewed, both aspects had been overwhelmed by the severity of problems yet both showed ultimate recovery.

We have never argued that early experience is unimportant; we (1992) have regarded development as a series of linkages in which characteristics in each period have a probability of linking with those in another period. But probabilities are not certainties, and deflections of the life path, for good or ill, are possible, although always within the powerful limits imposed by genetic, constitutional and social trajectories. So for the majority of people the effects of early life experience represent no more than an initial step in an ongoing life path. Depending on biosocial interactions and transactions, such a path may be straight or winding, incremental or decremental, or merely fluctuant.

In one of a number of notable contributions, Rutter (1989) points out that "chain" effects during development are common. "Life transitions have to be considered both as end products of past processes and as instigators of future ones . . . as both independent and dependent variables" (p. 46). Details of some personal and social factors operative in vulnerability and resilience have been reviewed by several researchers (e.g. Rutter, 1989; Clarke and Clarke, 1992); space precludes their elaboration here.

The fact that children rescued from adversity progress on average to normality has considerable implications. For example, some (perhaps many) of the children languishing in Eastern European orphanages have the potential for normality, a potential most unlikely to be realized for a variety of political and economic reasons, so for them a doom-laden life path is to be envisaged. The few who are adopted will have a far better outcome.

Powerful support for this argument has just been provided by Rutter et al. (1998) in a very important study of 111 Romanian children adopted in the UK before the age of two years. From severe developmental impairment on arrival (about half being below the third percentile for height, weight, head circumference and general cognitive level), by four years their physical and cognitive catch-up is described as dramatic and, in some cases, spectacular.

It is of interest that Bowlby (1988), in what may have been his last paper, responded to research findings of which we have offered only a small sample. He wrote that: "The central task . . . is to study the endless interactions of internal and external (factors), and how the one is influencing the other, not only during childhood but during adolescence and adult life as well . . . present knowledge requires that a theory of developmental pathways should replace theories that a person is fixated or to which [*sic*] he may regress" (pp. 1, 2). Schaffer (1992) takes a similar view: "The idea that specific experiences, occurring at specific points of time . . . can in themselves have long-term consequences must be rejected in favour of a much more complicated, multi-determined and continuing process' (p. 51).

Experience which has anything greater than transitory effects must involve learning in its broadest sense. While we have indicated that early learning effects can fade and disappear, there remains a possibility (to which we alluded in our 1968 paper) that under later stress such effects might be reactivated. In other words, there might remain a greater than usual vulnerability in such persons. Only careful longitudinal studies could answer this question. Apart from this problem, the research findings are clear.

In summary, for most children "good" early experiences tend to be reinforced during development, and "bad" likewise. Especially where a sharp and continuing break occurs, one can estimate the consequences, or lack of them, of the earlier period. This also applies to those cases where early educational intervention sets off a sequence of positive, enduring parental and other effects. The evidence is firm; while there is a range of outcomes, early social experience *by itself* does not predestine the future.

There are two reasons for a wider acceptance of this view. First, models of development which ascribe disproportionate long-term effects to the early years are clearly erroneous. Second, an acceptance of the early years as critical can carry with it subtle lowered expectancies for psychologically damaged children and hence less than desirable interventions.

References

Bowlby, J. (1951). *Maternal Care and Mental Health*. Geneva: World Health Organization.

Bowlby, J. (1988). Developmental psychiatry comes of age. *American Journal of Psychiatry*, 45, 1–10.

Bowlby, J., Ainsworth, M., Boston, M. and Rosenbluth, D. (1956). The effects of mother–child separation: a follow-up study. *British Journal of Medical Psychology*, 29, 211–47.

Clarke, A. D. B. (1968). Learning and human development – the 42nd Maudsley Lecture. *British Journal of Psychiatry*, 114, 1061–77.

Clarke, A. D. B. and Clarke, A. M. (1954). Cognitive changes in the feeble minded. *British Journal of Psychology*, 45, 173–9.

Clarke, A. D. B. and Clarke, A. M. (1984). Constancy and change in the growth of human characteristics. *Journal of Child Psychology and Psychiatry*, 25, 191–210.

Clarke, A. D. B., Clarke, A. M. and Reiman, S. (1958). Cognitive and social changes in the feeble minded – three further studies. *British Journal of Psychology*, 49, 144–57.

Clarke, A. M. and Clarke A. D. B. (eds) (1976). *Early Experience: Myth and Evidence*. London: Open Books.

Clarke, A. M. and Clarke A. D. B. (1992). How modifiable is the human life path? *International Review of Research in Mental Retardation*, 18, 137–57.

Curtiss, G. (1977). *Genie: A Psycholinguistic Study of a Modern-Day "Wild Child"*. New York: Academic Press.

Davis, K. (1947). Final note on a case of extreme isolation. *American Journal of Sociology*, 45, 554–65.

Ferguson, D. M., Horwood, L. J. and Lynskey, M. (1994). The childhood of multiple problem adolescents: a 15-year longitudinal study. *Journal of Child Psychology and Psychiatry*, 35, 1123–40.

Hodges, J. and Tizard, B. (1989). Social and family relationships of ex-institutional adolescents. *Journal of Child Psychology and Psychiatry*, 30, 77–98.

Kadushin, L. A. (1970). *Adopting Older Children*. New York: Columbia University Press.

Kagan, J. (1992). Yesterday's premises, tomorrow's promises. *Developmental Psychology*, 28, 990–7.

Koluchova, J. (1972). Severe deprivation in twins: a case study. *Journal of Child Psychology and Psychiatry*, 13, 107–11.

Koluchova, J. (1976). A report on the further development of twins after severe and prolonged deprivation. *Journal of Child Psychology and Psychiatry*, 17, 181–8.

Koluchova, J. (1991). Severely deprived twins after 22 years' observation. *Studia Psychologica*, 33, 23–8.

Kolvin, I., Miller, F. J. W., Scott, D. McL., Gatzanis, S. R. M. and Fleeting, M. (1990). *Continuities of Deprivation?: The Newcastle Thousand Family Study*. Aldershot: Gower House.

Lewis, H. (1954). *Deprived Children*. London: Oxford University Press.

Rutter, M. (1989). Pathways from childhood to adult life. *Journal of Child Psychology and Psychiatry*, 30, 23–51.

Rutter, M., Quinton, D. and Hill, J. (1990). Adult outcome of institution-reared children: males and females compared. In L. N. Robins and M. Rutter (eds), *Straight and Devious Pathways from Childhood to Adulthood*. Cambridge: Cambridge University Press.

Rutter, M. and the English and Romanian Adoptees (ERA) Study Team (1998). Developmental catch-up, and deficit, following adoption after severe global early privation. *Journal of Child Psychology and Psychiatry*, 39, 465–76.

Schaffer, H. R. (1992). Early experience and the parent–child relationship: genetic and environmental interactions as developmental determinants. In B. Tizard and V. Varma (eds), *Vulnerability and Resilience in Human Development*. London: Jessica Kingsley.

Skeels, H. (1966). Adult status of children with contrasting early life experiences. *Monographs of the Society for Research on Child Development*, 31, no. 105.

Skuse, D. (1984). Extreme deprivation in childhood. II. Theoretical issues and a comparative review. *Journal of Child Psychology and Psychiatry*, 25, 543–72.

Skuse, D., Pickles, A., Wolke, D. and Reilly, S. (1994). Postnatal growth and mental development: evidence for a "sensitive period'. *Journal of Child Psychology and Psychiatry*, 35, 521–45.

Sroufe, L. A., Egeland, B. and Kreutzer, T. (1990). The fate of early experience following developmental change. *Child Development*, 61, 1363–73.

Thompson, A. (1986). Adam – a severely deprived Colombian orphan. *Journal of Child Psychology and Psychiatry*, 27, 689–95.

Tizard, B. (1977). *Adoption: A Second Chance*. London: Open Books.

Tonge, W. L., Lunn, J. E., Greathead, M., McLaren, S. and Bosanko, C. (1983). Generations of problem families in Sheffield. In N. Madge (ed.), *Families at Risk*. London: Heinemann.

Triseliotis, J. and Russell, J. (1984). *Hard to Place: The Outcome of Adoption and Residential Care*. London: Heinemann.

Waddington, G. E. (1966). *Principles of Development and Differentation*. New York: Macmillan.

Prevention of Intellectual Disabilities: Early Interventions to Improve Cognitive Development

Introduction

Ramey and Ramey report on their methodologically and substantively ambitious studies on the effect of early enrichment on preschoolers' IQ performance. Intensive early intervention during the first three years of life resulted in significant IQ gains for low birth-weight children. Children from the poorest backgrounds experienced anywhere from 13 to 17 IQ-point gains by age three in all three intervention studies reported by these researchers. How long these gains will be maintained may determine society's willingness to pay for such expensive interventions. But for now, the Rameys have provided direct and convincing evidence that IQ scores are highly malleable at this early age if programs are appropriately intensive.

In figure 6 of their article, Ramey and Ramey reveal a linear increase in IQ scores with each additional level of maternal education for the untreated control-group children. This means that children's IQ scores remained very high even if they were not subjected to intensive enrichment *if* their mothers were highly educated. Intensive enrichment produced little IQ gain for children born to mothers with a college education. Thus, maternal education functions as its own form of early intervention. Educated mothers provide ongoing intellectual stimulation for their children that obviates the need for out-of-home enrichment.

Further reading

Ramey, C. T., Ramey, S. L., Gaines, R., and Blair, C. (1995). Two-generation early interventions: a child development perspective. In S. Smith (ed.), *Two-Generation Programs: A New Intervention Strategy. Vol. 9: Advances in Applied Developmental Psychology*. Norwood, NJ: Ablex.

TEN

Prevention of Intellectual Disabilities: Early Interventions to Improve Cognitive Development

Craig T. Ramey and
Sharon Landesman Ramey

Introduction

Each year thousands of children enter kindergarten unprepared to meet the intellectual demands of school. Lack of cognitive readiness bodes ill for future school performance. Poor school readiness predicts increased likelihood of low levels of academic achievement and high levels of retention in grade, of special education placement, and ultimately of school dropout. In turn, school dropouts are at much elevated risk for unemployment, teen pregnancy, juvenile delinquency, social dependency, and poor parenting practices. Their children all too frequently repeat this pattern (cf. [2]).

Poor school performance is foreshadowed by subaverage performance on cognitive and social functioning during the years prior to kindergarten. The Centers for Disease Control and Prevention now estimate that over 300,000 individuals under 21 years of age in the United States are so poorly developed cognitively as to have mental retardation (IQ < 70) that could have been prevented through early and continuing intervention. The full cost of this lack of prevention has yet to be determined. Epidemiological catchment area surveys reveal that risk for both mental retardation and poor school readiness is highest among children from the lowest socioeconomic status families (e.g., [12]).

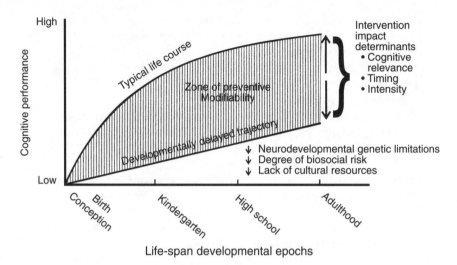

Figure 1 Hypothetical range of reaction for experience-driven cognitive neurodevelopment

Remedial special education to improve cognitive development and academic achievement that is begun in the elementary school years faces an enormous challenge. In essence, the rate of cognitive development must be altered if the progressive gap between normal and subaverage cognitive development is to be arrested and intellectual development is to be returned to normative trajectories. If genuine *catch-up* is to occur, then for a given period of intervention, the rate must actually exceed the normative rate. This point is illustrated in figure 1.

Little is known about how to accelerate cognitive development beyond normative or typical rates. Unfortunately, the hopes and expectations for remedially oriented special education often go unmet.

A policy alternative to remedial and special education is primary prevention. Primary prevention entails the identification of high-risk individuals among the general population and the provision of the hypothesized missing essential experiences for normative development.

A large body of observational research suggests that children who evidence delayed cognitive development have insufficient frequency of exposure to particular adult–child transactional experiences (e.g., [1]). These transactional experiences are particularly lacking in low socioeconomic status families and are reliably missing beginning in the

Table 1 Developmental priming mechanisms

1 Encouragement of exploration
To be encouraged by adults to explore and to gather information about their environments.
2 Mentoring in basic skills
To be mentored (especially by trusted adults) in basic cognitive skills, such as labeling, sorting, sequencing, comparing, and noting means–ends relationships.
3 Celebration of developmental advances
To have their developmental accomplishments celebrated and reinforced by others, especially those with whom they spend a lot of time.
4 Guided rehearsal and extension of new skills
To have responsible others help them in rehearsing and then elaborating upon (extending) their newly acquired skills.
5 Protection from inappropriate disapproval, teasing, or punishment
To avoid negative experiences associated with adults' disapproval, teasing, or punishment for those behaviors that are normative and necessary in children's trial-and-error learning about their environments (e.g., mistakes in trying out a new skill, unintended consequences of curious exploration or information seeking). *Note.* This does not mean that constructive criticism and negative consequences cannot be used for other behaviors that children have the ability to understand are socially unacceptable.
6 A rich and responsive language environment
To have adults provide a predictable and comprehensible communication environment, in which language is used to convey information, provide social rewards, and encourage learning of new materials and skills. *Note.* Although language to the child is the most important early influence, the language environment may be supplemented in valuable ways by the use of written materials.

second year of life and sometimes earlier [14]. These transactional experiences have been summarized by Ramey and Ramey [9] and are presented in table 1. These so-called developmental priming mechanisms are part of a theoretical framework derived from General Systems Theory and applied to two-generational early intervention programs by Ramey et al. [10]. This conceptual framework is presented schematically in figure 2. Insufficient exposure to these developmental priming mechanisms is hypothesized to negatively affect developmentally appropriate cortical neuronal connections and synaptic efficiency associated with cognitive development.

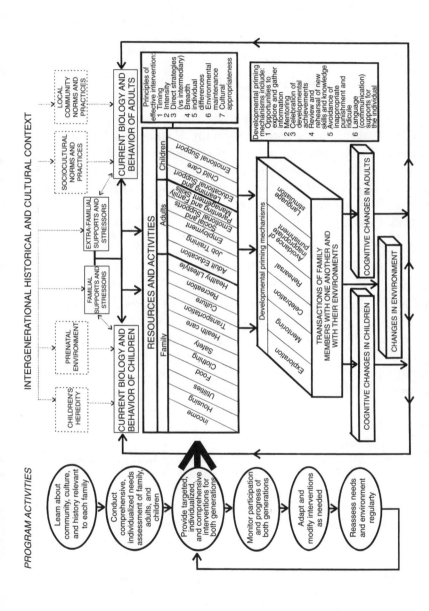

Figure 2 A conceptual framework for early intervention programs

To test the hypothesis that provision of theoretically critical experiences can potentially prevent progressive cognitive delay, we have conducted two single-site randomized trials and one multisite randomized controlled trial with high-risk children and their families. These projects and their cognitive outcomes are described below.

The Early Intervention Programs

Certain programmatic commonalities run throughout the Abecedarian Project, Project CARE, and the Infant Health and Development Program. These early intervention programs were multidisciplinary, intergenerational, individualized for children and their families, contextually embedded in local service delivery systems, research oriented, and organized around key concepts undergirding randomized controlled trials. We will briefly elaborate on these key concepts.

Multidisciplinary

The Early Intervention Programs consisted of a compound of services that included early childhood education, family counseling and home visits, health services, medical services, nursing services, nutrition services, service coordination services, social work services, special instruction, speech–language services, and transportation. Many of these services were forerunners of those services specified under Part H (Birth to 3 Years) of the Individuals with Disabilities Education Act.

Intergenerational

The Early Intervention programs focused on the household(s) in which the children resided with a special emphasis on the child's caregivers. These caregivers were typically parents but were sometimes grandparents, other relatives, foster parents, or others. A dual emphasis was maintained on the needs and goals of the adults and the health and developmental needs of the children, particularly those directly germane to the developmental priming mechanisms.

Individualized

Key to the Early Intervention Programs was the philosophy that it was crucial to tailor the social and health services as well as the early childhood educational program to be developmentally appropriate and in explicit recognition of meaningful individual and family differences. This "individual tailoring" was done in the context of a matrix of services potentially available to all participants. Similarly, the particular educational program for each child was continuously documented using procedures developed within the educational curriculum that is known as *Partners for Learning: Birth to 36 Months* [13]. Together this family and child individualization foreshadowed the now mandated Individual Family Service Plan and Individual Education Plan required under the IDEA legislation. (See [8] for a fuller discussion of the provisions of this legislation for children under the age of 5 years.) Extensive records of service utilization were kept and plans were reviewed and updated at frequent intervals.

Contextually embedded and cooperative

The Early Intervention Programs sought to use existing health, social, and other human services to the extent that they could be drawn upon for the potential benefit of children and families. Extensive records of local service availability and service usage were kept.

Research oriented

This Early Intervention Program was designed to better understand how specific risk factors affect the course of cognitive development and to determine whether a comprehensive and high-intensity intervention program can minimize the impact of those risk factors and if so, by how much. The research teams for these programs have included many senior investigators, postdoctoral fellows, and graduate students. Disciplines prominently represented include clinical psychology, developmental psychology, early childhood education, epidemiology, pediatrics, neonatology, nursing, psychiatry, public health, social work, special education, and speech and language.

The research design and associated key concepts that have guided our efforts have derived from the evolving literature on randomized controlled trials concerned with efficacy of treatments. Guiding concepts worthy of special mention include:

1 recruitment from prespecified populations to enhance generality of findings;
2 random assignment to treatment and control groups to establish initial group equivalence;
3 application and documentation of receipt of a replicable compound of services;
4 minimization of attrition to prevent biased estimates of treatment effects, if any;
5 independent assessment of outcomes by observers masked to treatment conditions of participants;
6 preplanned statistical analyses of hypothesized outcomes with adequate sample sizes for appropriate statistical power to detect statistically and practically meaningful group differences;
7 replication of key findings;
8 publication of findings in peer-reviewed journals; and
9 dissemination of findings to key policy-makers and the general public after publication in peer-reviewed journals.

Participants and Services

The first two projects [the Abecedarian Project ($n = 111$ children) and Project CARE ($n = 63$ children) were single-site randomized controlled trials that enrolled children at birth who were biologically healthy but who came from very poor and undereducated families. The criterion for admission was a score indicating extreme risk on a 13-item high risk index [11]. For example, the mean maternal education was 10 years, and the mean maternal IQ was 85. Approximately three-quarters of the mothers were unmarried. Control group families (sometimes referred to as follow-up families) were not a totally untreated group. Rather, those children received pediatric follow-up services on a schedule recommended by the American Academy of Pediatrics. In addition, the children were provided unlimited iron-fortified formula. Families of control group children also received social work services and home visits.

The Early Intervention groups received the same services just mentioned for the control groups plus they received an early childhood education program known as *Partners for Learning* [13] within the context of a specially developed child development center. This center admitted children after 6 weeks of age and maintained low child/teacher ratios (e.g., 3 : 1 for children <1 year and 4 : 1 for children between 1 and 3 years) and an ongoing inservice training and technical assistance program for teachers and other staff. Parent involvement was facilitated by home visits and parent groups. A fuller description of the program can be found in an article by Ramey and Campbell [7]. In general, program features in the Abecedarian and CARE projects foreshadowed those that are now recommended by the National Association for the Education of Young Children.

Partners for Learning is an educational program focused on the first 36 months of life; it has these basic features: (1) divided into game-like learning episodes, (2) integrated into all aspects of the day, and (3) focused on both specific skills and general principles. The games and activities for children cover 31 developmental skill areas. The areas, organized into four broad themes and two age groups, are presented in table 2.

The 31 skill areas are further divided into skill goals, each related to one of the 265 specific learning activities that make up *Partners for Learning*.

In summary, *Partners for Learning* can be described as an educational resource that is cyclic, game-like, integral to home and child developmental centers, covering 31 child development areas, and consistently oriented toward adult–child transactions involving language. *Partners for Learning* acts both as a child program resource and as a staff development resource. It contains all of the materials needed for implementation (activity cards, newsletters, picture cards, posters, record sheets, assessment instrument, handbooks, etc.) and its simple reading level plus cartoon format make it easy to use.

The Infant Health and Development Program (IHDP) was a modified version of that used in the Abecedarian and CARE projects. Modifications included: (1) establishing the program as an eight-site randomized controlled trial, (2) limiting enrollment to infants who were born at <2,500 g and <37 weeks gestational age; thus, all child participants were to varying degrees of low birth-weight and prematurity; and (3) making weekly home visits the main early intervention

Table 2   Developmental domains embedded in *Partners for Learning*

For infants/toddlers	For 2-year-olds
Cognitive/fine motor	
1 Object permanence	2 Number concepts
3 Objects in space	
4 Matching	5 Matching/visual perception
6 Cause and effect	7 Reasoning
8 Sensory awareness	
Social/self	
9 Self-image	
10 Sharing with adult	
11 Children together	
12 Imitating gestures	13 Creative play
14 Self-help	
15 Needs/feelings	
Motor	
16 Rhythm	
17 Balance	18 Balance/motion
19 Throw/pull/push	
Language	
20 Dialogue	
21 Books	
22 Picture–object words	23 Reporting
24 Words as concepts	25 Predicting
26 Action words	27 Imaging
28 Words for things	29 Giving/following directions
30 Position words	31 Sorting/classifying

component until children were 12 months of age (corrected for prematurity). At 12 months of age children began attending child development centers that were replicas of the one used for the Abecedarian and CARE projects. (Fuller descriptions of IHDP can be found in [3, 5].)

Results

Consistent with the General Systems Theory conceptual framework, multiple measures of cognitive and social functioning have been collected at periodic intervals during the first three years of life. In this paper we report Bayley mental development indices (MDIs) and Stanford-Binet (S-B) IQ scores during the first three years. These scores have been presented in detail in previous publications and for the sake of brevity will be present here only graphically. All descriptions that mention differences are significant by statistical comparisons with a probability level of $P \leq 0.05$.

Figure 3 shows Bayley MDIs and S-B IQ scores by age and treatment conditions during the first three years of life for both the Abecedarian Project (top) and Project CARE (bottom). In both of these graphs there is a divergence of the curves favoring the early intervention groups over the control groups during the first 18 months. Consistent with the random assignment of children to treatment and control conditions, a strong causal inference is justified concerning the preventive power of the early intervention. By 36 months the mean IQ scores in the Abecedarian Project are 101 and 84 for the early intervention and control group, respectively [6]. In Project Care the comparable 36-month scores are 105 and 93 [4].

Figure 4 contains plots for the IHDP children most comparable with the Abecedarian and CARE children – those closest to full birth weight (2,001–500 g) at each of the eight sites. These eight graphs all show similar divergence to 36 months with an overall mean difference of 13.2 IQ points favoring the early intervention groups at 36 months. Comparable plots (figure 5) for the lighter low-birth-weight groups (<2,001 g) reveal similar trends in seven of the eight comparisons (the Harvard site being the exception)[1] but with a somewhat diminished magnitude of difference between the early intervention and the control (follow-up) groups (overall mean difference 6.6 IQ points at 36 months). Thus 17 of the 18 comparisons at 36 months across the Abecedarian, CARE, and IHDP projects support the hypothesis that intensive early intervention is associated with higher cognitive performance relative to randomized controls.

Figure 6 illustrates that children's cognitive performance at 36 months is positively related to mother's education levels in the control groups and that the positive effects of the early intervention are greater for the children of lesser educated mothers. That is, those children at greatest cognitive risk due to low family educational resources benefit the most.

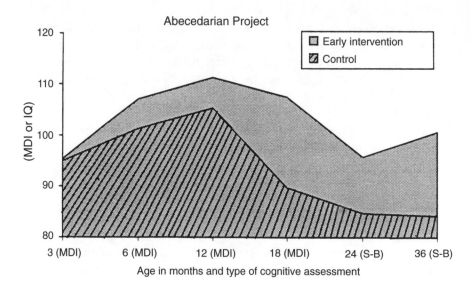

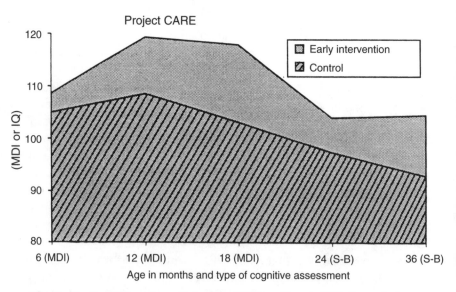

Figure 3 Cognitive scores during the first three years of life for early intervention and control group participants in the Abecedarian Project (top) and Project CARE (bottom)

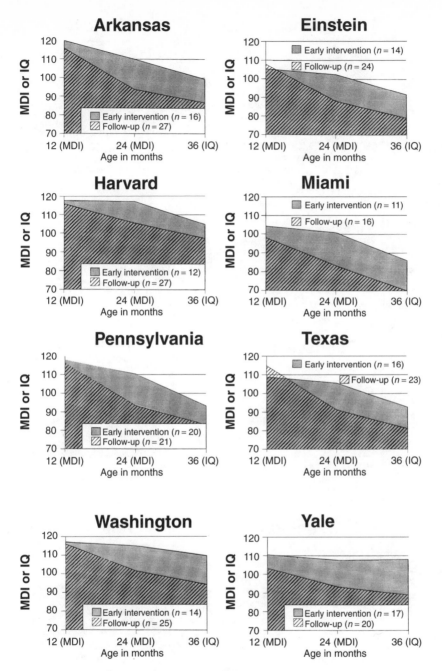

Figure 4 Cognitive scores for early intervention (gray) and control group (follow-up) (lined) participants in the Infant Health and Development Program by site for infants 2,001–500 g at birth

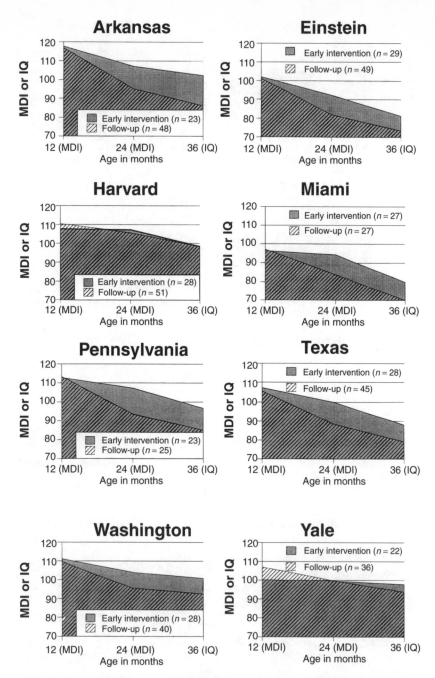

Figure 5 Cognitive scores for early intervention (gray) and control group (follow-up) (lined) participants in the Infant Health and Development Program by site for infants <2,001 g at birth

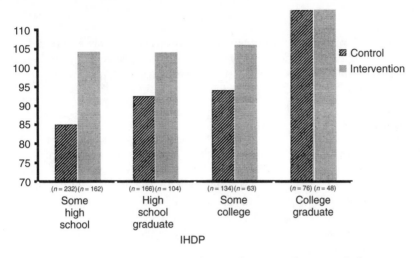

Figure 6   Children's IQ at 36 months as a function of maternal education level and early intervention of control group status from the Infant Health and Development Program

Discussion

That intensive early intervention can positively alter the cognitive developmental trajectories of socially and biologically vulnerable young children has now been demonstrated and replicated in diverse samples. In principle, therefore, the issue of the efficacy of early intervention is answered in the affirmative for both biologically and socially at-risk infants. Intensive early intervention can have a meaningful positive impact on the cognitive development of vulnerable young children. Importantly, those infants from families with the least formal education derive the greatest cognitive benefits. This finding is an important piece of information in this era of reform concerning health care, education, and welfare. Many important research issues, however, remain to be addressed. Salient among those issues is the optimal timing of early intervention services and, therefore, their costs. In our opinion, systematic research is likely to lead to cost reductions as particularly vulnerable children are targeted with effective interventions. It is our belief that scientific policy and social responsibility can be conjoined for the benefit of such vulnerable children and their families.

Notes

1   It is noteworthy that children in Massachusetts were eligible for other early intervention services if they were born at <2,000 g. Thus, many children in the control condition actually received early intervention services.

References

1   Bradley R. H., Caldwell B. M., Rock S. L., Ramey C. T., Barnard K. E., Gray A., Hammond M. A., Gottfried A., Siegel L. S., Johnson D. L. Home environment and cognitive development in the first 3 years of life: a collaborative study involving six sites and three ethnic groups in North America. *Dev Psychol* 1989;25:217–35.
2   *Years of Promise: A Comprehensive Learning Strategy for America's Children.* New York: Carnegie Corp. 1995.
3   The Infant Health and Development Program. Enhancing the outcomes of low-birth-weight, premature infants. *JAMA* 1990;263:3035–42.
4   Ramey C. T., Bryant D. M., Sparling J. J., Wasik B. H. Project CARE: a comparison of two early intervention strategies to prevent retarded development. *Top Early Child Spec Educ* 1985;5:12–25.
5   Ramey C. T., Bryant D. M., Wasik B. H., Sparling J. J., Fendt K. H., LaVange L. M. Infant Health and Development Program for low birth weight, premature infants: program elements, family participation, and child intelligence. *Pediatrics* 1992;89:454–65.
6   Ramey C. T., Campbell F. A. Preventive education for high-risk children: cognitive consequences of the Carolina Abecedarian Project. *Am J Ment Defic* 1984;88:(5):515–23.
7   Ramey C. T., Campbell F. A. Poverty, early childhood education, and academic competence: the Abecedarian experiment. In: Huston A., editor. *Children in Poverty.* New York: Cambridge University Press, 1992:190–221.
8   Ramey C. T., Ramey S. L. Early intervention: optimizing development for children with disabilities and risk conditions. In: Wolraich M., editor. *Disorders of Development and Learning: A Practical Guide to Assessment and Management.* 2nd edn. Philadelphia: Mosby, 1996;141–58.
9   Ramey S. L., Ramey C. T. Early educational intervention with disadvantaged children – to what effect? *Appl Prev Psychol* 1992;1:131–40.
10 Ramey C. T., Ramey S. L., Gaines R., Blair C. Two-generation early interventions: a child development perspective. In Siegel I., series editor, and Smith S., volume editor. *Two-Generation Programs: A New Intervention Strategy. Vol. 9: Advances in Applied Developmental Psychology.* Norwood (NJ): Ablex Publ., 1995:199–228.

11 Ramey C. T., Smith B. J. Assessing the intellectual consequences of early intervention with high-risk infants. *Am J Ment Defic* 1977;8(4):318–24.

12 Ramey C. T., Stedman D. S., Borders-Patterson A., Mengel W. Predicting school failure from information available at birth. *Am J Ment Defic* 1978;82:525–34.

13 Sparling J. J., Lewis I., Ramey C. T. *Partners for Learning: Birth to 36 Months.* Lewisville (NC): Kaplan Press, 1995.

14 Yeates K. O., MacPhee D., Campbell F. A., Ramey C. T. Maternal IQ and home environment as determinants of early childhood intellectual competence: developmental analysis. *Dev Psychol* 1983;19:731–9.

Part V

Later Influences on IQ Development

Schooling and Intelligence

Introduction

It was once thought that an IQ test measured native intelligence in a manner that was not "contaminated" by differences in social advantage. According to this view, differences in IQ scores reflected true differences in inherent intelligence that were not the product of differences in schooling, parenting, and so on. In the next article, Ceci provides a brief of the evidence against this position. He shows that if two children have the identical IQ at age 14 and the same grades in school, but one of them ceases schooling at age 15 while the other continues until age 18, they will no longer have identical IQs. In fact, they will differ by approximately 1.8 IQ points for each year that schooling was terminated for one child. Ceci provides eight classes of such evidence, none of which by itself can provide definitive proof for the power of schooling, but which together provide strong support for the effects of schooling on IQ. It appears that schooling prevents large drops in IQ rather than causing rises in IQ; that is, staying in school prevents your IQ from dropping rather than elevating it.

Further reading

Ceci, S. J. (1991). How much does schooling influence general intelligence and its cognitive components?: A reassessment of the evidence. *Developmental Psychology, 27,* 703–22. Also Winship, C. and Korenman, S. (1998). Does staying in school make you smarter? In S. Devlin, D. Resnick, and K. Roeder (eds), *Intelligence, Genes, and Success.* New York: Copernicus. (This chapter provides a statistical test of the claim that it is schooling as opposed to other forces that is responsible for maintenance of IQ. It is beyond the grasp of readers lacking a strong statistics background, but readers can skip the math.)

ELEVEN

Schooling and Intelligence

Stephen J. Ceci

What are the consequences of not attending school? This question is as alluringly simple as it is complex. A complete answer is not within the scope of this *Science Brief*, as it would entail a consideration of the social and emotional developments that accrue as a result of missed schooling and the economic implications of early school termination. Here I address only part of this question, namely, *What are the intellectual consequences of school attendance?* The influence of schooling on intellectual development has been the subject of much confusion and mistaken belief.

Those familiar with the history of psychometric testing may know that many early testing proponents argued that intelligence was unaffected by schooling, because by intelligence they meant the inborn, native capacity – something that neither schooling nor training was thought to affect. For instance, Cyril Burt, in a 1933 radio interview on BBC, asserted that "By intelligence the psychologist understands inborn, all-around intellectual ability . . . inherited, not due to teaching or training . . . uninfluenced by industry or zeal." The best-known and most thoroughly validated measure of intelligence was, then as now, the IQ test.

Yet, today, many of us would argue that schooling *does* influence intelligence, if by the latter we mean IQ scores. I do not regard IQ scores as adequate indices of intelligence, but *if* one does view them as such, then schooling exerts an influence on them. Notwithstanding past claims, there is an inextricable relationship between schooling and IQ performance. Simply put, the less one attends school, the more IQ will decline. The strongest type of support for this statement would be data on the development of children who were known to be similar at the start of schooling but whose schooling and IQ were systematically covaried to demonstrate the decline of the latter as a function of reductions in the former. Although such support is in short supply, there is nevertheless a wealth of data that converge on the view that schooling influences IQ scores. Below, I shall present only a glimpse of this evidence. Readers who wish to examine the totality of data should consult my 1991 article in *Developmental Psychology* (Vol. 27, pp. 703–22).

IQ, Cognitive Processing, Cultural Knowledge, and Achievement

During the past decade, all of us have been made painfully aware of the declining SAT scores of American youth, the large percentage of high-school graduates who are unable to read or "reckon" on even a ninth-grade level, and the cultural ignorance of the modal teenager. A seldom realized paradox in the story of the decline of American schooling, however, is that while schooling increasingly has failed to guarantee an adequate level of basic skills among its graduates, it is nevertheless associated with many cognitive accomplishments. The easiest accomplishment to document is the steady, linear trend for years of schooling to be correlated with IQ scores. For each year of missed or abbreviated schooling, there is a commensurate decline in IQ. For instance, if you take two boys who at age 13 have identical IQs and grades and then retest these two boys five years later, after one has finished high school or gymnasium while the other had dropped out in ninth grade, you discover that the latter boy has lost around 1.8 IQ points for every year of missed school, thus differing from his former classmate by approximately a half standard deviation by the age of 18. This is an enormous gap for two children who were at one time equated on IQ, and it cannot be due to any factor except the lost years of school attendance.

A similar story can be told for children who begin school late or who miss school a lot. The less one attends school, the more her IQ decreases. The same applies for changes in IQ score across cohorts that differ in their level of school attendance; each added year of school attainment is associated with an increase in IQ over older sibs who attended school less. And there are even small drops in IQ that befall those whose summer vacations are less academically-oriented. In my recent article I reviewed eight classes of evidence for the link between attending school and IQ scores, and argued that alternative explanations for changes in IQ scores fail to account for the full panoply of findings. Only one explanation fits the entire data corpus, namely, each lost opportunity for schooling conveys a decrement on IQ.

The eight classes of evidence I discussed included large intergenerational changes in IQ scores that are related to the availability of schooling within a region, and the systematic alterations in IQ scores that are associated with increases or decreases in formal schooling within a generation. I reviewed evidence showing that starting school late or leaving school early (before graduation from high school) resulted in decrements in IQ, *vis-à-vis* a matched peer who received more schooling. In families of children who attended school intermittently, there is a high negative correlation between chronological age and IQ, implying that as these children got older their IQ scores dropped commensurately. For instance, children of gypsies and canal boat pilots began school in England around the turn of this century with IQs in the low average range (mean = 90), whereas by the time their sibs had reached adolescence, their IQs had presumably plummeted to the retarded range, $r = 0.75$ between age and IQ.

The most parsimonious explanation of the full corpus of data and findings that I reviewed is that schooling helps prop up IQ because much of what is tapped by IQ tests is either directly taught in school (e.g., information questions on popular IQ tests, such as "Who wrote Hamlet?", and "What are hieroglyphics?" are taught in school or confronted in school-related activities such as plays and class trips, as are vocabulary items such as "What is espionage?") or else indirectly taught by schools (e.g., modes of cognizing that emphasize one form of conceptual organization over another). In addition, schooling fosters disembedded ways of construing the world in terms of hypotheticals, and inculcates attitudes toward testing that may be favored by test manufacturers, such as sitting still for prolonged periods, trying hard, and making certain assumptions about the purposes of testing.

Let me give an example of what I mean by fostering certain "modes of cognizing." Around the age of 7 or 8 most schools begin to encourage taxonomic sorting, not as an end in itself but as a means of classifying materials in history, social studies, and geography (e.g., "these are the grain states, these are the dairy states, these are the manufacturing states, etc."). It is not a coincidence that the developers of IQ tests reward children of this age for using precisely these same taxonomic organizations when they answer IQ questions such as "How are an apple and on orange alike?" (e.g., giving a taxonomic answer such as "they are both fruit") instead of a perceptually-based answer (e.g., "they are all round") or a functionally-based answer ("they both can be eaten"). That children who do not attend school perform worse on such subtests of IQ items ought not surprise anyone, given the content of most IQ tests. Unschooled adults also have a tendency to employ the same non-taxonomic (i.e., perceptual and functional) organizations as younger children. But non-taxonomic modes of cognizing are not inherently less abstract or complex than taxonomic modes, and examples of perceptual/functional organizations can be found that are more complex than taxonomic ones. But there is no eschewing the fact that schooling conveys an advantage as far as IQ performance is concerned because it encourages the type of taxonomic organization that is rewarded on the IQ test.

Having said the above, it is important to make a disclaimer: although schooling helps prop up IQ scores, this is not equivalent to claiming that it props up *intelligence*. The latter entails more than the acquisition of certain modes of cognizing that are valued by a test manufacturer, or the acquisition of cultural artifacts – no matter how important some may regard such shared knowledge as being. While intelligence has as many definitions as there are knowledgeable respondents, most researchers agree that it includes some element of novel problem solving. If intelligence is defined as the ability to solve novel problems, then nothing in the literature indicates that schooling actually increases intelligence. Individuals who have never set foot in a school are often capable of engaging in high levels of cognitively complex problem solving, while those who graduate with advanced degrees often cannot. Schooling may make it more likely that one will engage in complex thought processes, but the relationship is imperfect at best. So, while schooling seems to prop up IQ test performance, it does not seem as obvious that it increases intellectual development, particularly if we conceptualize the latter in terms of novel problem solving.

Why Does Schooling Assist IQs but not SATs?

If you accept my argument that staying in school is the best way to prevent a decline in IQ, then why is it that staying in school is not associated with a similar benefit for SATs? Well, the technical answer to the question is that it is associated with such a benefit. To see this one needs only administer the SAT to pairs of youngsters who were similar on their cognitive profiles at age 13 but who differed in their subsequent level of schooling. Being out of school hurts SAT performance, too. The confusion comes when we are told that SAT scores have been declining in recent decades, even as the mean level of schooling has been increasing. But keep in mind that the sample taking the SAT is always comprised of high-school seniors; thus, there is no difference in the level of schooling of today's SAT takers from those of an earlier generation. So, the decline in SATs may reflect a comparative failure among today's high-school graduates to go as far beyond the basics as was formerly true of high-school graduates. Since the number of years of completed schooling is constant among SAT takers, it cannot be blamed or credited with SAT fluctuations. (It also deserves to be noted that today's cohort of SAT takers is more economically and culturally diverse than earlier cohorts taking the SAT, and this factor accounts for approximately 25 percent of the drop in scores over the past 30 years.) Therefore, while the level of schooling among IQ takers is related to changes in their scores, the level of schooling among SAT takers is not because there is no variation in quantity of schooling completed. Of course, there may be large variation in the *quality* of schooling, but so far I have said nothing about *quality* of education, restricting all of my arguments to quantity or number of years of education.

Why Increasing Resources Alone is Not the Answer

There is a lot research showing that various educational techniques, ways of organizing classrooms, and philosophies of teaching can improve educational outcomes. These effective innovations are mostly non-economic in nature. The data are lacking that could support the claim for greater economic resources to improve educational outcomes. Almost without fail, the large meta-analyses have not found a relationship between teacher salaries, class size, per-pupil expenditures, teacher credentials, etc. and those outcomes we as a nation are most concerned about, namely performance in the areas of math, science, and language arts. There are lots of problems with the way data are aggregated in the published meta-analyses, and one could argue that district-wide aggregation fails to detect relationships between economic resources and educational outcomes that exist within individual school buildings, or that within-building aggregations of educational data mask what could be going on within a single grade in that building. Finally, one can rightfully claim, as Gerald Bracey, a former senior policy analyst at NEA, did, that the dependent measure we are studying is wrong: if we expect a relationship to exist between finances and medical outcomes, then we would be disappointed to find none, or perhaps even a negative one. This is because those most of need of intensive medical resources – the cancer patients – have the poorest prognosis. We devote more resources to them even though more of them will die. By analogy the educationally needy may require the most resources despite their poor prognosis. If so, then schools comprised of many poor children will not show large improvements *vis-à-vis* middle-class schools as a linear function of added resources.

There is sense to such criticisms, I think, but they ought not lead to the conclusion that the case for greater financial resources in education has been made, because it has not. The medical analogy can be turned on its heels to argue that schools catering to wealthier families will achieve good outcomes regardless of their level of resources, therefore we can safely provide less per-pupil expenditures there. All that I am trying to say is that it is one thing to criticize studies that show no relationship between financial resources and educational outcomes, but it is quite another to see in this criticism support for a *positive* relation between resources and outcome. To my knowledge, there is no clear evidence in the scientifically reviewed evaluation literature that demonstrates that adding financial resources will improve math, science, or language achievement, beyond the minimum level that we would all agree is necessary, but below which only a small fraction of schools in industrial nations actually fall.

The case is far different in developing nations like Brazil where municipal and state schools are frequently so poor that obvious remedies such as allowing a child to attend two 3-hour school sessions per day instead of the customary single session cannot be adopted because it would require an extra snack per day – something the state schools in many *favelas* (shanty-towns) are unable to do because they lack the extra food. Clearly, nothing I am saying ought to be construed as claiming financial resources never matter. In extremely impoverished schools, some added finances are sorely needed to help achieve educational goals, not to mention humanitarian ones.

What *is* clear in the scientific literature is that American schools spend less of their school day on those substantive subjects that are assessed in the large transnational comparisons (especially science and math) in which our children perform poorly. American teachers spend more time telling children what they are going to teach them and less time actually teaching them; they also spend more time trying to get control of their classes; and they spend more time than competitor countries on subjects that are not tested, but which *may* be important for us as a people (e.g., AIDS awareness, drug refusal training, sexual health, etc.). I underscore the word *may* because, again, there is no credible scientific literature that I am aware of to support many of the programs that can be found in most American elementary schools. As an occasional reviewer for federal agencies that fund such programs, I am often surprised at the willingness of agencies to do something to show they are serious about AIDS, drug usage, teen pregnancy, child abuse, etc. Yet, it is precisely because these are such serious problems that those advocating prevention programs should be required to show that the programs work. For example, we need to ensure that a drug refusal training program in which the local police officer visits the third grade to discourage drug use will not have the opposite effect from what is hoped for. In short, educators need to be more critical about their consumption of programs and ask what evidence there is to recommend their adoption, as well as the costs of doing nothing.

I began this *Science Brief* by noting that if we conceive of intelligence as an IQ score, then the evidence is persuasive that staying in school props up intelligence. Next, I commented that I personally conceive of intelligence as more than an IQ score, and in this regard the evidence is less persuasive that schooling matters. Finally, I noted that my entire argument was based on the relationship between the *quantity* of schooling (highest grade completed) and IQ, and I had said little about the relationship between the *quality* of schooling, especially quality indicators such as teachers' salaries, class size (within the limits found in indus-trialized nations), and per-pupil expenditures. Here the evidence is incomplete, but there is no support for the claim that adding more funds to schools, with the exception of the poorest schools in our country, will raise the level of outcomes, at least beyond the first three grades.

The Genetics of Cognitive Abilities and Disabilities

Introduction

In the next article, two eminent behavior-genetic researchers, Plomin and DeFries, review evidence from the Hawaii Family Study of Cognition (a large-scale study of resemblances among family members on verbal and spatial tests), and the Colorado Adoption Project, a large-scale study of resemblances among adopted children and their birth mothers and adoptive mothers and sibs.

Plomin and DeFries show that the heritability for general intellectual skills measures around 0.5, meaning that 50 percent of the differences among individuals are accounted for by genetic differences among them. Similarly, the heritability for traditional academic skills runs around 0.4. Importantly, the contribution of genes is not fully apparent during infancy, and only comes to fruition during adolescence.

The final point worth noting in this article is the sage advice these authors give concerning the mutability of heritability estimates. They correctly note that heritability estimates (h^2) are not carved in stone, and they can and do change with changes in the environment. Keep the following point in mind: if the environment was equated for everyone, then h^2 would have to be 1.0, because the only source of differences among individuals would have to be genes. Similarly, if we studied only individuals who were genetic clones of each other, then any differences among them would have to result from differences in their environments.

Further reading

Plomin, R., and McClearn, G. E. (1995). *Nature, Nurture, and Psychology.* Washington, DC: American Psychological Association Books.

For a cautionary statement about the separation of nature–nurture effects, see: Wahlsten, D., and Gottlieb, G. (1997). The invalid separation of effects of nature and nurture: lessons from animal experimentation. In R. J. Sternberg and E. Grigorenko (eds), *Intelligence, Heredity, and Environment.* NY: Cambridge University Press.

TWELVE

The Genetics of Cognitive Abilities and Disabilities

Robert Plomin and John C. DeFries

People differ greatly in all aspects of what is casually known as intelligence. The differences are apparent not only in school, from kindergarten to college, but also in the most ordinary circumstances: in the words people use and comprehend, in their differing abilities to read a map or follow directions, or in their capacities for remembering telephone numbers or figuring change. The variations in these specific skills are so common that they are often taken for granted. Yet what makes people so different?

It would be reasonable to think that the environment is the source of differences in cognitive skills – that we are what we learn. It is clear, for example, that human beings are not born with a full vocabulary; they have to learn words. Hence, learning must be the mechanism by which differences in vocabulary arise among individuals. And differences in experience – say, in the extent to which parents model and encourage vocabulary skills or in the quality of language training provided by schools – must be responsible for individual differences in learning.

Earlier in this century psychology was in fact dominated by environmental explanations for variance in cognitive abilities. More recently, however, most psychologists have begun to embrace a more balanced view: one in which nature and nurture interact in cognitive development. During the past few decades, studies in genetics have pointed to a substantial role for heredity in molding the components of intellect, and researchers have even begun to track down the genes involved in cognitive function. These findings do not refute the notion that environmental factors shape the learning process. Instead they suggest that differences in people's genes affect how easily they learn.

Just how much do genes and environment matter for specific cognitive abilities such as vocabulary? That is the question we have set out to answer. Our tool of study is quantitative genetics, a statistical approach that explores the causes of variations in traits among individuals. Studies comparing the performance of twins and adopted children on certain tests of cognitive skills, for example, can assess the relative contributions of nature and nurture.

In reviewing several decades of such studies and conducting our own, we have begun to clarify the relations among specialized aspects of intellect, such as verbal and spatial reasoning, as well as the relations between normal cognitive function and disabilities, such as dyslexia. With the help of molecular genetics, we and other investigators have also begun to identify the genes that affect these specific abilities and disabilities. Eventually, we believe, knowledge of these genes will help reveal the biochemical mechanisms involved in human intelligence. And with the insight gained from genetics, researchers may someday develop environmental interventions that will lessen or prevent the effects of cognitive disorders.

Some people find the idea of a genetic role in intelligence alarming or, at the very least, confusing. It is important to understand from the outset, then, what exactly geneticists mean when they talk about genetic influence. The term typically used is "heritability": a statistical measure of the genetic contribution to differences among individuals.

Verbal and Spatial Abilities

Heritability tells us what proportion of individual differences in a population – known as variance – can be ascribed to genes. If we say, for example, that a trait is 50 percent heritable, we are in effect saying that half of the variance in that trait is linked to heredity. Heritability, then, is a way of explaining what makes people different, not what constitutes a given individual's intelligence. In general, however, if

Twins are common research subjects in studies of specific cognitive abilities. The identical (above) and fraternal (opposite page) pairs depicted here are participants in the authors' research. They are performing a task in a test of spatial ability, trying to reconstruct a block model with their own toy building

blocks. On such tests, which are given to each child individually, the scores of identical twins (who have all the same genes) are more similar than the scores of fraternal twins (who share about half their genes) – a sign that genetic inheritance exerts an influence on spatial ability.

heritability for a trait is high, the influence of genes on the trait in individuals would be strong as well.

Attempts to estimate the heritability of specific cognitive abilities began with family studies. Analyses of similarities between parents and their children and between siblings have shown that cognitive abilities run in families. Results of the largest family study done on specific cognitive abilities, which was conducted in Hawaii in the 1970s, helped to quantify this resemblance.

The Hawaii Family Study of Cognition was a collaborative project between researchers at the University of Colorado at Boulder and the University of Hawaii and involved more than 1,000 families and sibling pairs. The study determined correlations (a statistical measure of resemblance) between relatives on tests of verbal and spatial ability. A correlation of 1.0 would mean that the scores of family members were identical; a correlation of zero would indicate that the scores were no more similar than those of two people picked at random. Because children on average share half their genes with each parent and with siblings, the highest correlation in test scores that could be expected on genetic grounds alone would be 0.5.

The Hawaii study showed that family members are in fact more alike than unrelated individuals on measures of specific cognitive skills. The actual correlations for both verbal and spatial tests were, on average, about 0.25. These correlations alone, however, do not disclose whether cognitive abilities run in families because of genetics or because of environmental effects. To explore this distinction, geneticists rely on two "experiments": twinning (an experiment of nature) and adoption (a social experiment).

Twin studies are the workhorse of behavioral genetics. They compare the resemblance of identical twins, who have the same genetic makeup, with the resemblance of fraternal twins, who share only about half their genes. If cognitive abilities are influenced by genes, identical twins ought to be more alike than fraternal twins on tests of cognitive skills. From correlations found in these kinds of studies, investigators can estimate the extent to which genes account for variances in the general population. Indeed, a rough estimate of heritability can be made by doubling the difference between identical-twin and fraternal-twin correlations.

Adoption provides the most direct way to disentangle nature and nurture in family resemblance, by creating pairs of genetically related individuals who do not share a common family environment. Corre-lations among these pairs enable investigators to estimate the con-tribution of genetics to family resemblance. Adoption also produces pairs of genetically unrelated individuals who share a family environ-ment, and their correlations make it possible to estimate the contri-bution of shared environment to resemblance.

Twin studies of specific cognitive abilities over three decades and in four countries have yielded remarkably consistent results (see top illus-tration on p. 185). Correlations for identical twins greatly exceed those for fraternal twins on tests of both verbal and spatial abilities in chil-dren, adolescents and adults. Results of the first twin study in the elderly – reported last year by Gerald E. McClearn and his colleagues at Pennsylvania State University and by Stig Berg and his associates at the Institute for Gerontology in Jönköping, Sweden – show that the resemblances between identical and fraternal twins persist even into old age. Although gerontologists have assumed that genetic differences become less important as experiences accumulate over a lifetime, research on cognitive abilities has so far demonstrated otherwise. Calculations based on the combined findings in these studies imply that in the general population, genetics accounts for about 60 percent of the variance in verbal ability and about 50 percent of the variance in spatial ability.

Investigations involving adoptees have yielded similar results. Two recent studies of twins reared apart – one by Thomas J. Bouchard, Jr., Matthew McGue, and their colleagues at the University of Minnesota, the other an international collaboration headed by Nancy L. Pedersen at the Karolinska Institute in Stockholm – have implied heritabilities of about 50 percent for both verbal and spatial abilities.

In our own Colorado Adoption Project, which we launched in 1975, we have used the power of adoption studies to further characterize the roles of genes and environment, to assess developmental trends in cognitive abilities and to explore the extent to which specific cognitive skills are related to one another. The ongoing project compares the correlations between more than 200 adopted children and their birth and adoptive parents with the correlations for a control group of children raised by their biological parents (see lower illustration on p. 185).

These data provide some surprising insights. By middle childhood, for example, birth mothers and their children who were adopted by others are just as similar as control parents and their children on

TESTS OF VERBAL ABILITY

1. VOCABULARY: In each row, circle the word that means the same or nearly the same as the underlined word. There is only one correct choice in each line.

a. <u>arid</u>	coarse	clever	modest	dry
b. <u>piquant</u>	fruity	pungent	harmful	upright

2. VERBAL FLUENCY: For the next three minutes, write as many words as you can that start with F and end with M.

3. CATEGORIES: For the next three minutes, list all the things you can think of that are FLAT.

TESTS OF SPATIAL ABILITY

1. IMAGINARY CUTTING: Draw a line or lines showing where the figure on the left should be cut to form the pieces on the right. There may be more than one way to draw the lines correctly.

2. MENTAL ROTATIONS: Circle the two objects on the right that are the same as the object on the left.

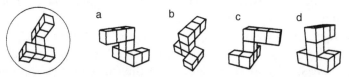

3. CARD ROTATIONS: Circle the figures on the right that can be rotated (without being lifted off the page) to exactly match the one on the left.

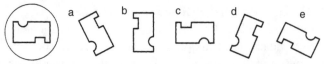

4. HIDDEN PATTERNS: Circle each pattern below in which the figure ⌐ appears. The figure must always be in this position, not upside down or on its side.

Tests of specific abilities administered to adolescents and adults include tasks resembling the ones listed here. The tests gauge each cognitive ability in several ways, and multiple tests are combined to provide a reliable measure of each skill. (Answers appear on p. 195.)

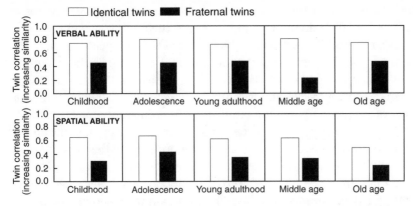

Twin studies have examined correlations in verbal (top) and in spatial (bottom) skills of identical twins and of fraternal twins. When the results of the separate studies are put side by side, they demonstrate a substantial genetic influence on specific cognitive abilities from childhood to old age; for all age groups, the scores of identical twins are more alike than those of fraternal twins. These data seem to counter the long-standing notion that the influence of genes wanes with time.

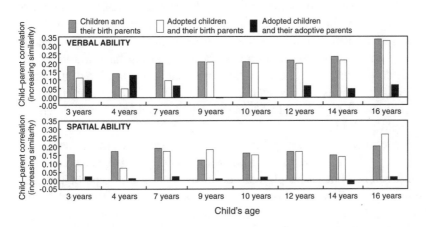

Colorado Adoption Project, which followed subjects over time, finds that for both verbal (top) and spatial (bottom) abilities, adopted children come to resemble their birth parents (white bars) as much as children raised by their birth parents do (gray bars). In contrast, adopted children do not end up resembling their adoptive parents (black bars). The results imply that most of the family resemblance in cognitive skills is caused by genetic factors, not environment.

measures of both verbal and spatial ability. In contrast, the scores of adopted children do not resemble those of their adoptive parents at all. These results join a growing body of evidence suggesting that the common family environment generally does not contribute to similarities in family members. Rather family resemblance on such measures seems to be controlled almost entirely by genetics, and environmental factors often end up making family members different, not the same.

The Colorado data also reveal an interesting developmental trend. It appears that genetic influence increases during childhood, so that by the mid-teens, heritability reaches a level comparable with that seen in adults. In correlations of verbal ability, for example, resemblance between birth parents and their children who were adopted by others increases from about 0.1 at age three to about 0.3 at age 16. A similar pattern is evident in tests of spatial ability. Some genetically driven transformation in cognitive function seems to take place in the early school years, around age seven. The results indicate that by the time people reach age 16, genetic factors account for 50 percent of the variance for verbal ability and 40 percent for spatial ability – numbers not unlike those derived from twin studies of specific cognitive abilities.

The Colorado Adoption Project and other investigations have also helped clarify the differences and similarities among cognitive abilities. Current cognitive neuroscience assumes a modular model of intelligence, in which different cognitive processes are isolated anatomically in discrete modules in the brain. The modular model implies that specific cognitive abilities are also genetically distinct – that genetic effects on verbal ability, say, should not overlap substantially with genetic effects on spatial ability.

Psychologists, however, have long recognized that most specialized cognitive skills, including verbal and spatial abilities, intercorrelate moderately. That is, people who perform well on one type of test also tend to do well on other types. Correlations between verbal and spatial abilities, for example, are usually about 0.5. Such intercorrelation implies a potential genetic link.

From Abilities to Achievement

Genetic studies of specific cognitive abilities also fail to support the modular model. Instead it seems that genes are responsible for most of the overlap between cognitive skills. Analysis of the Colorado project data, for example, indicates that genetics governs 70 percent of the correlation between verbal and spatial ability. Similar results have been found in twin studies in childhood, young adulthood and middle age. Thus, there is a good chance that when genes associated with a particular cognitive ability are identified, the same genes will be associated with other cognitive abilities.

Research into school achievement has hinted that the genes associated with cognitive abilities may also be relevant to academic performance. Studies of more than 2,000 pairs of high-school-age twins were done in the 1970s by John C. Loehlin of the University of Texas at Austin and Robert C. Nichols, then at the National Merit Scholarship Corporation in Evanston, Ill. In these studies the scores of identical twins were consistently and substantially more similar than those of fraternal twins on all four domains of the National Merit Scholarship Qualifying Test: English usage, mathematics, social studies and natural sciences. These results suggest that genetic factors account for about 40 percent of the variation on such achievement tests.

Genetic influence on school achievement has also been found in twin studies of elementary-school-age children as well as in our work with the Colorado Adoption Project. It appears that genes may have almost as much effect on school achievement as they do on cognitive abilities. These results are surprising in and of themselves, as educators have long believed that achievement is more a product of effort than of ability. Even more interesting, then, is the finding from twin studies and our adoption project that genetic effects overlap between different categories of achievement and that these overlapping genes are probably the very same genetic factors that can influence cognitive abilities.

This evidence supports a decidedly nonmodular view of intelligence as a pervasive or global quality of the mind and underscores the relevance of cognitive abilities in real-world performance. It also implies that genes for cognitive abilities are likely to be genes involved in school achievement, and vice versa.

Given the evidence for genetic influence on cognitive abilities and achievement, one might suppose that cognitive disabilities and poor academic achievement must also show genetic influence. But even if genes are involved in cognitive disorders, they may not be the same genes that influence normal cognitive function. The example of mental

What Heritability Means

The implications of heritability data are commonly misunderstood. As the main text indicates, heritability is a statistical measure, expressed as a percentage, describing the extent to which genetic factors contribute to variations on a given trait among the members of a population.

The fact that genes influence a trait does not mean, however, that "biology is destiny." Indeed, genetics research has helped confirm the significance of environmental factors, which generally account for as much variance in human behavior as genes do. If intelligence is 50 percent heritable, then environmental factors must be just as important as genes in generating differences among people.

Moreover, even when genetic factors have an especially powerful effect, as in some kinds of mental retardation, environmental interventions can often fully or partly overcome the genetic "determinants." For example, the devastating effects of phenylketonuria, a genetic disease that can cause mental retardation, can often be nullified by dietary intervention.

Finally, the degree of heritability for a given trait is not set in stone. The relative influence of genes and environment can change. If, for instance, environmental factors were made almost identical for all the members of a hypothetical population, any differences in cognitive ability in that population would then have to be attributed to genetics, and heritability would be closer to 100 percent than to 50 percent. Heritability describes what is, rather than what can (or should) be.

R. P. and J. C. D.

retardation illustrates this point. Mild mental retardation runs in families, but severe retardation does not. Instead severe mental retardation is caused by genetic and environmental factors – novel mutations, birth complications and head injuries, to name a few – that do not come into play in the normal range of intelligence.

Researchers need to assess, rather than assume, genetic links between the normal and the abnormal, between the traits that are part of a continuum and true disorders of human cognition. Yet genetic studies of verbal and spatial disabilities have been few and far between.

Genetics and Disability

Most such research has focused on reading disability, which afflicts 80 percent of children diagnosed with a learning disorder. Children with reading disability, also known as dyslexia, read slowly, show poor comprehension and have trouble reading aloud (see "Dyslexia," by Sally E. Shaywitz, *Scientific American*, November 1996). Studies by one of us (DeFries) have shown that reading disability runs in families and that genetic factors do indeed contribute to the resemblance among family members. The identical twin of a person diagnosed with reading disability, for example, has a 68 percent risk of being similarly diagnosed, whereas a fraternal twin has only a 38 percent chance.

Is this genetic effect related in any way to the genes associated with normal variation in reading ability? That question presents some methodological challenges. The concept of a cognitive disorder is inherently problematic, because it treats disability qualitatively – you either have it or you don't – rather than describing the degree of disability in a quantitative fashion. This focus creates an analytical gap between disorders and traits that are dimensional (varying along a continuum), which are by definition quantitative.

During the past decade, a new genetic technique has been developed that bridges the gap between dimensions and disorders by collecting quantitative information about the relatives of subjects diagnosed qualitatively with a disability. The method is called DF extremes analysis, after its creators, DeFries and David W. Fulker, a colleague at the University of Colorado's Institute for Behavioral Genetics.

For reading disability, the analysis works by testing the identical and fraternal twins of reading-disabled subjects on quantitative measures of reading, rather than looking for a shared diagnosis of dyslexia (see illustration on p. 190). If reading disability is influenced by genes that also affect variation within the normal range of reading performance, then the reading scores of the identical twins of dyslexic children should be closer to those of the reading-disabled group than the scores of

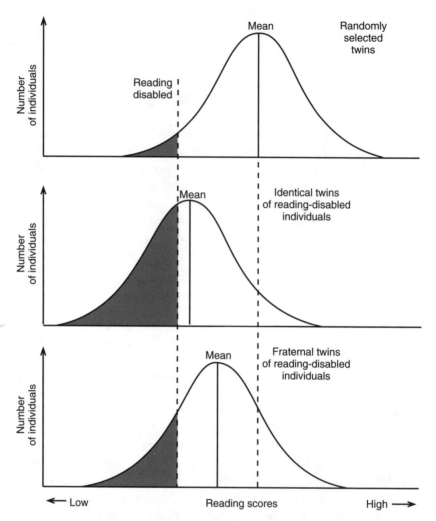

Mean

Randomly
selected
twins

Number
of individuals

Reading
disabled

Mean

Identical twins
of reading-disabled
individuals

Number
of individuals

Mean

Fraternal twins
of reading-disabled
individuals

Number
of individuals

← Low   Reading scores   High →

Reading scores of twins suggest a possible genetic link between normal and
abnormal reading skills. In a group of randomly selected members of twin
pairs (top), a small fraction of children were reading disabled (gray). Identical
(middle) and fraternal (bottom) twins of the reading-disabled children scored
lower than the randomly selected group, with the identical twins performing
worse than the fraternal ones. Genetic factors, then, are involved in reading
disability. The same genes that influence reading disability may underlie
differences in normal reading ability.

fraternal twins are. (A single gene can exert different effects if it occurs in more than one form in a population, so that two people may inherit somewhat different versions. The genes controlling eye color and height are examples of such variable genes.)

It turns out that, as a group, identical twins of reading-disabled subjects do perform almost as poorly as dyslexic subjects on these quantitative tests, whereas fraternal twins do much better than the reading-disabled group (though still significantly worse than the rest of the population). Hence, the genes involved in reading disability may in fact be the same as those that contribute to the quantitative dimension of reading ability measured in this study. DF extremes analysis of these data further suggests that about half the difference in reading scores between dyslexics and the general population can be explained by genetics.

For reading disability, then, there could well be a genetic link between the normal and the abnormal, even though such links may not be found universally for other disabilities. It is possible that reading disability represents the extreme end of a continuum of reading ability, rather than a distinct disorder – that dyslexia might be quantitatively rather than qualitatively different from the normal range of reading ability. All this suggests that if a gene is found for reading disability, the same gene is likely to be associated with the normal range of variation in reading ability. The definitive test will come when a specific gene is identified that is associated with either reading ability or disability. In fact, we and other investigators are already very close to finding such a gene.

The Hunt for Genes

Until now, we have confined our discussion to quantitative genetics, a discipline that measures the heritability of traits without regard to the kind and number of genes involved. For information about the genes themselves, researchers must turn to molecular genetics – and increasingly, they do. If scientists can identify the genes involved in behavior and characterize the proteins that the genes code for, new interventions for disabilities become possible.

Research in mice and fruit flies has succeeded in identifying single genes related to learning and spatial perception, and investigations of naturally occurring variations in human populations have found mutations in single genes that result in general mental retardation. These include the genes for phenylketonuria and fragile X syndrome, both causes of mental retardation. Single-gene defects that are associated with Duchenne's muscular dystrophy, Lesch-Nyhan syndrome, neurofibromatosis type 1 and Williams syndrome may also be linked to the specific cognitive disabilities seen in these disorders (see "Williams Syndrome and the Brain," by Howard M. Lenhoff, Paul P. Wang, Frank Greenberg and Ursula Bellugi; *Scientific American*, December 1997).

In fact, more than 100 single-gene mutations are known to impair cognitive development. Normal cognitive functioning, on the other hand, is almost certainly orchestrated by many subtly acting genes working together, rather than by single genes operating in isolation. These collaborative genes are thought to affect cognition in a probabilistic rather than a deterministic manner and are called quantitative trait loci, or QTLs. The name, which applies to genes involved in a complex dimension such as cognition, emphasizes the quantitative nature of certain physical and behavioral traits. QTLs have already been identified for diseases such as diabetes, obesity and hypertension as well as for behavioral problems involving drug sensitivity and dependence.

But finding QTLs is much more difficult than identifying the single-gene mutations responsible for some cognitive disorders. Fulker addressed this problem by developing a method, similar to DF extremes analysis, in which certain known variations in DNA are correlated with sibling differences in quantitative traits. Because genetic effects are easier to detect at the extremes of a dimension, the method works best when at least one member of each sibling pair is known to be extreme for a trait. Investigators affiliated with the Colorado Learning Disabilities Research Center at the University of Colorado first used this technique, called QTL linkage, to try to locate a QTL for reading disability – and succeeded. The discovery was reported in 1994 by collaborators at Boulder, the University of Denver and Boys Town National Research Hospital in Omaha.

Like many techniques in molecular genetics, QTL linkage works by identifying differences in DNA markers: stretches of DNA that are known to occupy particular sites on chromosomes and that can vary somewhat from person to person. The different versions of a marker, like the different versions of a gene, are called alleles. Because people have

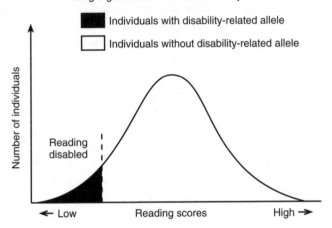

SINGLE-GENE MODEL
Single-gene variant causes disability

■ Individuals with disability-related allele

□ Individuals without disability-related allele

Number of individuals

Reading
disabled

← Low   Reading scores   High →

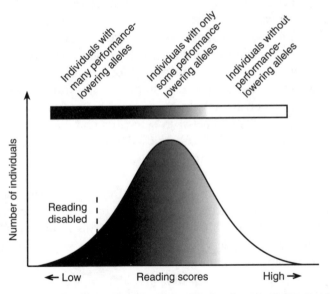

QUANTITATIVE-TRAIT MODEL
Variants of multiple reading-related genes combine to lower scores

Individuals with many performance-lowering alleles

Individuals with only some performance-lowering alleles

Individuals without performance-lowering alleles

Number of individuals

Reading
disabled

← Low   Reading scores   High →

Two models illustrate how genetics may affect reading disability. In the classic view (*top*), a single variant, or allele, of a gene is able to cause the disorder; everyone who has that allele becomes reading disabled (*graph*). But evidence points to a different model (*bottom*), in which a single allele cannot produce the disability on its own. Instead variants of multiple genes each act subtly but can combine to lower scores and increase the risk of disability.

two copies of all chromosomes (except for the gender-determining X and Y chromosomes in males), they have two alleles for any given DNA marker. Hence, siblings can share one, two or no alleles of a marker. In other words, for each marker, siblings can either be like identical twins (sharing both alleles), like fraternal twins (sharing half their alleles) or like adoptive siblings (sharing no alleles).

The investigators who found the QTL for reading disability identified a reading-disabled member of a twin pair and then obtained reading scores for the other twin – the "co-twin." If the reading scores of the co-twins were worse when they shared alleles of a particular marker with their reading-disabled twins, then that marker was likely to lie near a QTL for reading disability in the same chromosomal region. The researchers found such a marker on the short arm of chromosome 6 in two independent samples, one of fraternal twins and one of non-twin siblings. The findings have since been replicated by others.

It is important to note that whereas these studies have helped point to the location of a gene (or genes) implicated in reading disability, the gene (or genes) has not yet been characterized. This distinction gives a sense of where the genetics of cognition stand today: poised on the brink of a new level of discovery. The identification of genes that influence specific cognitive abilities will revolutionize researchers' understanding of the mind. Indeed, molecular genetics will have far-ranging consequences for the study of all human behavior. Researchers will soon be able to investigate the genetic connections between different traits and between behaviors and biological mechanisms. They will be able to better track the developmental course of genetic effects and to define more precisely the interactions between genes and the environment.

The discovery of genes for disorders and disabilities will also help clinicians design more effective therapies and to identify people at risk long before the appearance of symptoms. In fact, this scenario is already being enacted with an allele called Apo-E4, which is associated with dementia and cognitive decline in the elderly. Of course, new knowledge of specific genes could turn up new problems as well: among them, prejudicial labeling and discrimination. And genetics research always raises fears that DNA markers will be used by parents prenatally to select "designer babies."

We cannot emphasize too much that genetic effects do not imply genetic determinism, nor do they constrain environmental interventions. Although some readers may find our views to be controversial, we believe the benefits of identifying genes for cognitive dimensions and disorders will far outweigh the potential abuses.

Test answers

Verbal:
1a   dry
1b   pungent
Spatial:

1

2   b, c
3   a, c, d
4   a, b, f

Part VI

Becoming an Expert – Training or Talent?

Expert Performance: Its Structure and Acquisition

Introduction

In the next article, Anders Ericsson and Neil Charness rebut the widely accepted notion that expert performance results from innate or genetic abilities. The authors argue that, in fact, expert performance reflects the acquisition of complex learned skills and physiological adaptations that result from a substantial amount of deliberate practice. This type of focused practice is seen as the primary cause of expert-level performance. Differences in the levels of performance of elite performers are attributed to differences in the amount of time dedicated to deliberate practice, rather than to innate gifts.

For example, the authors note that in their empirical research, top violinists by age 20 had practiced more than 10,000 total hours, and the less successful violinists had practiced only 5,000 total hours. This practice across domains was found to begin as early as age 4 or 6 for international performers, and to occupy approximately four concentrated hours per day. The authors show that fully a decade of such sustained practice is necessary for an individual to achieve top-level performance in our competitive world.

As part of their refutation of the innate ability or genetic hypothesis, the authors note that the winning time of the first Olympic marathon was comparable to the qualifying time met by thousands of runners in today's Boston Marathon. These dramatic increases in runners' capacity are seen as a result of more knowledge about running, better nutrition and medical care, and better training techniques, which have combined to create a backdrop for daily training that enables runners to practice for superior benefits. The authors believe that innate genetic talent for running is not responsible for creating the world-class runner, but rather, sustained training and practice beginning early in life. As with the top violinists, the authors believe that differences among world-class athletes reflect differences in amount of practice, and not genetic differences.

The authors hold an extreme environmentalist view about the relative unimportance of genes in expert performance. Their data are fascinating and deserve close attention from anyone interested in the nature–nurture debate. We hope readers will be provoked by this article to examine their own biases about the origins of exceptional abilities.

Further reading

Ericcson, K. A., Krampe, T., and Heizman, S. (1993). Can we create gifted people? In G. R. Bock and K. Ackrill (eds), *The Origins and Development of High Ability*. Chichester: Wiley.

THIRTEEN

Expert Performance: Its Structure and Acquisition

K. Anders Ericsson and Neil Charness

In nearly every field of human endeavor, the performance of the best practitioners is so outstanding, so superior even to the performance of other highly experienced individuals in the field, that most people believe a unique, qualitative attribute, commonly called innate talent, must be invoked to account for this highest level of performance. Although these differences in performance are by far the largest psychologists have been able to reliably measure among healthy adults, exceptional performance has not, until recently, been extensively studied by scientists.

In the last decade, interest in outstanding and exceptional achievements and performance has increased dramatically. Many books have been recently published on the topic of genius (for example, Gardner, 1993a; Murray, 1989a; Simonton, 1984, 1988b; Weisberg, 1986, 1993), exceptionally creative individuals (D. B. Wallace and Gruber, 1989), prodigies (Feldman, 1986; A. Wallace, 1986), and exceptional performance and performers (Howe, 1990; Radford, 1990; Smith, 1983). Of particular interest to the general public has been the remarkable ability of idiot savants or savants, who in spite of a very low general intellectual functioning display superior performance in specific tasks and domains, such as mental multiplication and recall of music (Howe, 1990; Treffert, 1989). The pioneering research comparing the performance of experts and beginners (novices) by de Groot (1978) and Chase and Simon (1973) has generated a great deal of research (Chi, Glaser, and Farr, 1988; Ericsson and Smith, 1991b). A parallel development in computer science has sought to extract the knowledge of experts by interviews (Hoffman, 1992) to build expert systems, which are computer models that are designed to duplicate the performance of these experts and make their expertise generally available. These efforts at artificial intelligence have been most successful in domains that have established symbolic representations, such as mathematical calculation, chess, and music (Barr and Feigenbaum, 1981–2; Cohen & Feigenbaum, 1982), which incidentally are the main domains in which prodigies and savants have been able to display clearly superior performance (Feldman, 1980, 1986).[1]

The recent advances in our understanding of exceptional performance have had little impact on general theories in psychology. The new knowledge has not fulfilled the humanistic goals of gaining insights from the lives of outstanding people about how people might improve their lives. Maslow (1971) long ago eloquently expressed these goals:

> If we want to know how fast a human being can run, then it is no use to average out the speed of a "good sample" of the population; it is far better to collect Olympic gold medal winners and see how well they can do. If we want to know the possibilities for spiritual growth, value growth, or moral development in human beings, then I maintain that we can learn most by studying our moral, ethical, or saintly people. . . . Even when "good specimens," the saints and sages and great leaders of history, have been available for study, the temptation too often has been to consider them not human but supernaturally endowed. (p. 7)

The reasons for the lack of impact become clear when we consider the two most dominant approaches and their respective goals. The human information-processing approach, or the skills approach, has attempted to explain exceptional performance in terms of knowledge and skills acquired through experience. This approach, originally developed by Newell and Simon (1972), has tried to show that the basic information-processing system with its elementary information processes and basic capacities remains intact during skill acquisition and that outstanding performance results from incremental increases in knowledge and skill due to the extended effects of experience. By constraining the changes to acquired knowledge and skill, this approach has been able to account for exceptional performance within existing general theories of human cognition. According to this approach the mechanisms identified in laboratory studies of learning can be extrapolated to account for expertise and expert performance by an incremental accumulation of knowledge and skill over a decade of intense experience in the domain. The long duration of the necessary period of experience and the presumed vast complexity of the accumulated knowledge have discouraged investigators from empirically studying the acquisition of expert performance. Similarly, individual differences in expert performanue, when the amount of experience is controlled, have not been of major interest and have been typically assumed to reflect differences in the original structure of basic processes, capacities, and abilities.

The other major approach focuses on the individual differences of exceptional performers that would allow them to succeed in a specific domain. One of the most influential representatives of this approach is Howard Gardner, who in 1983 presented his theory of multiple intelligence in his book *Frames of Mind: The Theory of Multiple Intelligences* (hereinafter referred to as *Frames of Mind*). Gardner (1983, 1993a, 1993b) drew on the recent advances in biology and brain physiology about neural mechanisms and localization of brain activity to propose an account of the achievements of savants, prodigies, and geniuses in specific domains. He argued that exceptional performance results from a close match between the individual's intelligence profile and the demands of the particular domain. A major concern in this approach is the early identification and nurturing of children with high levels of the required intelligence for a specific domain. Findings within this approach have limited implications for the lives of the vast majority of children and adults of average abilities and talents.

In this article we propose a different approach to the study of exceptional performance and achievement, which we refer to as the study of expert performance. Drawing on our earlier published research, we focus on reproducible, empirical phenomena of superior performance. We will thus not seriously consider anecdotes or unique events, including major artistic and scientific innovations, because they cannot be repeatedly reproduced on demand and hence fall outside the class of phenomena that can be studied by experimental methods. Our approach involves the identification of reproducible superior performance in the everyday life of exceptional performers and the capture of this performance under laboratory conditions. Later we show that the analysis of captured superior performance reveals that extended training alters the cognitive and physiological processes of experts to a greater degree than is commonly believed possible. In the final section of the article we review results from studying the lives of expert performers and identify the central role of large amounts of focused training (deliberate practice), which we distinguish from other forms of experience in a domain. The recent evidence for far-reaching effects of training leads us to start by reexamining the available evidence for innate talent and specific gifts as necessary conditions for attaining the highest levels of performance in a domain.

Traditional View of the Role of Talent in Exceptional Performance

Since the emergence of civilization, philosophers have speculated about the origin of highly desirable individual attributes, such as poetic ability, physical beauty, strength, wisdom, and skill in handiwork (Murray, 1989b). It was generally believed that these attributes were gifts from the gods, and it was commonly recognized that "On the whole the gods do not bestow more than one gift on a person" (Murray, 1989b, p. 11). This view persisted in early Greek thought, although direct divine intervention was replaced by natural causes. Ever since, there has been a bias toward attributing high abilities to gifts rather than experience; as expressed by John Stuart Mill, there is "a common tendency among mankind to consider all power which is not visibly the effect of practice, all skill which is not capable of being reduced to mechanical rules, as the result of a particular gift" (quoted in Murray, 1989b, p. 12).

One important reason for this bias in attribution, we believe, is linked to immediate legitimatization of various activities associated with the gifts. If the gods have bestowed a child with a special gift in a given art form, who would dare to oppose its development, and who would not facilitate its expression so everyone could enjoy its wonderful creations? This argument may appear strange today, but before the French Revolution the privileged status of kings and nobility and the birthright of their children were primarily based on such claims.

The first systematic development of this argument for gaining social recognition to artists can be found in the classic work on *The Lives of the Artist* by Vasari (Bull, 1987), originally published in 1568. This book provided the first major biography of artists and is generally recognized as a major indirect influence on the layman's conceptions of artists even today (Barolsky, 1991). Although Vasari's expressed goal was simply to provide a factual history of art, modern scholars argue that "the *Lives* were partly designed to propagate ideas of the artist as someone providentially born with a vocation from heaven, entitled to high recognition, remuneration and respect" (Bull, 1987, Vol. 2, p. xxvi). To support his claim, Vasari tried to identify early signs of talent and ability in the lives of the artists he described. When facts were missing, he is now known to have added or distorted material (Barolsky, 1991). For example, Vasari dated his own first public demonstration of high ability to the age of 9, although historians now know that he was 13 years old at that event (Boase, 1979). His evaluations of specific pieces of art expressed his beliefs in divine gifts. Michelangelo's famous painting in the Sistine Chapel, the *Final Judgment*, was described by Vasari as "the great example sent by God to men so that they can perceive what can be done when intellects of the highest grade descend upon the earth" (quoted in Boase, 1979, pp. 251–2). Vasari also tried to establish a link between the noble families and the families of outstanding artists by tracing the heritage and family trees of the artists of his time to the great families of antiquity and to earlier great artists. However, much of the reported evidence is now considered to have been invented by Vasari (Barolsky, 1992). In the centuries following Vasari, our civilization underwent major social changes leading to a greater social mobility through the development of a skilled middle class and major progress in the accumulation of scientific knowledge. It became increasingly clear that individuals could dramatically increase their performance though education and training, if they had the necessary drive and motivation. Speculation on the nature of talent started to distinguish achievements due to innate gifts from other achievements resulting from learning and training. In 1759 Edward Young published a famous book on the origin of creative products, in which he argued that "An *Original* may be said to be of *vegetable* nature: it rises spontaneously from the vital root of Genius; it *grows*, it is not *made*" (quoted with original italics in Murray, 1989b, p. 28). Hence, an important characteristic of genius and talent was the apparent absence of learning and training, and thus talent and acquired skill became opposites (Bate, 1989). A century later Galton (1979) presented a comprehensive scientific theory integrating talent and training that has continued to influence the conception of exceptional performance among the general population.

Sir Francis Galton was the first scientist to investigate empirically the possibility that excellence in diverse fields and domains has a common set of causes. On the basis of an analysis of eminent men in a wide range of domains and of their relatives, Galton (1979) argued that three factors had to be present: innate ability, eagerness to work, and "an adequate power of doing a great deal of very laborious work" (p. 37). Because the importance of the last two factors – motivation and effort – had already been recognized (Ericsson, Krampe, and Heizmann, 1993), later investigators concentrated primarily on showing that innate abilities and capacities are necessary to attain the highest levels of performance.

Galton (1979) acknowledged a necessary but not sufficient role for instruction and practice in achieving exceptional performance. According to this view, performance increases monotonically as a function of practice toward an asymptote representing a fixed upper bound on performance. Like Galton, contemporary researchers generally assume that training can affect some of the components mediating performance but cannot affect others. If performance achieved after extensive training is limited by components that cannot be modified, it is reasonable to assert that stable, genetically determined factors determine the ultimate level of performance. If all possible changes in performance related to training are attained after a fairly limited period of practice, this argument logically implies that individual differences in final performance must reflect innate talents and natural abilities.

The view that talent or giftedness for a given activity is necessary to attain the highest levels of performance in that activity is widely held among people in general. This view is particularly dominant in such domains of expertise as chess, sports, music, and visual arts, where millions of individuals are active but only a very small number reach the highest levels of performance.

One of the most prominent and influential scientists who draw on evidence from exceptional performance of artists, scientists, and athletes for a biological theory of talent is Howard Gardner. In *Frames of Mind*, Gardner (1983) proposed seven intelligences: linguistic, musical, spatial, logical–mathematical, bodily kinesthetic, and interpersonal and intrapersonal intelligence – each an independent system with its own biological bases (p. 68). This theory is a refinement and development of ideas expressed in an earlier book (Gardner, 1973), in which the talent position was more explicitly articulated, especially in the case of music. Gardner (1973) wrote,

Further evidence of the strong hereditary basis of musical talent comes
from a number of sources. Most outstanding musicians are discovered
at an early age, usually before 6 and often as early as 2 or 3, even in
households where relatively little music is heard. Individual differences
are tremendous among children, and training seems to have comparatively little effect in reducing these differences. (p. 188)

He discussed possible mechanisms for talent in the context of music
savants, who in spite of low intellectual functioning display impressive
music ability as children: "it seems possible that the children are
reflecting a rhythmic and melodic capacity that is primarily hereditary,
and which needs as little external stimulation as does walking and
talking in the normal child" (Gardner, 1973, p. 189). Although Gardner
(1983) did not explicitly discuss his earlier positions, the evidence from
prodigies and savants remains central. *Frames of Mind* contains a careful
review of the then available research on the dramatic effects of training
on performance. In particular, he reviewed the exceptional music
performance of young children trained with the Suzuki method
and noted that many of these children who began training without
previous signs of musical talent attained levels comparable to music
prodigies of earlier times and gained access to the best music teachers
in the world. The salient aspect of talent, according to Gardner (1983),
is no longer the innate structure (gift) but rather the potential for
achievement and the capacity to rapidly learn material relevant to one
of the intelligences. Gardner's (1983) view is consistent with Suzuki's
rejection of inborn talent in music and Suzuki's (1981a) early belief
in individual differences in innate general ability to learn, although
Suzuki's innate abilities were not specific to a particular domain, such
as music. However, in his later writings, Suzuki (1981b) argued that
"every child can be highly educated if he is given the proper training"
(p. 233), and he blamed earlier training failures on incorrect training
methods and their inability to induce enthusiasm and motivation in
the children. The clearest explication of Gardner's (1983) view is
found when he discussed his proposal for empirical assessments of
individuals' profiles in terms of the seven intelligences. He proposed
a test in which "individuals were given the opportunity to learn to
recognize certain patterns [relevant to the particular domain] and were
tested on their capacities to remember these from one day to the next"
(p. 385). On the basis of tests for each of the intelligences, "intellectual

profiles could be drawn up in the first year or two of life" (p. 386), although reliable assessments may have to wait until the preschool years because of "early neural and functional plasticity" (p. 386). Gardner's own hunch about strong intellectual abilities was that "an individual so blessed does not merely have an easy time learning new patterns; he learns them so readily that *it is virtually impossible for him to forget them*" (pp. 385–6).

Our reading of Gardner's (1993a, 1993b)[2] most recent books leads us to conclude that his ideas on talent have not fundamentally changed. According to Gardner's (1983) influential view, the evidence for the talent view is based on two major sources of data on performance: the performance of prodigies and savants and the ability to predict future success of individuals on the basis of early test results. Given that our knowledge about the exceptional performance of savants and prodigies and the predictive validity of tests of basic abilities and talents have increased considerably in the past decade, we briefly review the evidence or rather the lack of evidence for innate abilities and talent.

Performance of prodigies and savants

When the large collection of reports of amazing and inexplicable performance is surveyed, one finds that most of them cannot even be firmly substantiated and can only rarely be replicated under controlled laboratory conditions. Probably the best established phenomenon linked to talent in music is perfect pitch, or more accurately absolute pitch (AP). Only approximately 0.01 percent of the general population have AP and are able to correctly name each of the 64 different tones, whereas average musicians without AP can distinguish only approximately five or six categories of pitches when the pitches are presented in isolation (Takeuchi and Hulse, 1993). Many outstanding musicians display AP, and they first reveal their ability in early childhood. With a few exceptions, adults appear to be unable to attain AP in spite of extended efforts. Hence the characteristics of absolute pitch would seem to meet all of the criteria of innate talent, although there is some controversy about how useful this ability is to the expert musicians. In a recent review of AP, Takeuchi and Hulse (1993) concluded that the best account of the extensive and varied evidence points toward a theory that "states AP can be *acquired by anyone* [italics added], but only during a limited period of development" (p. 355). They found that all individuals with AP had started with music instruction early – nearly always before age five or six – and that several studies had been successful in teaching AP to three- to six-year-old children. At older ages children perceive relations between pitches, which leads to accurate relative pitch, something all skilled musicians have. "Young children *prefer* to process absolute rather than the relative pitches of musical stimuli" (p. 356). Similar developmental trends from individual features to relational attributes are found in other forms of perception during the same age period (Takeuchi & Hulse, 1993). Rather than being a sign of innate talent, AP appears to be a natural consequence of appropriate instruction and of ample opportunities to interact with a musical instrument, such as a piano, at very young ages.

Other proposed evidence for innate talent comes from studies of prodigies in music and chess who are able to attain high levels of performance even as young children. In two influential books, Feldman (1980, 1986) showed that acquisition of skills in prodigies follows the same sequence of stages as in other individuals in the same domain. The primary difference is that prodigies attain higher levels faster and at younger ages. For example, an analysis of Picasso's early drawings as a child shows that he encountered and mastered problems in drawing in ways similar to less gifted individuals (Pariser, 1987). Feldman (1986) also refuted the myth that prodigies acquire their skills irrespective of the environment. In fact, he found evidence for the exact opposite, namely that "the more powerful and specific the gift, the more need for active, sustained and specialized intervention" (p. 123) from skilled teachers and parents. He described the classic view of gifts, in which parents are compelled to support their development, when he wrote, "When extreme talent shows itself it demands nothing less than the willingness of one or both of the parents to give up almost everything else to make sure that the talent is developed" (p. 122). A nice case in point is the child art prodigy Yani (Ho, 1989), whose father gave up his own painting career so as not to interfere with the novel style that his daughter was developing. Feldman (1980, 1986) argued that prodigious performance is rare because extreme talent for a specific activity in a particular child and the necessary environmental support and instruction rarely coincide.

Contrary to common belief, most child prodigies never attain exceptional levels of performance as adults (Barlow, 1952; Feldman,

1986). When Scheinfeld (1939) examined the reported basis of the initial talent assessment by parents of famous musicians, he found signs of interest in music rather than objective evidence of unusual capacity. For example, Fritz Kreisler was "playing violin" (p. 239) with two sticks at age four, and Yehudi Menuhin had a "response to violins at concerts" (p. 239) at the age of one and a half years. Very early start of music instruction would then lead to the acquisition of absolute pitch. Furthermore, the vast majority of exceptional adult performers were never child prodigies, but instead they started instruction early and increased their performance due to a sustained high level of training (Bloom, 1985). The role of early instruction and maximal parental support appears to be much more important than innate talent, and there are many examples of parents of exceptional performers who successfully designed optimal environments for their children without any concern about innate talent (see Ericsson, Krampe, and Tesch-Römer, 1993; Howe, 1990). For example, as part of an educational experiment, Laslo and Klara Polgar (Forbes, 1992) raised one of their daughters to become the youngest international chess grand master ever – she was even younger than Bobby Fischer, who was the youngest male achieving that exceptional level of chess-playing skill. In 1992 the three Polgar daughters were ranked first, second, and sixth in the world among women chess players, respectively.

Although scientists and the popular press have been interested in the performance of prodigies, they have been especially intrigued by so-called savants. Savants are individuals with a low level of general intellectual functioning who are able to perform at high levels in some special tasks. In a few cases the parents have reported that these abilities made their appearances suddenly, and they cited them as gifts from God (Ericsson and Faivre, 1988; Feldman, 1986). More careful study of the emergence of these and other cases shows that their detection may in some cases have been sudden, but the opportunities, support, and encouragement for learning had preceded the original performance by years or even decades (Ericsson and Faivre, 1988; Howe, 1990; Treffert, 1989). Subsequent laboratory studies of the performance of savants have shown them to reflect acquired skills. For example, savants who can name the day of the week of an arbitrary date (e.g., November 5, 1923) generate their answers using instructable methods that allow their performance to be reproduced by a college student after a month of training (for a review see Ericsson and Faivre,

1988). The only ability that cannot be reproduced after brief training concerns some savants' reputed ability to play a piece of music after a single hearing.

However, in a carefully controlled study of a music savant (J.L.), Charness, Clifton, and MacDonald (1988) showed that reproduction of short (2- to 12-note) tonal sequences and recall of from two to four chords (4 notes each) depended on whether the sequences or chords followed Western scale structure. Unfamiliar sequences that violated musical conventions were poorly recalled past 6 notes. Short, familiar sequences of notes and chords were accurately recalled, although recall dropped with length of sequence so that only 3 (of 24) 12-note familiar sequences were completely correct. Attempts to train J.L. to learn temporally static 16-note melodies were unsuccessful. Even in the case of the musical savant studied by Sloboda, Hermelin, and O'Connor (1985), who was able to memorize a new piece of music, there was a marked difference in success with a conventional versus a tonally unconventional piece. Thus, music savants, like their normally intelligent expert counterparts, need access to stored patterns and retrieval structures to enable them to retain long, unfamiliar musical patterns. Given that savants cannot read music – most of them are blind – they have to acquire new music by listening, which would provide motivation and opportunities for the development of domain-specific memory skills.

In summary, the evidence from systematic laboratory research on prodigies and savants provides no evidence for giftedness or innate talent but shows that exceptional abilities are acquired often under optimal environmental conditions.

Prediction of future success based on innate abilities and talent

The importance of basic processes and capacities is central to many theorists in the human information-processing tradition. In conceptual analogies with computers, investigators often distinguish between hardware (the physical components of the computer) and software (computer programs and stored data). In models of human performance, "software" corresponds to knowledge and strategies that can be readily changed as a function of training and learning, and "hardware" refers to the basic elements that cannot be changed through training. Even theorists such as Chase and Simon (1973), who acknowledge that "practice is the major independent variable in the acquisition of skill" (p. 279), argue in favor of individual differences in talent that predispose people to be successful in different domains: "Although there clearly must be a set of specific aptitudes (e.g., aptitudes for handling spatial relations) that together comprise a talent for chess, individual differences in such aptitudes are largely overshadowed by immense differences in chess experience" (p. 297). Bloom (1985) went through many different domains to point out some necessary qualities that are likely to be mostly inborn, such as "*motor coordination, speed of reflexes* and *hand–eye coordination*" (p. 546). These views were consistent with the available information at the time, such as high heritabilities for many of these characteristics. In their review of sport psychology, Browne and Mahoney (1984) argued for the importance of fixed physiological traits for elite performance of athletes and wrote that "there is good evidence that the limits of physiological capacity to become more efficient with training is determined by genetics" (p. 609). They cited research reporting that percentage of muscle fibers and aerobic capacity "are more than 90% determined by heredity for both male and female" (p. 609). However, more recent reviews have shown that heritabilities in random samples of twins are much lower and range between zero and 40 percent (Malina and Bouchard, 1991).

It is curious how little empirical evidence supports the talent view of expert and exceptional performance. Ever since Galton, investigators have tried to measure individual differences in unmodifiable abilities and basic cognitive and perceptual capacities. To minimize any influence from prior experience, they typically base their tests on simple tasks. They measure simple reaction time and detection of sensory stimuli and present meaningless materials, such as nonsense syllables and lists of digits, in tests of memory capacity. A recent review (Ericsson, Krampe, and Tesch-Römer, 1993) showed that efforts to measure talent with objective tests for basic cognitive and perceptual motor abilities have been remarkably unsuccessful in predicting final performance in specific domains. For example, elite athletes are able to react much faster and make better perceptual discriminations to representative situations in their respective domains, but their simple reaction times and perceptual acuity to simple stimuli during laboratory tests do not differ systematically from those of other athletes or control subjects (for reviews see

Regnier, Salmela, and Russell, 1993, and Starkes and Deakin, 1985). Chess players' and other experts' superior memory for brief presentation of representative stimuli from their domains compared with that of novices is eliminated when the elements of the same stimuli are presented in a randomly arranged format (Chase and Simon, 1973; see Ericsson and Smith, 1991a, for a review). The performance of elite chess players on standard tests of spatial ability is not reliably different from control subjects (Doll and Mayr, 1987). The domain specificity of superior performance is striking and is observed in many different domains of expertise (Ericsson, Krampe, and Tesch-Römer, 1993).

This conclusion can be generalized with some qualifications to current tests of such general abilities as verbal and quantitative intelligence. These tests typically measure acquired knowledge of mathematics, vocabulary, and grammar by successful performance on items testing problem solving and comprehension. Performance during and immediately after training is correlated with IQ, but the correlations between this type of ability test and performance in the domain many months and years later is reduced (even after corrections for restriction of range) to such low values that Hulin, Henry, and Noon (1990) questioned their usefulness and predictive validity. At the same time, the average IQ of expert performers, especially in domains of expertise requiring thinking, such as chess, has been found to be higher than the average of the normal population and corresponds roughly to that of college students. However, IQ does not reliably discriminate the best adult performers from less accomplished adult performers in the same domain.

Even physiological and anatomical attributes can change dramatically in response to physical training. Almost everyone recognizes that regular endurance and strength training uniformly improves aerobic endurance and strength, respectively. As the amount and intensity of physical training are increased and maintained for long periods, far-reaching adaptations of the body result (see Ericsson, Krampe, & Tesch-Römer, 1993, for a review). For example, the sizes of hearts and lungs, the flexibility of joints, and the strength of bones increase as the result of training, and the nature and extent of these changes appear to be magnified when training overlaps with physical development during childhood and adolescence. Furthermore, the number of capillaries supplying blood to trained muscles increases, and muscle fibers can change their metabolic properties from fast twitch to slow twitch. With the clear exception of height, a surprisingly large number of anatomical characteristics show specific changes and adaptations to the specific nature of extended intense training, which we describe in more detail later in this article.

If one accepts the necessity of extended intense training for attaining expert performance – a claim that is empirically supported later in this article – then it follows that currently available estimates of heritability of human characteristics do not generalize to expert performance. An estimate of heritability is valid only for the range of environmental effects for which the studied subjects have been exposed. With a few exceptions, studies of heritabilities have looked only at random samples of subjects in the general population and have not restricted their analyses to individuals exposed to extended training in a domain. The remaining data on exceptional and expert performers have not been able to demonstrate systematic genetic influences. Explanations based on selective access to instruction and early training in a domain provide as good or in some cases better accounts of familial relations of expert performers, such as the lineage of musicians in the Bach family (see Ericsson, Krampe, and Tesch-Römer, 1993, for a review).

In summary, we argue that the traditional assumptions of basic abilities and capacities (talent) that may remain stable in studies of limited and short-term practice do not generalize to superior performance acquired over years and decades in a specific domain. In addition, we will later review evidence showing that acquired skill can allow experts to circumvent basic capacity limits of short-term memory and of the speed of basic reactions, making potential basic limits irrelevant. Once the potential for change through practice is recognized, we believe that a search for individual differences that might be predictive of exceptional and expert performance should refocus on the factors advocated by Charles Darwin (quoted in Galton, 1908) in a letter to Galton after reading the first part of Galton's (1979) book: "You have made a convert of an opponent in one sense, for I have always maintained that excepting fools, men did not differ much in intellect, only in zeal and hard work; I still think this is an *eminently* important difference" (p. 290). In commenting on Darwin's remark, Galton (1908) agreed but argued that "character, including the aptitude for work, is heritable" (p. 291). On the basis of their review, Ericsson, Krampe, and Tesch-Römer (1993) found that motivational factors are more likely to be the locus of heritable influences than is innate talent. We explicate the connection between these "motivational" factors and the rate of improving performance in a specific domain in the last section of this article.

There are two parts to the remaining portion of this article. First, we show that it is possible to study and analyze the mechanisms that mediate expert performance. We also show that the critical mechanisms reflect complex, domain-specific cognitive structures and skills that performers have acquired over extended periods of time. Hence, individuals do not achieve expert performance by gradually refining and extrapolating the performance they exhibited before starting to practice but instead by restructuring the performance and acquiring new methods and skills. In the final section, we show that individuals improve their performance and attain an expert level, not as an automatic consequence of more experience with an activity but rather through structured learning and effortful adaptation.

The Study of Expert Performance

The conceptions of expert performance as primarily an acquired skill versus a reflection of innate talents influence how expert performance and expert performers are studied. When the goal is to identify critical talents and capacities, investigators have located experts and then compared measurements of their abilities with those of control subjects on standard laboratory tests. Tests involve simple stimuli and tasks in order to minimize any effects of previously acquired knowledge and skill. Given the lack of success of this line of research, we advocate a different approach that identifies the crucial aspects of experts' performance that these experts exhibit regularly at a superior level in their domain. If experts have acquired their superior performance by extended adaptation to the specific constraints in their domains, we need to identify representative tasks that incorporate these constraints to be able to reproduce the natural performance of experts under controlled conditions in the laboratory. We illustrate this method of designing representative test situations with several examples later in this section. Once the superior performance of experts can be reliably reproduced in a test situation, this performance can then be analyzed to assess its mediating acquired mechanisms. Following Ericsson and Smith

(1991a), we define expert performance as consistently superior performance on a specified set of representative tasks for the domain that can be administered to any subject. The virtue of defining expert performance in this restricted sense is that the definition both meets all the criteria of laboratory studies of performance and comes close to meeting those for evaluating performance in many domains of expertise.

Perceived experts versus consistent expert performance

In many domains, rules have evolved and standardized conditions, and fair methods have been designed for measuring performance. The conditions of testing in many sports and other activities, such as typing competitions, are the same for all participating individuals. In other domains, the criteria for expert performance cannot be easily translated into a set of standardized tasks that captures and measures that performance. In some domains, expert performance is determined by judges or by the results of competitive tournaments. Psychometric methods based on tournament results, most notably in chess (Elo, 1986), have successfully derived latent measures of performance on an interval scale. In the arts and sciences, selected individuals are awarded prizes and honors by their peers, typically on the basis of significant achievements such as published books and research articles and specific artistic performances.

Some type of metric is of course required to identify *superior performance*. The statistical term *outlier* may be a useful heuristic for judging superior performance. Usually, if someone is performing at least two standard deviations above the mean level in the population, that individual can be said to be performing at an expert level. In the domain of chess (Elo, 1986), the term *expert* is defined as a range of chess ratings (2,000–199) approximately two to three standard deviations (200 rating points) above the mean (1,600 rating points) and five to six standard deviations above the mean of chess players starting to play in chess tournaments.

In most domains it is easier to identify individuals who are socially recognized as experts than it is to specify observable performance at which these individuals excel. The distinction between the perception of expertise and actual expert performance becomes increasingly important as research has shown that the performance of some individuals who are nominated as experts is not measurably superior. For example, studies have found that financial experts' stock investments yield returns that are not consistently better than the average of the stock market, that is, financial experts' performance does not differ from the result of essentially random selection of stocks. When successful investors are identified and their subsequent investments are tracked, there is no evidence for sustained superiority. A large body of evidence has been accumulated showing that experts frequently do not outperform other people in many relevant tasks in their domains of expertise (Camerer and Johnson, 1991). Experts may have much more knowledge and experience than others, yet their performance on critical tasks may not be reliably better than that of nonexperts. In summary, researchers cannot seek out experts and simply assume that their performance on relevant tasks is superior; they must instead demonstrate this superior performance.

Identifying and capturing expert performance

For most domains of expertise, people have at least an intuitive conception of the kind of activities at which an expert should excel. In everyday life, however, these activities rarely have clearly defined starting and end points, nor do the exact external conditions of a specific activity reoccur. The main challenge is thus to identify particular well-defined tasks that frequently occur and that capture the essence of expert performance in a specific domain. It is then possible to determine the contexts in which each task naturally occurs and to present these tasks in a controlled context to a larger group of other experts.

De Groot's (1978) research on expertise in chess is generally considered the pioneering effort to capture expert performance. Ability in chess playing is determined by the outcomes of chess games between opponents competing in tournaments. Each game is different and is rarely repeated exactly except for the case of moves in the opening phase of the game. De Groot, who was himself a chess master, determined that the ability to play chess is best captured in the task of selecting the next move for a given chess position taken from the middle of the game between two chess masters. Consistently superior performance on this task for arbitrary chess positions logically implies a very high level of skill. Researchers can therefore elicit experts' superiority in performing a critical task by presenting the same unfamiliar chess position to any number of chess players and asking them to find the best next move. De Groot demonstrated that performance on this task discriminates well between chess players at different levels of skill and thus captures the essential phenomenon of ability to play this game.

In numerous subsequent studies, researchers have used a similar approach to study the highest levels of thinking in accepted experts in various domains of expertise (Chi et al., 1988; Ericsson and Smith, 1991b). If expert performance reflects extended adaptation to the demands of naturally occurring situations, it is important that researchers capture the structure of these situations in order to elicit maximal performance from the experts. Furthermore, if the tasks designed for research are sufficiently similar to normal situations, experts can rely on their existing skills, and no experiment-specific changes are necessary. How similar these situations have to be to real-life situations is an empirical question. In general, researchers should strive to define the simplest situation in which experts' superior performance can still be reliably reproduced.

Description and analysis of expert performance

The mere fact that it is possible to identify a set of representative tasks that can elicit superior performance from experts under standardized conditions is important. It dramatically reduces the number of contextual factors that can logically be essential for reproducing that superior performance. More important, it allows researchers to reproduce the phenomenon of expert performance under controlled conditions and in a reliable fashion. Researchers can thus precisely describe the tasks and stimuli and can theoretically determine which mechanisms are capable of reliably producing accurate performance across the set of tasks. Part of the standard methodology in cognitive psychology is to analyze the possible methods subjects could use to generate the correct response to a specific task, given their knowledge about procedures and facts in the domain. The same methodology can be applied to tasks that capture expert performance. Because, however, the knowledge experts may apply to a specific task is quite extensive and complex, it is virtually impossible for nonexperts to understand an analysis of such a task. Instead of describing such a case, we illustrate the methodology and related issues with a relatively simple skill, mental multiplication.

Mental multiplication: an illustration of text analysis

In a study of mental multiplication, the experimenter typically reads a problem to a subject: what is the result of multiplying 24 by 36? The subject then reports the correct answer – 864. It may be possible that highly experienced subjects recognize that particular problem and retrieve the answer immediately from memory. That possibility is remote for normal subjects, and one can surmise that they must calculate the answer by relying on their knowledge of the multiplication table and familiar methods for complex multiplication. The most likely method is the paper-and-pencil method taught in the schools, where 24×36 is broken down into 24×6 and 24×30 and the products are added together (illustrated as case B in table 1). Often students are told to put the highest number first. By this rule, the first step in solving 24×36 is to rearrange it as 36×24 and then to break it down as 36×4 and 36×20 (case A). More sophisticated subjects may recognize that 24×36 is equivalent to $(30 - 6) \times (30 + 6)$ and use the formula $(a - b) \times (a + b) = a^2 - b^2$, thus calculating 24×36 as $30^2 - 6^2 = 900 - 36 = 864$ (case C). Other subjects may recognize other short cuts, such as $24 \times 36 = (2 \times 12) \times (3 \times 12) = 6 \times 12^2 = 6 \times 144$ (case D). Skilled mental calculators often prefer to calculate the answer in the reverse order, as is illustrated in case E. Especially for more complex problems this procedure allows them to report the first digit of the final result long before they have completed the calculation of the remaining digits. Because most people expect that the entire answer has to be available before the first digit can be announced, the last method gives the appearance of faster calculation speeds.

An investigator cannot determine on which of the methods in table 1 a subject relied. However, if the subject was instructed to think aloud (see Ericsson and Simon, 1993, for the detailed procedure) while completing the mental multiplication, the investigator could record in detail the mediating sequences of the subject's thoughts, as is illustrated in the right panel of table 1. Although methodologically rigorous methods for encoding and evaluating think-aloud protocols are avail-

Table 1 Five possible methods of mentally multiplying 24 by 36 and a think-aloud protocol from a subject generating the correct answer

Mental multiplication	Think-aloud protocol
Method A	36 times 24
$$\begin{array}{r} 24 \\ \times\,36 \\ \hline 144 \\ 72 \\ \hline 864 \end{array}$$	4 carry the – no wait 4 carry the 2 14 144
Method B	0 36 times 2 is
$$\begin{array}{r} 36 \\ \times\,24 \\ \hline 144 \\ 72 \\ \hline 864 \end{array}$$	12 6 72 720 plus 144 4 uh, uh
Method C	6 8
$$\begin{aligned} 24 \times 36 &= \\ &= (30-6) \times (30+6) = \\ &= 30^2 - 6^2 = \\ &= 900 - 36 = 864 \end{aligned}$$	uh, 864
Method D	
$$\begin{aligned} 24 \times 36 &= 2 \times 12 \times 3 \times 12 = \\ &= 6 \times 12^2 = 6 \times 144 = 864 \end{aligned}$$	
Method E	
$$\begin{array}{rr} AB & 24 \\ \times\,CD & \times\,36 \\ \hline 100 \times A \times C & 600 \\ 10 \times A \times D & 120 \\ 10 \times C \times B & 120 \\ B \times D & 24 \\ \hline & 864 \end{array}$$	

able (Ericsson and Simon, 1993), the visual match between case B and the protocol in table 1 is sufficiently clear for the purposes of our illustration. Even with a less detailed record of the verbalized intermediate products in the calculation, it is possible to reject most of the alternative methods as being inconsistent with a recorded protocol.

Think-aloud protocols and task analysis in research on expert performance

Since the demise of introspective analysis of consciousness around the turn of the century, investigators have been reluctant to consider any type of verbal report as valid data on subjects' cognitive processes. More recently investigators have been particularly concerned that having subjects generate verbal reports changes the underlying processes. In a recent review of more than 40 experimental studies comparing performance with and without verbalization, Ericsson and Simon (1993) showed that the structure of cognitive processes can change if subjects are required to explain their cognitive processes. In contrast, if subjects were asked simply to verbalize the thoughts that come to their attention (think aloud), Ericsson and Simon found no reliable evidence that structural changes to cognitive processing occurred. Thinking aloud appears only to require additional time for subjects to complete verbalization and therefore leads to somewhat longer solution times in some cases.

A critical concern in applying this methodology to expert performance is how much information the thinkaloud protocols of experts contain about the mediating cognitive processes. Obviously many forms of skilled perceptual–motor performance are so rapid that concurrent verbalization of thought would seem impossible. We later consider alternative methodologies for such cases; but for a wide range of expert performance, think-aloud protocols have provided a rich source of information on expert performance. In his work on chess masters, de Groot (1978) instructed his subjects to think aloud as they identified the best move for chess positions. From an analysis of the verbal reports, de Groot was able to describe how his subjects selected their moves. First they familiarized themselves with the position and extracted the strengths and weaknesses of its structure. Then they systematically explored the consequences of promising moves and the opponent's likely countermoves by planning several moves ahead. From subjects' verbalizations, de Groot and subsequent investigators (Charness, 1981a) have been able to represent the sequences of moves subjects explored as search trees and to measure the amount and depth of planning for chess players at different levels of expertise (see figure 1). The results of these analyses show that the amount and depth of search increase as a function of chess expertise to a given point (the level of chess experts); thereafter, no further systematic differences were found (Charness, 1989). That the very best chess players still differ in their ability to find and selectively explore the most promising moves suggests that the structure of their internal representation of chess positions differs.

The central importance of experts' representation of solutions is revealed by verbal reports in other domains such as physics and medical diagnosis. When novices in physics solve a problem, they typically start with the question that asks for, say, a velocity; then they try to recall formulas for calculating velocities and then construct step by step a sequence of formulas by reasoning backward from the goal to the information given in the problem. In contrast, more experienced subjects proceed by forward reasoning. As they read the description of the problem situation, an integrated representation is generated and updated, so when they finally encounter the question in the problem text, they simply retrieve a solution plan from memory (Larkin, McDermott, Simon, and Simon, 1980). This finding suggests that experts form an immediate representation of the problem that systematically cues their knowledge, whereas novices do not have this kind of orderly and efficient access to their knowledge. Similarly, medical experts comprehend and integrate the information they receive about patients to find the correct diagnosis by reasoning forward, whereas less accomplished practitioners tend to generate plausible diagnoses that aid their search for confirming and disconfirming evidence (Patel and Groen, 1991).

Experts' internal representation of the relevant information about the situation is critical to their ability to reason, to plan out, and to evaluate consequences of possible actions. Approximately 100 years ago Binet was intrigued by some chess players' claims that they could visualize chess positions clearly when they played chess games without a visible chessboard (blindfold chess). Binet (1894) and subsequently Luria (1968) studied individuals with exceptional memory abilities,

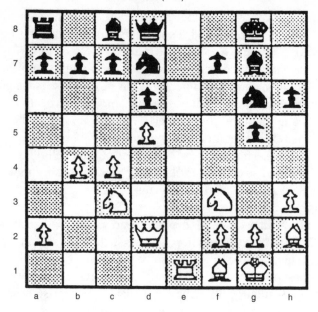

White to move (P-c5)

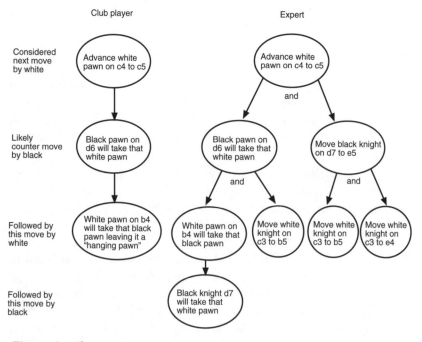

Figure 1 Chess position presented to players with instruction to select best next move by white (top panel)

who claimed to visualize as a mental image the information presented to them. These claims, if substantiated, would imply that some individuals have a sensory-based memory akin to a photographic memory, making them qualitatively different from the vast majority of human adults. To gain understanding of these processes and capacities, investigators have turned to tests of perception and memory.

Immediate memory of perceived situations

To study subjects' immediate perception of chess positions, de Groot (1978) restricted the presentation to 2–15 seconds and then removed the chess position from view. Even after such a brief exposure, the best chess players were able to describe the structure of the chess position and could reproduce the locations of all the chess pieces almost perfectly. Weaker chess players' memory was much worse, and generally the amount of information chess players could recall was found to be a function of skill. In a classic study Chase and Simon (1973) studied subjects' memory for briefly presented chess positions and replicated de Groot's findings under controlled conditions. To the same subjects Chase and Simon also presented chess positions with randomly rearranged chess pieces. Memory for these scrambled positions was uniformly poor and did not differ as a function of skill. This finding has been frequently replicated and shows that the superior memory for briefly presented chess positions is not due to any general memory ability, such as photographic memory, but depends critically on subjects' ability to perceive meaningful patterns and relations between chess pieces. Originally Chase and Simon proposed that experts' superior short-term memory for chess positions was due to their ability to recognize configurations of chess pieces on the basis of their knowledge of vast numbers of specific patterns of pieces. With greater Knowledge of more complex and larger configurations of chess pieces (chunks), an expert could recall more individual chess pieces with the same number of chunks. Hence Chase and Simon could account for very large individual differences in memory for chess positions within the limits of the capacity of normal short-term memory (STM), which is approximately seven chunks (Miller, 1956).

The Chase–Simon theory has been very influential. It gives an elegant account of experts' superior memory only for representative stimuli from their domain, and not even for randomly rearranged versions of the same stimuli (see Ericsson and J. Smith, 1991a, for a summary of the various domains of expertise in which this finding has been demonstrated). At that time Chase and Simon (1973) believed that storage of new information in long-term memory (LTM) was quite time consuming and that memory for briefly presented information could be maintained only in STM for experts and nonexperts alike. However, subsequent research by Chase and Ericsson (1982) on the effects of practice on a specific task measuring the capacity of STM has shown that through extended practice (more than 200 hours), it is possible for subjects to improve performance by more than 1,000 percent. These improvements are not mediated by increasingly larger chunks in STM but reflect the acquisition of memory skills that enable subjects to store information in LTM and thereby circumvent the capacity constraint of STM. Hence with extensive practice it is possible to attain skills that lead to qualitative, not simply quantitative, differences in memory performance for a specific type of presented information.

From experimental analyses of their trained subjects and from a review of data on other individuals with exceptional memory, Chase and Ericsson (1982; Ericsson, 1985) extracted several genera findings of skilled memory that apply to all subjects. Exceptional memory is nearly always restricted to one type of material, frequently random sequences of digits. The convergence of acquired memory skills and alleged exceptional memory was demonstrated when the trained subjects performed tasks given previously to "exceptional" subjects. Figure 2 (middle panel) shows a matrix that Binet presented visually to his subjects. Below the matrix are several orders in which the same subjects were asked to recall the numbers from the matrix that they memorized. Ericsson and Chase (1982) found that their subjects matched or surpassed the exceptional subjects both in the speed of initial memorization and in the speed of subsequent recall. A detailed analysis contrasting the speed for different orders of recall showed the same pattern in trained and exceptional subjects, both of whom recalled by rows faster than by columns. Consistent with their acquired memory skill, the trained subjects encoded each row of the matrix as a group by relying on their extensive knowledge of facts relevant to numbers. They then associated a cue corresponding to the spatial location of each row with a retrieval structure illustrated in the top panel of figure 2. To recall numbers in flexible order, subjects retrieved the relevant row using the

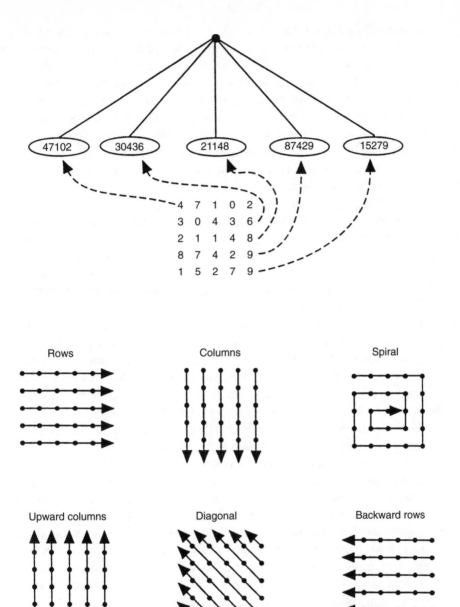

Figure 2 Twenty-five-digit matrix used by Binet to test memory experts

corresponding retrieval cue and then extracted the desired next digit or digits. The high correlation between the recall times predicted from this method and the recall times observed for both exceptional and trained subjects imply that these groups have a similar memory representation. When the biographical background of individuals exhibiting exceptional memory performance was examined, Ericsson (1985, 1988) found evidence for extended experience and practice with related memory tasks. Hence, these exceptional individuals and the trained college students should be viewed as expert performers on these laboratory tasks, where the same type of memory skills has been acquired during extended prior experience.

Acquired memory skill (skilled memory theory, Ericsson and Staszewski, 1989; and long-term working memory, Ericsson and Kintsch, 1994) accounts well even for the superior memory of experts. In many types of expert performance, research has shown that working memory is essentially unaffected by interruptions, during which the experts are forced to engage in an unrelated activity designed to eliminate any continued storage of information is STM. After the interruption and after a brief delay involving recall and reactivation of relevant information stored in LTM, experts can resume activity without decrements in peformance. Storage in LTM is further evidenced by experts' ability to recall relevant information about the task even when they are unexpectedly asked for recall after the task has been completed. The amount recalled is found to increase as a function of the level of expert performance in chess (Charness, 1991).

The critical aspect of experts' working memory is not the amount of information stored per se but rather how the information is stored and indexed in LTM. In support of this claim, several cases have been reported in which nonexperts have been able to match the amount of domain-specific information recalled by experts, but without attaining the expert's sophisticated representation of the information. After 50 hours of training on memory for presented chess positions, a college student with minimal knowledge of chess was able to match the performance of chess masters (Ericcson and Harris, 1990). However, an analysis of how the chess position was encoded revealed that the trained subject focused on perceptually salient patterns in the periphery of the chessboard, whereas the chess master attended to the central aspects critical to the selection of the next moves (Ericsson and Harris, 1990). When told explicitly to memorize presented medical information, medical students match or even surpass medical experts (Patel and Groen, 1991; Schmidt and Boshuizen, 1993). However, the medical experts are more able than medical students to identify and recall the important pieces of presented information. Medical experts also encode more general clinical findings, which are sufficient for reasoning about the case but not specific enough to recall or reconstruct the detailed facts presented about the medical patient (Boshuizen and Schmidt, 1992; Groen and Patel, 1988).

Experts acquire skill in memory to meet specific demands of encoding and accessibility in specific activities in a given domain. For this reason their skill does not transfer from one domain to another. The demands for storage of intermediate products in mental calculation differ from the demands of blindfold chess, wherein the chess master must be able not simply to access the current position but also to plan and accurately select the best chess moves. The acquisition of memory skill in a domain is integrated with the acquisition of skill in organizing acquired knowledge and refining of procedures and strategies, and it allows experts to circumvent limits on working memory imposed by the limited capacity of STM.

Perceptual–motor skill in expert performance

In many domains it is critical that experts respond not just accurately but also rapidly in dynamically changing situations. A skilled performer needs to be able to perceive and encode the current situation as well as to select and excecute an action or a series of actions rapidly. In laboratory studies of skill acquisition, investigators have been able to demonstrate an increase in the speed of perceptual–motor reactions as a direct function of practice. With extensive amounts of practice, subjects are able to evoke automatically the correct reaction to familiar stimulus situations. This analysis of perceived situations and automatically evoked responses is central to our understanding of skilled performance, yet it seems to be insufficient to account for the speeds observed in many types of expert performance. The time it takes to respond to a stimulus even after extensive training is often between 0.5 and 1.0 seconds, which is too slow to account for a return of a hard tennis serve, a goalie's catching a hockey puck, and fluent motor activities in typing and music.

The standard paradigm in laboratory psychology relies on independent trials in which the occurrence of the presented stimulus, which the subject does not control, defines the beginning of a trial. In contrast, in the perceptual environment in everyday life, expert performance is continuous and changing, and experts must be able to recognize if and when a particular action is required. Most important, it is possible for the expert to analyze the current situation and thereby anticipate future events. Research on the return of a tennis serve shows that experts do not wait until they can see the ball approaching them. Instead they carefully study the action of the server's racquet and are able to predict approximately where in the service area the tennis ball will land even before the server has hit the ball. Abernethy (1991) has recently reviewed the critical role of anticipation in expert performance in many recquet sports. Similarly, expert typists are looking well ahead at the text they are typing in any particular instant. The difference between the text visually fixated and the letters typed in a given instant (eye–hand span) increases with the typists' typing speed. High-speed filming of the movements of expert typists' fingers shows that their fingers are simultaneously moved toward the relevant keys well ahead of When they are actually struck. The largest differences in speed between expert and novice typists are found for successive keystrokes made with fingers of different hands because the corresponding movements can overlap completely after extended typing practice. When the typing situation is artificially changed to eliminate looking ahead at the text to be typed, the speed advantage of expert typists is virtually eliminated (Salthouse, 1991a). Similar findings relating the amount of looking ahead and speed of performance apply to reading aloud (Levin and Addis, 1979) and sight-reading in music (Sloboda, 1985).

In summary, by successfully anticipating future events and skillfully coordinating overlapping movements, the expert performer is able to circumvent potential limits on basic elements of serial reactions.

General comments on the structure of expert performance

Recent studies of expert performance have questioned the talent-based view that expert performance becomes increasingly dependent on unmodifiable innate components. Although these studies have revealed how beginners acquire complex cognitive structures and skills that circumvent the basic limits confronting them, researchers have not uncovered some simple strategies that would allow nonexperts to rapidly acquire expert performance, except in a few isolated case, such as the sexing of chickens (Biederman and Shiffrar, 1987). Aanalyses of exceptional performance, such as exceptional memory and absolute pitch, have shown how it differs from the performance of beginners and how beginners can acquire skill through instruction in the correct general strategy and corresponding training procedures (Howe, 1990). However, to attain exceptional levels of performance, subjects must in addition undergo a very long period of active learning, during which they refine and improve their skill, ideally under the supervision of a teacher or coach. In the following section we describe the particular activities (deliberate practice) that appear to be necessary to attain these improvements (Ericsson, Krampe, and Tesch-Römer, 1993).

By acquiring new methods and skills, expert performers are able to circumvent basic, most likely physiological, limits imposed on serial reactions and working memory. The traditional distinction between physiological (unmodifiable physical) and cognitive (modifiable mental) factors that influence performance does not seem valid in studies of expert performance. For the purposes of the typical one-hour experiment in psychology, changes in physiological factors might be negligible; but once we consider extended activities, physiological adaptations and changes are not just likely but virtually inevitable. Hence we also consider the possibility that most of the physiological attributes that distinguish experts are not innately determined characteristics but rather the results of extended, intense practice.

Acquisition of Expert Performance

A relatively uncontroversial assertion is that attaining an expert level of performance in a domain requires mastery of all of the relevant knowledge and prerequisite skills. Our analysis has shown that the central mechanisms mediating the superior performance of experts are acquired; therefore acquisition of relevant knowledge and skills may be the major limiting factor in attaining expert performance. Some of the strongest evidence for this claim comes from a historical description of how domains of expertise evolved with increased specialization within each domain. To measure the duration of the acquisition process, we analyze the length of time it takes for the best individuals to attain the highest levels of performance within a domain. Finally we specify the type of practice that seems to be necessary to acquire expert performance in a domain.

Evolution of domains of expertise and the emergence of specialization

Most domains of expertise today have a fairly long history of continued development. The knowledge in natural science and calculus that represented the cutting edge of mathematics a few centuries ago and that only the experts of that time were able to master is today taught in high school and college (Feldman, 1980). Many experts today are struggling to master the developments in a small sub-area of one of the many natural sciences. Before the twentieth century it was common for musicians to compose and play their own music; since then, distinct career patterns have emerged for composers, solo performers, accompanists, teachers, and conductors. When Tchaikovsky asked two of the greatest violinists of his day to play his violin concerto, they refused, deeming the score unplayable (Platt, 1966). Today, elite violinists consider the concerto part of their standard repertory. The improvement in music training has been so considerable that according to Roth (1982), the virtuoso Paganini "would indeed cut a sorry figure if placed upon the modern concert stage" (p. 23). Paganini's techniques and Tchaikovsky's concerto were deemed impossible until other musicians figured out how to master and describe them so that students could learn them as well. Almost 100 years ago the first Olympic Games were held, and results on standardized events were recorded. Since then records for events have been continuously broken and improved. For example, the winning time for the first Olympic Marathon is comparable to the current qualifying time for the Boston Marathon, attained by many thousands of amateur runners every year. Today amateur athletes cannot successfully compete with individuals training full time, and training methods for specific events are continuously refined by professional coaches and trainers.

In all major domains there has been a steady accumulation of knowledge about the domain and about the skills and techniques that mediate superior performance. This accumulated experience is documented and regularly updated in books, encyclopedias, and instructional material written by masters and professional teachers in the domain. During the last centuries the levels of performance have increased, in some domains dramatically so. To attain the highest level of performance possible in this decade, it is necessary both to specialize and to engage in the activity full time.

Minimum period of attainment of expert performance

Another measure of the complexity of a domain is the length of time it takes an individual to master it and attain a very high level of performance or make outstanding achievements. Of particular interest is how fast the most "talented" or best performers can attain an international level of performance. In their classic study on chess, Simon and Chase (1973) argued that a 10-year period of intense preparation is necessary to reach the level of an international chess master and suggested similar requirements in other domains. In a review of subsequent research, Ericsson, Krampe, and Tesch-Römer (1993) showed that the 10-year rule is remarkably accurate, although there are at least some exceptions. However, even those exceptions, such as Bobby Fischer, who started playing chess very early and attained an international level at age 15, are only about a year shy of the 10-year requirement. Winning international competitions in sports, arts, and science appears to require at least 10 years of preparation and typically substantially longer. In the sciences and some of the arts, such as literature, the necessary preparation overlaps so much with regular education that it is often difficult to determine a precise starting point. However, when the time interval between scientists' and authors' first accepted publication and their most valued publication is measured, it averages more than 10 years and implies an even longer preparation period (Raskin, 1936). Even for the most successful ("talented") individuals, the major domains of expertise are sufficiently complex that mastery of them requires approximately 10 years of essentially full-time preparation, which corresponds to several thousands of hours of practice.

Practice activities to attain expert performance

In almost every domain, methods for instruction and efficient training have developed in parallel with the accumulation of relevant knowledge and techniques. For many sports and performance arts in particular, professional teachers and coaches monitor training programs tailored to the needs of individuals ranging from beginners to experts. The training activities are designed to improve specific aspects of performance through repetition and successive refinement. To receive maximal benefit from feedback, individuals have to monitor their training with full concentration, which is effortful and limits the duration of daily training. Ericsson, Krampe, and Tesch-Römer (1993) referred to individualized training on tasks selected by a qualified teacher as deliberate practice. They argued that the amount of this type of practice should be closely related to the level of acquired performance.

From surveys of the kinds of activities individuals engage in for the popular domains, such as tennis and golf, it is clear that the vast majority of active individuals spend very little if any time on deliberate practice. Once amateurs have attained an acceptable level of performance, their primary goal becomes inherent enjoyment of the activity, and most of their time is spent on playful interaction. The most enjoyable states of play are characterized as flow (Csikszentmihalyi, 1990), when the individual is absorbed in effortless engagement in a continuously changing situation. During play even individuals who desire to improve their performance do not encounter the same or similar situations on a frequent and predictable basis. For example, a tennis player wanting to improve a weakness, such as a backhand volley, might encounter a relevant situation only once per game. In contrast, a tennis coach would give that individual many hundreds of opportunities to improve and refine that type of shot during a training session.

Work, another type of activity, refers to public performances, competitions, and other performances motivated by external social and monetary rewards. Although work activities offer some opportunities for learning, they are far from optimal. In work activities, the goal is to generate a quality product reliably. In several domains, such as performance arts and sports, there is a clear distinction between training before a performance and the performance itself. During the performance itself, opportunities for learning and improvements are minimal, although the problems encountered can be addressed during training following the performance. Most occupations and professional domains pay individuals to generate efficiently services and products of consistently high quality. To give their best performance in work activities, individuals rely on previously well-entrenched methods rather than exploring new methods with unknown reliability. In summary, deliberate practice is an effortful activity motivated by the goal of improving performance. Unlike play, deliberate practice is not inherently motivating; and unlike work, it does not lead to immediate social and monetary rewards (Ericsson, Krampe, and Tesch-Römer 1993).

Individualized training of students, who begin as very young children under the supervision of professional teachers and coaches, is a relatively recent trend in most major domains. It was only in 1756, for example, that Wolfgang Amadeus Mozart's father published the first book in German on teaching students to play the violin. Before organized education became the norm, people acquired skill through apprenticeship, working as adolescents with a skilled performer, frequently one of their parents. Recently there has been a lot of interest in this type of learning environment within the framework of situated cognition (Lave, 1988; Lave and Wenger, 1991). A significant element of apprenticeship is the imitation of skilled performers and careful study and copying of their work. In the arts the study and imitation of masterpieces has a long history. For example, Benjamin Franklin (1986) described in his autobiography how he tried to learn to write in a clear and logical fashion. He would read through a passage in a good book to understand it rather than memorize it and Then try to reproduce its structure and content. Then he would compare his reproduction with the original to identify differences. By repeated application of this cycle of study, reproduction, and comparison with a well-structured original, Franklin argued that he acquired his skill in organizing thoughts for speaking and writing.

With the advent of audio and video recording, which have opened new possibilities for repeated study of master artists' performance, reproduction and comparison have been extended to allow individualized study and improvement of performance. This general method is central to achieving expert performance in chess. Advanced chess players spend as many as four hours a day studying published games between international chess masters (Forbes, 1992). The effective component of this type of study is predicting the chess master's next move without looking ahead. If the prediction is wrong, the advanced player examines the chess position more deeply to identify the reasons for the chess master's move. The activity of planning and extended evaluation of chess games is likely to improve a player's ability to internally represent chess positions, a memory skill that we discussed earlier in this article. This form of self-directed study has most of the characteristics of deliberate practice, but it is probably not as effective as individualized study guided by a skilled teacher. It is interesting to note that most of the recent world champions in chess were at one time tutored by chess masters (Ericsson, Krampe, and Tesch-Römer, 1993).

Deliberate practice differs from other domain-related activities because it provides optimal opportunities for learning and sill acquisition. If the regular activities in a domain did not offer accurate and preferably immediate feedback or opportunities for corrected repetitions, improvements in performance with further experience would not be expected from learning theory. Most amateurs and employees spend a very small amount of time on deliberate efforts to improve their performance, once it has reached an acceptable level. Under these conditions only weak relations between amount of experience and performance would be predicted, which is consistent with the empirical data. Recent research has explored the question whether deliberate practice can account for the attainment of elite performance levels and for individual differences among expert-level performers. According to the framework proposed by Ericsson, Krampe, and Tesch-Römer (1993), the primary mechanism creating expert-level performance in a domain is deliberate practice.

Acquiring elite performance

Why do individuals even begin to engage in deliberate practice, when this activity is not inherently enjoyable? From many interviews, Bloom (1985) found that international-level performers in several domains start out as children by engaging in playful activities in the domain (see phase 1 in figure 3). After a period of playful and enjoyable experience they reveal "talent" or promise. At this point parents typically suggest that their children take lessons from a teacher and engage in limited amounts of deliberate practice. The parents help their children acquire regular habits of practice and teach them that this activity has

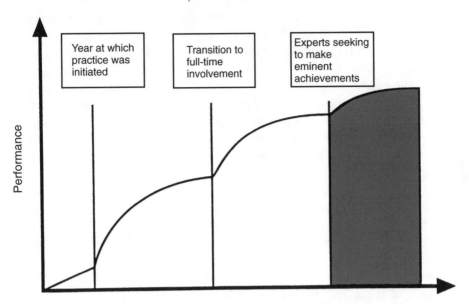

Figure 3 Phases of development of expert performance followed by a qualitatively different phase of efforts to attain eminent achievements

instrumental value by noticing improvements in performance. The next phase (Bloom, 1985) is an extended period of preparation and ends with the individual's commitment to pursue activities in the domain on a full-time basis. During this period the daily amounts of deliberate practice are increased, and more advanced teachers and training facilities are sought out. Occasionally parents even move to a different region of the country to provide their children with the best training environment. In the next phase, the individual makes a full-time commitment to improving performance. This phase ends when the individual either can make a living as a professional performer in the domain or terminates full-time engagement in the activity. Bloom (1985) found that during this phase nearly all of the individuals who ultimately reach an international level performance work with master teachers who either themselves had reached that level or had previously trained other individuals to that level. All through their development, international-level performers are provided with the best teachers for their current level of performance and engage in a great amount of deliberate practice.

The dilemma in most domains of expertise is that millions of young individuals enter these domains with aspirations to reach the highest levels of performance, but by definition only a very small number can succeed. Given the low probability of ultimate success, parents and coaches have been very much interested in identifying these select individuals as early as possible and giving them encouragement, support, and the best learning opportunities. The consistent failures to identify specific "talents" in children is not surprising when one considers the qualitative changes occurring during the long period of development. In many domains international performers start practice at age 4 to 6, when it is unclear what kind of objective evidence of talent and promise they could possibly display. Available descriptions suggest that children this young display interest and motivation to practice rather than exceptional performance. Once deliberate practice has begun, the primary measure of acquired skill and talent is the current level of performance compared with that of other children of comparable ages in the neighborhood. Only later at age 10 to 12 do the children typically start participating in competitions, where their performance is compared with that of other successful children from a larger geographical area. As performance level and age increase, the criteria for evaluating performance also change. In the arts and sciences, technical proficiency is no longer enough, and adult criteria of abstract understanding and artistic expression are applied.

During the first three phases of development, individuals master the knowledge and skills that master teachers and coaches know how to convey. To achieve the highest level (eminent performance), individuals must enter a fourth phase, going beyond the available knowledge in the domain to produce a unique contribution to the domain. Eminent scientists make major discoveries and propose new theories that permanently change the concepts and knowledge in the domain. Similarly eminent artists generate new techniques and interpretations that extend the boundaries for future art. The process of generating innovations differs from the acquisition of expertise and mastery. Major innovations by definition go beyound anything even the master teachers know and could possibly teach. Furthermore, innovations are rare, and it is unusual that eminent individuals make more than a single major innovation during their entire lives. Unlike consistently superior expert performance, innovation occurs so infrequently and unpredictably that the likelihood of its ever being captured in the laboratory is small.

However, it is still possible through retrospective analysis of concurrent records, such as notebooks and diaries (Gruber, 1981; D. B. Wallace and Gruber, 1989), to reconstruct the processes leading up to major discoveries. Once the context of a particular discovery has been identified, it is possible to reconstruct the situation and study how other naive subjects with the necessary knowledge can uncover the original discovery (Qin and Simon, 1990). Let us now turn back to expert performance, which we consider both reproducible and instructable.

Individual differences in expert performance

Biographies of international-level performers indicate that a long period of intense, supervised practice preceded their achievements. The simple assumption that these levels of deliberate practice are necessary accounts for the fact that the vast majority of active individuals who prematurely stop practicing never reach the highest levels of performance. However, in most major domains a relatively large number of individuals continue deliberate practice and thus meet the criterion of necessity. Within this group striking individual differences in adult performance nonetheless remain.

Ericsson, Krampe, and Tesch-Römer (1993) hypothesized that differences in the amount of deliberate practice could account for even the individual differences among the select group of people who continue a regimen of deliberate practice. The main assumption, which they called the *monotonic benefits assumption*, is that individuals' performances are a monotonic function of the amount of deliberate practice accumulated since these individuals began deliberate practice in a domain. The accumulated amount of deliberate practice and the level of performance an individual achieves at a given age are thus a function of the starting age for practice and the weekly amount of practice during the intervening years. This function is illustrated in figure 4. The second curve has been simply moved horizontally to reflect a later starting age, and the third curve reflects in addition a lower weekly rate of practice.

To evaluate these predictions empirically, it is necessary to measure the amount of time individuals spend on various activities, in particular deliberate practice. One way of doing so, which is to have them keep

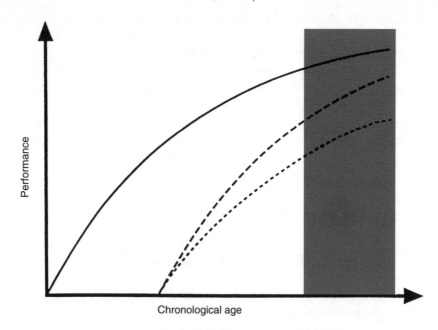

Figure 4   Relations between age and performance

detailed diaries, has a fairly long tradition in studies of time budgeting in sociology (Juster and Stafford, 1985). In most domains with teachers and coaches, deliberate practice is regularly scheduled on a daily basis, and advanced performers can accurately estimate their current and past amounts of practice as well as their starting ages and other character-istics of their practice history.

In a comprehensive review of studies comparing starting ages and amount of weekly practice for international, national, and regional-level performers in many different domains, Ericsson, Krampe, and Tesch-Römer (1993) found that performers who reached higher levels tended to start practicing as many as from two to five years earlier than did less accomplished performers. Individuals who attained higher levels of performance often spent more time on deliberate practice than did less accomplished individuals, even when there was no difference in the total time both groups spent on domain-related activities. Differences in the amount of deliberate practice accumulated during their development differentiated groups of expert performers at various current levels of performance. The three graphs in figure 4 illustrate how simple differences in starting ages and weekly amounts of practice can yield very stable differences in amounts of training and performance levels.

Everyone recognizes that maturational factors affect performance. For this reason competitions are nearly always structured by groups of contestants with the same ages. By the time individuals approach their middle to late teens (the shaded area in figure 4) and are applying for scholarships and admission to the studios of master teachers and the best training environments, large differences in past practice and acquired skill are already present. Ericsson, Krampe, and Tesch-Römer (1993) found that by age 20, the top-level violinists in their study had practiced an average of more than 10,000 hours, approximately 2,500 hours more than the next most accomplished group of expert violinists and 5,000 hours more than the group who performed at the lowest expert level.

In summary, evidence from a wide range of domains shows that the top-level experts have spent a very large amount of time improving their performance and that the total amount accumulated during development is several years of additional full-time practice more than that of other less accomplished performers. This difference is roughly equivalent to the difference between freshmen and seniors in a highly competitive college. In these environments, where the best opportunities for further development are offered only to the individuals with the best current performance, it may be difficult for individuals with less prior practice and lower levels of performance even to secure situations in which they can practice full time. It is virtually impossible for them to catch up with the best performers because those performers maintain their lead through continuous practice at optimal levels.

Structure of practice in the daily lives of elite performers

From analyses of diaries and other sources of biographical material, Ericsson, Krampe, and Tesch-Römer (1993) concluded that expert performers design their lives to optimize their engagement in deliberate practice. Expert musicians in their study spent approximately four hours a day – every day including weekends – on deliberate practice. Practice sessions were approximately one hour long, followed by a period of rest. Performers practiced most frequently during the morning, when independent research indicates that individuals have the highest capacity for complex, demanding activity during the day (Folkard and Monk, 1985). All the expert musicians reported on the importance of sleep and rest in maintaining their high levels of daily practice. The expert musicians in the two best groups, who practiced longer each day, slept more than those in the least accomplished group and also slept more than other reference groups of subjects of comparable age. The additional sleep was primarily from an afternoon nap. Expert subjects maximize the amount of time they can spend on deliberate practice when they can fully focus on their training goals without fatigue. Many master teachers and coaches consider practice while fatigued and unfocused not only wasteful but even harmful to sustained improvements.

Focused, effortful practice of limited duration has been found to be important in a wide range of domains of expertise. Interestingly the estimated amount of deliberate practice that individuals can sustain for extended periods of time does not seem to vary across domains and is close to four hours a day (Ericsson, Krampe, and Tesch-Römer, 1993).

The effort and intensity of deliberate practice are most readily observable for perceptual – motor behavior in sports and performance arts. One goal of most of the practice activities is to push the limits of performance to higher levels by, for example, stretching in ballet, or repeated maximal efforts until exhaustion during interval training in running and weight lifting. It is well known that intense exercise increases endurance and the size of muscles. However, recent research in sports physiology has shown that anatomical changes in response to extended intense exercise are more far-reaching than commonly believed. Within a few weeks of vigorous training, the number of capillaries supplying blood to the trained muscles increases. Longitudinal studies show that after years of "elite-level" endurance training, the heart adapts and increases in size to values outside the normal range for healthy adults. The metabolism and general characteristics of muscle fibers also change – from slow-twitch to fast-twitch or vice versa. Most interestingly these changes are limited only to those muscles that are trained and critical to the particular sports event for which the athlete is preparing. Many of these changes appear to increase when practice overlaps with the body's development during childhood and adolescence. For example the flexibility required for elite performance in ballet requires that dancers begin practicing before age 10 or 11. With the exception of height, the characteristics that differentiate elite athletes and performance artists from less accomplished performers in the same domains appear to reflect the successful adaptations of the body to intense practice activities extended over many years (Ericsson, Krampe, and Tesch-Römer, 1993).

These physiological adaptations are not unique to expert performers. Similar but smaller changes are found for individuals who train at less intense levels. Similar extreme adaptations are seen in individuals living under extreme environmental conditions, such as at very high altitudes, or coping with diseases, such as partial blockages of the blood supply to the heart. Many occupation-specific problems that expert performers experience in middle age also seem to result from related types of (mal)adaptive processes.

It is becoming increasingly clear that maximizing the intensity and duration of training is not necessarily good. Expert performers have a constant problem with avoiding strains and injuries and allowing the body enough time to adapt and recuperate. Even in the absence of physical injuries, an increasing number of athletes and musicians overtrain and do not allow themselves enough rest to maintain a stable equilibrium from day to day. Sustained overtraining leads to burnout, for which the only known remedy is to terminate practice completely for long periods. It appears that top-level adult experts practice at the highest possible level that can be sustained for extended periods without burnout or injury. Hence, it may be extremely difficult to consistently practice harder and improve faster than these individuals already do.

Expert performance from a life span perspective

Elite performers in most domains are engaged essentially full time from childhood and adolescence to late adulthood. The study of expert performers therefore offers a unique perspective on life span development and especially on the effects of aging. Many studies have examined the performance of experts as a function of age or of the ages when experts attained their best performance or their highest achievement. It is extremely rare for performers to attain their best performance before reaching adulthood, but it is not necessarily the case that performance continues to improve in those who keep exercising their skills across the life span. Rather, a peak age for performance seems to fall in the 20s, 40s, and 40s, as Lehman (1953) first noted. The age distributions for peak performance in vigorous sports are remarkably narrow and centered in the 20s with systematic differences between different types of sports (Schulz and Curnow, 1988). In vigorous sports it is rare for elite athletes above age 30 to reach their personal best or even in many cases remain competitive with younger colleagues. Although less pronounced, similar age distributions centered somewhere in the 30s are found for fine motor skills and even predominantly cognitive activities, such as chess, science, and the arts. Simonton (1988a) has argued that the relative decline with age may be slight and may be attributable to the fact that total creative output for artists and scientists declines, although the probability of achieving an outstanding performance remains constant. Thus the frequency of producing an outstanding work declines with age. Perhaps the best evidence for decline with age is Elo's (1965) analysis of the careers of grand master chess players. As seen in figure 5 (from Charness and Bosman, 1990), there is a peak for chess players in their 30s, although performance at 63 years of age is no worse than that at 21 years. The peak age for creative achievement differs considerably between domains. In pure mathematics, theoretical physics, and lyric poetry, the peak ages for contributions occur in the late 20s and early 30s. In novel writing, history, and philosophy, the peaks are less pronounced and occur in the 40s and early 50s (Simonton, 1988a). Even within domains the peak age for performance seems to vary systematically with the types of demands placed on the performer. In international-level tournament chess, individuals typically play chess games for four to five hours daily for more than a week. Furthermore, tournament chess makes strong demands on working memory and, to some extent, on speed of processing, when players attempt to choose the best move by searching through the problem space of possible moves. On average, a tournament chess player has approximately three minutes to consider each move (when normal time controls are used). In "postal chess," players have several days to make a move. Because deliberation times are longer and the players can use external memory to maintain the results of analysis, ascension to the world postal chess championship occurs much later, near 46 years of age as compared with 30 years of age for tournament chess (Charness and Bosman, 1990).

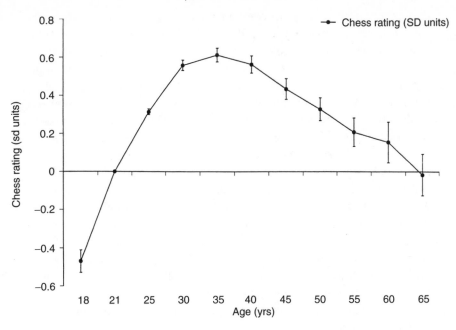

Figure 5 Grand master performance by age

To researchers on aging, the decline in expert performance in old age, which in many domains is often relatively slight, is less interesting than expert performers' ability to maintain a very high level of performance during ages when beginners and less accomplished performers display clear effects of aging. A common hypothesis related to the notion of innate talent is that experts generally age more slowly than other performers, and thus no observable impairments would be expected. However, this hypothesis is not consistent with recent research on expert performance in chess (Charness, 1981b), typing (Bosman, 1993; Salthouse, 1984), and music (Krampe, 1994). The superior performance of older experts is found to be restricted to relevant tasks in their domains of expertise. For unrelated psychometric tasks and some tasks related to occupational activities, normal age-related decline is observed (Salthouse, 1991b).

The mediating mechanisms in younger and older experts' performance have been examined in laboratory studies developed under the expert performance approach. In typing, older experts who type at the same speed as younger experts are found to have larger eye–hand spans that permit older experts to compensate through advance preparation (Bosman, 1993; Salthouse, 1984). Older chess experts' ability to select the best chess move is associated with less planning than that of younger experts at an equivalent skill level. This suggests that older chess experts compensate through more extensive knowledge of chess (Charness, 1981a). Comparisons of older and younger expert pianists' ability to perform simple and complex sequences of key strokes requiring bimanual coordination reveal no or small differences, whereas the same comparisons between older and younger amateur pianists reveal clear decrements with age that increase with the complexity of the tasks (Krampe, 1994). Such age effects require greater diversity in the models proposed to explain expertise. It is now evident that at least in typing and chess, two individuals at the same level of skill can achieve their performance through mechanisms with different structure. Although it is convenient to collapse a measure of expertise onto a unidimensional scale (such as chess rating or net words per minute for typing), this is an oversimplification that may obscure individual differences in the underlying processes that mediate same-level performance.

The role of deliberate practice

In the previous sections we described the evidence for the necessity of deliberate practice for initially acquiring expert performance. The maintenance of expert performance could be due to the unique structure of the mechanisms acquired in expert performance or to a level of deliberate practice maintained during adulthood or both.

The most marked age-related decline is generally observed in perceptual–motor performance displayed in many types of sports. High levels of practice are necessary to attain the physiological adaptations that are found in expert performers, and the effects of practice appear to be particularly large when intense practice overlaps with physical development during childhood and adolescence. Most of these adaptations require that practice is maintained; if not, the changes revert to normal values, although for some anatomical changes many years of no practice appear necessary before the reversion is completed. Hence, much of the age-related decline in performance may reflect the reduction or termination of practice. Studies of master athletes show that older athletes do not practice at the same intensity as the best young athletes. When older master athletes are compared with young athletes training at a similar level, many physiological measurements do not differ between them. However, at least some physiological functions, such as maximal heart rate, show an age-related decline independent of past or current practice. In summary, the ability to retain superior performance in sports appears to depend critically on maintaining practice during adulthood (Ericsson, 1990).

Evidence on the role of early and maintained practice in retaining cognitive aspects of expertise is much less extensive. Takeuchi and Hulse's (1993) recent review of absolute (perfect) pitch shows that children can easily acquire this ability at around the ages of three to five. Acquisition of the same ability during adulthood is very difficult and time consuming. Some other abilities, such as the acquisition of second languages (especially accents and pronunciation), appear easier to acquire at young rather than adult ages. Whether early acquisition of abilities, per se, translates into better retention into old age is currently not known.

Virtually by definition expert performers remain highly active in their domains of expertise. With increasing age, they typically reduce their intensive work schedules, a change in life style that is consistent with the decrease observed in their productivity (Simonton, 1988a). Roe (1953) found that eminent scientists reduce their level of work during evenings and weekends. Information about the distribution of time among different types of activities and especially the amount of time spent on maintaining and improving performance is essentially lacking. However, Krampe (1994) collected both diaries and retrospective estimates of past practice for older expert pianists. Consistent with the lack of performance differences between younger and older pianists in tasks relevant to piano playing, Krampe found that the older experts still practiced approximately 10 hours a week and spent more than 40 additional hours a week on other music-related activities. In addition he found that individual differences in performance among older pianists could be predicted well by the amount of practice during the past 10 years. Whether a reduction in practice by older chess players and typists accounts for the differences between younger and older experts in these fields cannot currently be answered, given the lack of longitudinal data on performance and practice.

The study of expert performance over the life span of the performers is needed. This perspective is quite likely to provide new insights into the plasticity of the structure of human performance as a function of different developmental phases. Through investigation of focused sustained practice, it may be possible to determine which aspects can and, at least with the current training methods, cannot be modified to enhance current and future performance. Of particular practical and theoretical interest are those factors that enable experts to retain and maintain superior performance into old age.

Summary and Conclusion

The differences in performance between experts and beginners are the largest that have been reliably reproduced with healthy, normal adults under controlled test conditions. From the life-long efforts of expert performers who continuously strive to improve and reach their best performance, one can infer that expert performance represents the highest performance possible, given current knowledge and training methods in the domain. Individuals' acquisition of expert performance is thus a naturally occurring experiment for identifying the limits of human performance. It is hard to imagine better empirical evidence on maximal performance except for one critical flaw. As children, future international-level performers are not randomly assigned to their training condition. Hence one cannot rule out the possibility that there is something different about those individuals who ultimately reach expert-level performance.

Nevertheless the traditional view of talent, which concludes that successful individuals have special innate abilities and basic capacities, is not consistent with the reviewed evidence. Efforts to specify and measure characteristics of talent that allow early identification and successful prediction of adult performance have failed. Differences between expert and less accomplished performers reflect acquired knowledge and skills or physiological adaptations effected by training, with the only confirmed exception being height.

More plausible loci of individual differences are factors that predispose individuals toward engaging in deliberate practice and enable them to sustain high levels of practice for many years. Differences in these factors clearly have, in part, an environmental origin and can be modified as the level of practice is slowly increased with further experience. However, some of these factors, such as preferred activity level and temperament, may have a large genetic component. Furthermore, there may need to be a good fit between such predisposing factors and the task environment (along the lines of Thomas and Chess's, 1984, temperament–environment fit model) for expert-level performance to develop.

For a long time the study of exceptional and expert performance has been considered outside the scope of general psychology because such performance has been attributed to innate characteristics possessed by outstanding individuals. A better explanation is that expert performance reflects extreme adaptations, accomplished through life-long effort, to demands in restricted, well-defined domains. By capturing and examining the performance of experts in a given domain, researchers have identified adaptive changes with physiological components as well as the acquisition of domain-specific skills that circumvent basic limits on speed and memory. Experts with different teachers and training histories attain their superior performance after many years of continued effort by acquiring skills and making adaptations with the same general structure. These findings imply that in each domain, there is only a limited number of ways in which individuals can make large improvements in performance. When mediating mechanisms of the same type are found in experts in very different domains that have evolved independently from each other, an account of this structure based on shared training methods is highly unlikely.

There is no reason to believe that changes in the structure of human performance and skill are restricted to the traditional domains of expertise. Similar changes should be expected in many everyday activities, such as thinking, comprehension, and problem solving, studied in general psychology. However, people acquire everyday skills under less structured conditions that lack strict and generalizable criteria for evaluation. These conditions also vary among individuals because of their specific living situations. In contrast, stable expert performance is typically restricted to standardized situations in a domain. Hence, the criteria for expert performance offer a shared goal for individuals in a domain that directs and constrains their life-long efforts to attain their maximal performance. Even when scientific investigators' ultimate goal is to describe and understand everyday skills, they are more likely to succeed by studying expert performance than by examining everyday skills because the former is acquired under much more controlled and better understood conditions and achieved at higher levels of proficiency in a specific domain.

We believe that studies of the acquisition and structure of expert performance offer unique evidence on many general theoretical and applied issues in psychology. Extended deliberate practice gives near maximal values on the possible effects of environmental variables (in interaction with developmental variables) relevant to theoretical claims for invariant cognitive capacities and general laws of performance. We will significantly advance our knowledge of the interaction between environment and development by observing the effects of training during the early development of expert performers and the effects of maintaining training for older experts in late adulthood. The study of expert performance complements cross-cultural studies of environmental influences on thinking and cognition. The relation between language and thinking, traditionally restricted to comparisons between different languages (Hunt and Agnoli, 1991), should be particularly suitable for study in the context of expertise, where domain-specific names, concepts, and knowledge are explicated in training manuals and books and subjects with differing levels of mastery of the vocabulary and where "language" of the domain can be easily found.

For applied psychologists the study of expert performers and their master teachers and coaches offers a nearly untapped reservoir of knowledge about optimal training and specific training methods that has been accumulated in many domains for a long time. Across very different domains of expert performance, Ericsson, Krampe, and Tesch-Römer (1993) uncovered evidence for intriguing invariances in the duration and daily scheduling of practice activities. Further efforts to investigate training and development of training methods and to derive principles that generalize across domains should be particularly fruitful. Most important, a better understanding of social and other factors that motivate and sustain future expert performers at an optimal level of deliberate practice should have direct relevance to motivational problems in education, especially in our school system.

In conclusion, an analysis of the acquired characteristics and skills of expert performers as well as their developmental history and training methods will provide us with general insights into the structure and limits of human adaptations.

Notes

1   The field of visual art may offer at least one recent exception (Feldman, 1986). The Chinese girl Yani produced some acclaimed paintings between the ages of three and six (Ho, 1989), but matters are complicated by the fact that these paintings were selected by her father (a professional painter) from more than 4,000 paintings completed by Yani during this three-year period (Feng, 1984).

2   In his recent book *Creating Minds*, Gardner (1993a) examined the lives of seven great innovators such as Einstein, Picasso, Stravinsky, and Gandhi. Each was selected to exemplify outstanding achievements in one of seven different intelligences. Gardner's careful analysis reveals that the achievements of each individual required a long period of intense preparation and required the coincidence of many environmental factors. Striking evidence for traditional talent, such as prodigious achievements as a child, is notably absent, with the exception of Picasso. The best evidence for talent, according to Gardner, is their rapid progress once they made a commitment to a particular domain of expertise. These findings are not inconsistent with Gardner's views on talent because innovation and creation of new ideas are fundamentally different from high achievements in a domain due to talent. Gardner wrote, "in the case of a universally acclaimed prodigy, the prodigy's talents mesh perfectly with current structure of the domain and the current tastes of the field. Creativity, however, does not result from such perfect meshes" (pp.40–1).

References

Abernethy, B. (1991). Visual search strategies and decision-making in sport. *International Journal of Sport Psychology, 22*, 189–210.

Barlow, F. (1952). *Mental Prodigies*. New York: Greenwood Press.

Barolsky, P. (1991). *Why Mona Lisa Smiles and Other Tales by Vasari*. University Park: Pennsylvania State University Press.

Barolsky, P. (1992). *Giotto's Father and the Family of Vasari's Lives*. University Park: Pennsylvania State University Press.

Barr, A., and Feigenbaum, E. A. (eds). (1981–2). *The Handbook of Artificial Intelligence* (Vols 1–2). Stanford, CA: HeurisTech Press.

Bate, J. (1989). Shakespeare and original genius. In P. Murray (ed.), *Genius: The History of an Idea* (pp. 76–97). Oxford, England: Basil Blackwell.

Biederman, I., and Shiffrar, M. M. (1987). Sexing day-old chicks: a case study and expert systems analysis of a difficult perceptual–learning task. *Journal of Experimental Psychology: Learning, Memory, and Cognition, 13*, 640–5.

Binet, A. (1894). *Psychologie des Grands Calculateurs et Joueurs d'Echecs* [Psychology of great mental calculators and chess players]. Paris: Libraire Hachette.

Bloom, B. S. (1985). Generalizations about talent development. In B. S. Bloom (ed.), *Developing Talent in Young People* (pp. 507–49). New York: Ballantine Books.

Boase, T. S. R. (1979). *Giorgio Vasari: The Man and the Book.* Princeton, NJ: Princeton University Press.

Boshuizen, H. P. A., and Schmidt, H. G. (1992). On the role of biomedical knowledge in clinical reasoning by experts, intermediates and novices. *Cognitive Science, 16,* 153–84.

Bosman, E. A. (1993). Age-related differences in motoric aspects of transcription typing skill. *Psychology and Aging, 8,* 87–102.

Browne, M. A., and Mahoney, M. J. (1984). Sport psychology. *Annual Review of Psychology, 35,* 605–25.

Bull, G. (1987). *A Translation of Giorgio Vasari's* Lives of the Artists (2 vols). New York: Viking Penguin.

Camerer, C. F., and Johnson, E. J. (1991). The process–performance paradox in expert judgment: how can the experts know so much and predict so badly? In K. A. Ericsson and J. Smith (eds), *Toward a General Theory of Expertise: Prospects and Limits* (pp. 195–217). Cambridge, England: Cambridge University Press.

Charness, N. (1981a). Search in chess: age and skill differences. *Journal of Experimental Psychology: Human Perception and Performance, 7,* 467–76.

Charness, N. (1981b). Visual short-term memory and aging in chess players. *Journal of Gerontology, 36,* 615–19.

Charness, N. (1989). Expertise in chess and bridge. In D. Klahr and K. Kotovsky (eds), *Complex Information Processing: The Impact of Herbert A. Simon* (pp. 183–208). Hillsdale, NJ: Erlbaum.

Charness, N. (1991). Expertise in chess: the balance between knowledge and search. In K. A. Ericsson and J. Smith (eds), *Toward a General Theory of Expertise: Prospects and Limits* (pp. 39–63). Cambridge, England: Cambridge University Press.

Charness, N., and Bosman, E. A. (1990). Expertise and aging: life in the lab. In T. H. Hess (ed.), *Aging and Cognition: Knowledge Organization and Utilization* (pp. 343–85). Amsterdam: Elsevier.

Charness, N., Clifton, J., and MacDonald, L. (1988). Case study of a musical mono-savant. In L. K. Obler and D. A. Fein (eds). *The Exceptional Brain: Neuropsychology of Talent and Special Abilities* (pp. 277–93). New York: Guilford Press.

Chase, W. G., and Ericsson, K. A. (1982). Skill and working memory. In G. H. Bower (ed.), *The Psychology of Learning and Motivation* (Vol. 16, pp. 1–58). New York: Academic Press.

Chase, W. G., and Simon, H. A. (1973). The mind's eye in chess. In W. G. Chase (ed.), *Visual Information Processing* (pp. 215–81). New York: Academic Press.

Chi, M. T. H., Glaser, R., and Farr, M. J. (eds). (1988). *The Nature of Expertise.* Hillsdale, NJ: Erlbaum.

Cohen, P. R., and Feigenbaum, E. A. (eds). (1982). *The Handbook of Artificial Intelligence* (Vol. 3). Stanford, CA: HeurisTech Press.

Csikszentmihalyi, M. (1990). *Flow: The Psychology of Optimal Experience*, New York: Harper & Row.

de Groot, A. (1978). *Thought and Choice and Chess.* The Hague, The Netherlands: Mouton. (Original work published 1946).

Doll, J., and Mayr, U. (1987). Intelligenz und Schachleistung – Eine Untersuchung an Schachexperten [Intelligence and achievement in chess: a study of chess masters]. *Psychologische Beitrdge, 29,* 270–89.

Elo, A. E. (1965). Age changes in master chess performances. *Journal of Gerontology, 20,* 289–99.

Elo, A. E. (1986). *The Rating of Chessplayers, Past and Present* (2nd edn). New York: Arco.

Ericsson, K. A. (1985). Memory skill. *Canadian Joural of Psychology, 39*(2), 188–231.

Ericsson, K. A. (1988). Analysis of memory performance in terms of memory skill. In R. J. Sternberg (ed.), *Advances in the Psychology of Human Intelligence* (Vol. 4, pp. 137–79). Hillsdale, NJ: Erlbaum.

Ericsson, K. A. (1990). Peak performance and age: an examination of peak performance in sports. In P. B. Baltes and M. M. Baltes (eds), *Successful Aging: Perspectives from the Behavioral Sciences* (pp. 164–95). New York: Cambridge University Press.

Ericsson, K. A., and Chase, W. G. (1982). Exceptional memory. *American Scientist, 70,* 607–15.

Ericsson, K. A., and Faivre, I. A. (1988). What's exceptional about exceptional abilities? In I. K. Obler and D. Fein (eds), *The Exceptional Brain: Neuropsychology of Talent and Special Abilities* (pp. 436–73). New York: Guilford Press.

Ericsson, K. A., and Harris, M. S. (1990, November). Expert chess memory without chess knowledge: a training study. Poster presented at the 31st Annual Meeting of the Psychonomic Society, New Orleans, LA.

Ericsson, K. A., and Kintsch, W. (1994). *Long-Term Working Memory* (ICS Tech. Report No. 94-01). Boulder: University of Colorado, Institute of Cognitive Science.

Ericsson, K. A., Krampe, R. Th., and Heizmann, S. (1993). Can we create gifted people? In CIBA Foundation Symposium 178. *The Origins and Development of High Ability* (pp. 222–49). Chichester, England: Wiley.

Ericsson, K. A., Krampe, R. Th., and Tesch-Römer, C. (1993). The role of deliberate practice in the acquisition of expert performance. *Psychological Review, 100,* 363–406.

Ericsson, K. A., and Simon, H. A. (1993). *Protocol Analysis: Verbal Reports as Data* (rev. edn). Cambridge, MA: MIT Press.

Ericsson, K. A., and Smith, J. (1991a). Prospects and limits of the empirical study of expertise: an introduction. In K. A. Ericsson and J. Smith (eds), *Toward a General Theory of Expertise: Prospects and Limits* (pp. 1–39). Cambridge, England: Cambridge University Press.

Ericsson, K. A., and Smith, J. (eds). (1991b). *Toward a General Theory of Expertise: Prospects and Limits.* Cambridge, England: Cambridge University Press.

Ericsson, K. A., and Staszewski, J. (1989). Skilled memory and expertise: mechanisms of exceptional performance. In D. Klahr and K. Kotovsky (eds), *Complex Information Processing: The Impact of Herbert A. Simon* (pp. 235–67). Hillsdale, NJ: Erlbaum.

Feldman, D. H. (1980). *Beyond Universals in Cognitive Development.* Norwood, NJ: Ablex.

Feldman, D. H. (1986). *Nature's Gambit: Child Prodigies and the Development of Human Potential.* New York: Basic Books.

Feng, J. (1984). Foreword. In L. Shufen and J. Cheng'an (eds), *Yani's Monkeys* (pp. 1–2). Beijing, China: Foreign Languages Press.

Folkard, S., and Monk, T. H. (1985). Circadian performance rhythms. In S. Folkard and T. H. Monk (eds), *Hours of Work* (pp. 37–52). Chichester, England: Wiley.

Forbes, C. (1992). *The Polgar Sisters: Training or Genius?.* New York: Henry Holt.

Franklin, B. (1986). *The Autobiography and Other Writings.* New York: Penguin Books. (Autobiography originally published 1788).

Galton, F. (1908). *Memories of My Life.* London: Methuen.

Galton, F. (1979). *Hereditary Genius: An Inquiry into its Laws and Consequences.* London: Julian Friedman. (Original work published 1869).

Gardner, H. (1973). *The Arts and Human Development.* New York: Wiley.

Gardner, H. (1983). *Frames of Mind: The Theory of Multiple Intelligences.* New York: Basic Books.

Gardner, H. (1993a). *Creating Minds.* New York: Basic Books.

Gardner, H. (1993b). *Multiple Intelligences: The Theory in Practice.* New York: Basic Books.

Groen, G. J., and Patel, V. L. (1988). The relationship between comprehension and reasoning in medical expertise. In M. T. H. Chi, R. Glaser. and M. J. Farr (eds), *The Nature of Expertise* (pp. 287–310). Hillsdale, NJ: Erlbaum.

Gruber, H. E. (1981). *Darwin on Man: A Psychological Study of Scientific Creativity* (2nd edn). Chicago: University of Chicago Press.

Ho, W.-C. (ed.). (1989). *Yani: The Brush Innocence.* New York: Hudson Hills.

Hoffman, R. R. (ed.). (1992). *The Psychology of Expertise: Cognitive Research and Empirical AI.* New York: Springer-Verlag.

Howe, M. J. A. (1990). *The Origins of Exceptional Abilities.* Oxford, England: Basil Blackwell.

Hulin, C. L., Henry, R. A., and Noon, S. L. (1990). Adding a dimension: time as a factor in the generalizability of predictive relationships. *Psychological Bulletin, 107,* 328–40.

Hunt, E., and Agnoli, F. (1991). The Whorfian hypothesis: a cognitive psychology perspective. *Psychological Review, 98,* 377–89.

Juster, F. T., and Stafford, F. P. (eds). (1985). *Time, Goods and Well-Being.* Ann Arbor: University of Michigan, Institute for Social Research.

Krampe, R. Th. (1994). *Maintaining Excellence: Cognitive–Motor Performance in Pianists Differing in Age and Skill Level.* Berlin. Germany: Edition Sigma.

Larkin, J. H., McDermott, J., Simon, D. P., and Simon, H. A. (1980). Models of competence in solving physics problems. *Cognitive Science, 4,* 317–45.

Lave, J. (1988). *Cognition in Practice.* Cambridge, England: Cambridge University Press.

Lave, J., and Wenger, E. (1991). *Situated Learning: Legitimate Peripheral Participation.* Cambridge, England: Cambridge University Press.

Lehman, H. C. (1953). *Age and Achievement.* Princeton, NJ: Princeton University Press.

Levin, H., and Addis, A. B. (1979). *The Eye–Voice Span.* Cambridge, MA: MIT Press.

Luria, A. R. (1968). *The Mind of a Mnemonist.* New York: Avon.

Malina, R. M., and Bouchard, C. (1991). *Growth, Maturity, and Physical Activity.* Champaign, IL: Human Kinetics.

Maslow, A. H. (1971). *The Farther Reaches of Human Nature.* New York: Viking.

Miller, G. A. (1956). The magical number seven, plus or minus two: some limits on our capacity for processing information. *Psychological Review, 63,* 81–97.

Murray, P. (ed.). (1989a). *Genius: The History of an Idea.* Oxford. England: Basil Blackwell.

Murray, P. (1989b). Poetic genius and its classic origins. In P. Murray (ed.), *Genius: The History of an Idea* (pp. 9–31). Oxford, England: Basil Blackwell.

Newell, A., and Simon, H. A. (1972). *Human Problem Solving.* Englewood Cliffs, NJ: Prentice-Hall.

Pariser, D. (1987). The juvenile drawings of Klee, Toulouse-Lautrec and Picasso. *Visual Arts Research, 13,* 53–67.

Patel, V. L., and Groen, G. J. (1991). The general and specific nature of medical expertise: a critical look. In K. A. Ericsson and J. Smith (eds), *Toward a General Theory of Expertise* (pp. 93–125). Cambridge, England: Cambridge University Press.

Platt, R. (1966). General introduction. In J. E. Meade and A. S. Parkes (eds), *Genetic and Environmental Factors in Human Ability* (pp. ix–xi). Edinburgh, Scotland: Oliver & Boyd.

Qin, Y., and Simon, H. A. (1990). Laboratory replication of scientific discovery processes. *Cognitive Science, 14*, 281–312.

Radford, J. (1990). *Child Prodigies and Exceptional Early Achievers*. New York: Free Press.

Raskin, E. (1936). Comparison of scientific and literary ability: a biographical study of eminent scientists and letters of the nineteenth century. *Journal of Abnormal and Social Psychology, 31*, 20–35.

Regnier, G., Salmela, J., and Russell, S. J. (1993). Talent detection and development in sport. In R. N. Singer, M. Murphy and L. K. Tennant (eds), *Handbook of Research in Sport Psychology* (pp. 290–313). New York: Macmillan.

Roe, A. (1953). A psychological study of eminent psychologists and anthropologists, and a comparison with biological and physical scientists. *Psychological Monographs: General and Applied, 67* (Whole No. 352), 1–55.

Roth, H. (1982). *Master Violinists in Performance*. Neptune City, NJ: Paganinia.

Salthouse, T. A. (1984). Effects of age and skill in typing. *Journal of Experimental Psychology: General, 13*, 345–71.

Salthouse, T. A. (1991a). Expertise as the circumvention of human processing limitations. In K. A. Ericsson and J. Smith (eds), *Toward a General Theory of Expertise: Prospects and Limits* (pp. 286–300). Cambridge, England: Cambridge University Press.

Salthouse, T. A. (1991b). *Theoretical Perspectives on Cognitive Aging*. Hillsdale, NJ: Erlbaum.

Scheinfeld, A. (1939). *You and Heredity*. New York: Frederick A. Stokes.

Schmidt, H. G., and Boshuizen, H. P. A. (1993). On the origin of intermediate effects in clinical case recall. *Memory and Cognition, 21*, 338–51.

Schulz, R., and Curnow, C. (1988). Peak performance and age among superathletes: track and field, swimming, baseball, tennis, and golf. *Journal of Gerontology: Psychological Sciences, 43*, 113–20.

Simon, H. A., and Chase, W. G. (1973). Skill in chess. *American Scientist, 61*, 394–403.

Simonton, D. K. (1984). *Genius, Creativity, and Leadership: Historiometric Inquiries*. Cambridge, MA: Harvard University Press.

Simonton, D. K. (1988a). Age and outstanding achievement: what do we know after a century of research? *Psychological Bulletin, 104*, 251–67.

Simonton, D. K. (1988b). *Scientific Genius: A Psychology of Science*. Cambridge, England: Cambridge University Press.

Sloboda, J. A. (1985). *The Musical Mind: The Cognitive Psychology of Music*. Oxford, England: Oxford University Press.

Sloboda, J. A., Hermelin, B., and O'Connor, N. (1985). An exceptional musical memory. *Music Perception, 3*, 155-70.

Smith, S. B. (1983). *The Great Mental Calculators*. New York: Columbia University Press.

Starkes, J. L., and Deakin, J. M. (1985). Perception in sport: a cognitive approach to skilled performance. In W. F. Straub and J. M. Williams (eds), *Cognitive Sport Psychology* (pp. 115–28). Lansing, NY: Sports Science Associates.

Suzuki, S. (1981a). Every child can become rich in musical sense. In E. Hermann (ed.), *Shinichi Suzuki: The Man and his Philosophy* (pp. 136–41). Athens, OH: Ability Development Associates. (Originally presented in 1963).

Suzuki, S. (1981b). Discovery of the law of ability and the principle of ability development: proof that talent is not inborn. In E. Hermann (ed.), *Shinichi Suzuki: The Man and his Philosophy* (pp. 233–46). Athens, OH: Ability Development Associates. (Originally presented in 1980).

Takeuchi, A. H., and Hulse, S. H. (1993). Absolute pitch. *Psychological Bulletin, 113*, 345–61.

Thomas, A., and Chess, S. (1984). Genesis and evolution of behavioral disorders: from infancy to early adult life. *American Journal of Psychiatry, 141*, 1–9.

Treffert, D. A. (1989). *Extraordinary People: Understanding "Idiot Savants.* "New York: Harper & Row.

Wallace, A. (1986). *The Prodigy.* New York: Dutton.

Wallace, D. B., and Gruber, H. E. (eds). (1989). *Creative People at Work.* New York: Oxford University Press.

Weisberg, R. W. (1986). *Creativity: Genius and Other Myths.* New York: Freeman.

Weisberg, R. W. (1993). *Creativity: Beyond the Myth of Genius.* New York: Freeman.

Innate Talents: Reality or Myth?

Introduction

Like reading 13, the article by Michael Howe, Jane Davidson, and John Sloboda attacks the notion that innate talent is responsible for expert performance. The authors argue that there is little or no basis for the concept of innate giftedness. To bolster their view that practice and not good genes gives rise to excellence, the authors note that even crude retrospective measures of practice are predictive of levels of performance and that so-called "talented" individuals do not reach high levels of expertise without substantial amounts of training. People assumed to possess no talent are seen as capable of very high levels of performance when given sufficient opportunities for training.

As evidence for their position, Howe et al. note that the same amount of practice time creates equivalent amounts of progress in the most and least successful musicians (in other words, very capable musicians do not profit more from practice time than do unsuccessful musicians, thus suggesting that the two groups do not differ in innate talent). The authors believe that, in addition to practice, other factors also contribute to variability in performance among individuals: opportunities, preparatory experiences, encouragement, support, motivation, self-confidence, perseverance, and single-minded concentration; plus differences in quality of instruction, effectiveness of practice strategy, and degree of enthusiasm.

Numerous examples are cited in support of the authors' arguments. Among them is the portrayal of high-performing children not as simply springing into being, but rather as benefitting from previous encouragement and training at the hands of their parents early in life. The authors' final point is that the concept of talent – and the identification of some children as possessing talent – is often used to justify selectivity and discrimination in education and training.

Further reading

The entire issue of the journal *Behavioral and Brain Sciences*, *21*(3), 1998, is devoted to Howe et al.'s target article. It contains 29 commentaries as well as Howe et al.'s response.

FOURTEEN

Innate Talents: Reality or Myth?

Michael J. A. Howe, Jane W. Davidson, and John A. Sloboda

1 Introduction

In many areas of expertise, ranging from music, dance, art, and literature to sports, chess, mathematics, science, and foreign-language acquisition, there is abundant evidence that young people differ from one another in their attainments and in the apparent ease with which they achieve them. Even within a family there may be marked differences: for example, a child who struggles at a musical instrument without much success may be overtaken by a younger sibling.

It is widely believed that the likelihood of becoming exceptionally competent in certain fields depends on the presence or absence of inborn attributes variously labelled "talents" or "gifts" or, less often, "natural aptitudes." According to an informal British survey, more than three-quarters of music educators who decide which young people are to receive instruction believe that children cannot do well unless they have special innate gifts (Davis 1994). The judgement that someone is talented is believed to help explain (as distinct from merely describing) that person's success. It is also widely assumed that the innate talent that makes it possible for an individual to excel can be detected in early childhood. We will refer to the view that exceptional accomplishments depend on a special biological potential that can be identified in some young children but not others as "the talent account." The purpose of this target article is to examine the evidence and arguments for and against this account.

The talent account has important social implications. A consequence of the belief that innate gifts are a precondition for high achievement is that young people who are not identified as having innate talents in a particular domain are likely to be denied the help and encouragement they would need to attain high levels of competence. Children's progress can be affected negatively as well as positively by adults' expectations (Brophy and Good 1973).

1.1 Agreeing on a definition of innate talent

Before considering evidence for and against the talent account, we should be as clear as possible about what is meant by "talent." People are rarely precise about what they mean by this term: users do not specify what form an innate talent takes or how it might exert its influence.

Certain pitfalls have to be avoided in settling on a definition of talent. A very restrictive definition could make it impossible for any conceivable evidence to demonstrate talent. For example, some people believe that talent is based on an inborn ability that makes it certain that its possessor will excel. This criterion is too strong. At the other extreme, it would be possible to make the definition of talent so vague that its existence is trivially ensured; talent might imply no more than that those who reach high levels of achievement differ biologically from others in some undefined way. No matter how talent is defined, those who believe that innate talent exists also assume that early signs of it can be used to predict future success.

For the purposes of this target article we will assign five properties to talent: (1) It originates in genetically transmitted structures and hence is at least partly innate. (2) Its full effects may not be evident at an early stage, but there will be some advance indications, allowing trained people to identify the presence of talent before exceptional levels of mature performance have been demonstrated. (3) These early indications of talent provide a basis for predicting who is likely to excel. (4) Only a minority are talented, for if all children were, there would be no way to predict or explain differential success. Finally, (5) talents are relatively domain-specific.

In principle, it is desirable to define precisely the indicators of talent, but in practice some imprecision is unavoidable, as in the phrase "relatively domain-specific" in (5). We would have preferred to be able to specify the boundaries between domains, but this is not currently possible. Nor can one specify just how much a trait should facilitate the acquisition of special abilities to qualify as a talent: the available empirical evidence is too coarse. We allow the possibility that an innate talent can take different forms. For example, saying that each of two children has "a talent for music" need not imply that both are advantaged in precisely the same way. A domain may draw on many different skills, and individuals' competence levels in them may not be highly intercorrelated (Sloboda et al. 1985; Sloboda and Howe 1991).

1.2 The talent concept in researchers' explanations

Our five properties are meant to provide a working definition that is acceptable to researchers and captures the intuitions of the lay public. Like laypersons, researchers typically believe that when they introduce the term "talent" they are predicting or explaining someone's performance, not just describing it. For example, Feldman (1988), writing about child prodigies, remarks that "it is not obvious what their talents will lead to" (p. 281): He insists that "the child must possess talent, and it must be very powerful" (p. 280). For Feldman, talents cannot be acquired; they must be "possessed" innately by prodigies. He believes that prodigies demonstrate "exceptional pretuning to an already existing body of knowledge, one that countless others had spent time and energy developing and refining" (p. 278). Similarly, Gardner (1993a) equates talent with early potential, noting that "a poignant state of affairs results when an individual of high talent and promise ends up failing to achieve that potential" (p. 176). For Gardner, talent is defined as a sign of precocious biopsychological potential in a particular domain (Gardner 1984; 1993b). The possession of "a strong gift in a specific domain, be it dance, chess or mathematics," is recognized by Gardner when there is a coincidence of factors, the first of which is "native talent" (1993b, p. 51). According to him, individuals who accomplish a great deal are people who were "at promise" in relevant areas from early in life.

For Heller (1993, p. 139) "scientific giftedness . . . can be defined as scientific thinking potential or as a special talent to excel in [natural sciences]." Detterman (1993, p. 234) likewise suggests that "innate ability is what you are talking about when you are talking about talent." Eysenck and Barrett (1993) claim that a strong genetic basis underlies all the variables associated with giftedness. Eysenck (1995) insists on the existence of genetically transmitted talents, which he regards as necessary but not sufficient for the emergence of genius. Benbow and Lubinski (1993) agree that talent is explicitly biological: they claim that "people are born into this world with some biological predispositions" (p. 65). Based on a survey of the use of terms such as "aptitude," "giftedness," and "talent" by experts and laypersons, Gagné (1993) concludes that a special ability must have a genetic basis to be defined as a gift or aptitude. Winner (1996) and Winner and Martino (1993) regard talents as unlearned domain-specific traits that may develop or "come to fruition" in favourable circumstances but cannot be manufactured. Talents are likely to be identified by parents or teachers or they may be discovered fortuitously (Winner and Martino 1993, p. 259), but many gifted children go unrecognized.

The above quotations make it clear that researchers and experts make extensive use of the concept of talent to predict exceptional abilities and to explain their causes. Because researchers as well as educators rely on the talent account, it is important to examine its validity.

Some previous challenges to the talent account have concentrated on the field of music. Sloboda et al. (1994a; 1994b) raised objections to the view that musical expertise arises from talent. They noted, for example, that in some non-Western cultures musical achievements are considerably more widespread than in our own (see section 3.3), that there are often no early signs of unusual excellence in outstanding adult instrumentalists (Sosniak 1985), and that very early experiences may be the real cause of what is interpreted as talent (Hepper 1991; Parncutt 1993). Others have challenged this analysis, arguing that the evidence of strong cultural influences on musicality can be reconciled with the existence of innate talent (Davies 1994; see also Hargreaves 1994; Radford 1994; Torff and Winner 1994).

Criticisms of the talent account in other domains have been raised by Ericsson and Charness (1994; 1995), who provide substantial evidence that the effects of extended, deliberate practice are more decisive than is commonly believed. They argue that although children undoubtedly differ in the ease with which they perform various skills (a fact to which Gardner [1995] has drawn attention in challenging their conclusions), no early predictors of adult performance have been found.

2 Evidence in Support of the Talent Account

Several findings appear to favour the talent account. (1) There are many reports of children acquiring impressive skills very early in life, in the apparent absence of opportunities for the kinds of learning experiences that would normally be considered necessary. (2) Certain relatively rare capacities that could have an innate basis (e.g., "perfect" pitch perception) appear to emerge spontaneously in a few children and may increase the likelihood of their excelling in music. (3) Biological correlates of certain skills and abilities have been reported. (4) Case histories of autistic, mentally handicapped people classified as "idiot savants" have yielded reports that appear to indicate impressive skills arising in the absence of learning opportunities.

2.1 Evidence of skills emerging unusually early

The literature on child prodigies (e.g., see Feldman 1980; Feldman and Goldsmith 1986; Fowler 1981; Freeman 1990; Goldsmith 1990; Gross 1993a; 1993b; Hollingworth 1942; Howe 1982; 1990a; 1993; 1995; Radford 1990) abounds with accounts of extraordinarily precocious development in the earliest years. Very early language skills are described by Fowler (1981) in a boy who was said to have begun speaking at 5 months of age, with a 50-word vocabulary 1 month later, and a speaking knowledge of 5 languages before the age of 3. Feldman and Goldsmith (1986) describe a boy whose parents said he began to speak in sentences at 3 months, to engage in conversations at 6 months, and to read simple books by his first birthday. Hollingworth (1942) writes that Francis Galton was reputed to be reading in his third year.

However, in none of these cases was the very early explosion of language skills observed directly by the investigator, and all the early studies were retrospective and anecdotal. Even the more recent studies have some of these limitations. For example, the boy described by Feldman and Goldsmith (1986) was not actually encountered by Feldman himself until he had reached the age of 3. Although the boy's parents claimed to be surprised by his swift progress, Feldman was astounded by their absolute dedication and "unending quest for stimulating and supportive environments" (Feldman and Goldsmith 1986, p. 36).

Fowler (1981) notes that the professed passivity of some parents is belied by their very detailed accounts. One pair of parents insisted that their daughter learned to read entirely unaided and claimed that they only realized this on discovering her reading *Heidi*. It turned out, however, that they had kept elaborate records of the child's accomplishments. Parents who keep such accounts cannot avoid becoming actively involved in the child's early learning.

Accounts of the early lives of musicians provide further anecdotes of the apparently spontaneous flowering of impressive abilities at remarkably early ages (Hargreaves 1986; Radford 1990; Shuter-Dyson and Gabriel 1981; Sloboda 1985; Winner and Martino 1993). A number of prominent composers were regarded as prodigies when they were young, and in some cases there are reports of unusual musical competence in their earliest years. Mozart's early feats are widely known. It is reported that the Hungarian music prodigy Erwin Nyiregyhazi was able to reproduce simple songs at the age of 2 and play tunes on a mouth organ at age 4 (Revesz 1925). Again, however, most of the reports are based on anecdotes reported many years after the early childhood events in question. Some of the accounts are auto-biographical, such as Stravinsky's description of having amazed his parents by imitating local singers as a 2-year-old (Gardner 1984) or Arthur Rubenstein's claim to have mastered the piano before he could speak. The accuracy of such autobiographical reports is questionable considering that childhood memories of the first three years are not at all reliable (e.g., see Usher and Neisser 1993). The early biographies of prominent composers have revealed that they all received intensive and regular supervised practice sessions over a period of several years (Lehmann 1997). The emergence of unusual skills typically followed rather than preceded a period during which unusual opportunities were provided, often combined with a strong expectation that the child would do well.

There are also some descriptions of precocious ability in the visual arts, and Winner (1996) has collected a number of drawings by 2- and 3-year-olds that are considerably more realistic than those of average children. Among major artists, however, few are known to have produced drawings or paintings that display exceptional promise prior to the age of 8 or so (Winner and Martino 1993).

2.2   Evidence of special capacities that facilitate acquisition of specific abilities

Some individuals acquire ability more smoothly and effortlessly than others, but that fact does not confirm the talent account. Differences between people in the ease with which a particular skill is acquired may be caused by any of a number of contributing factors. These include various motivational and personality influences as well as previous learning experiences that equip a person with knowledge, attitudes, skills, and self-confidence. Facility is often the outcome rather than the cause of unusual capabilities (Perkins 1981).

Perhaps the clearest indication of a special capacity that is displayed by a minority early in life in the apparent absence of deliberate efforts to acquire it, making further advances likely, is encountered in the field of music. A number of young children have "perfect" or "absolute" pitch perception. A child thus endowed can both name and sing specified pitches without being given a reference pitch (Takeuchi and Hulse 1993). Structural differences in brain morphology related to absolute pitch have been observed. Musicians who have absolute pitch show stronger leftward planum temporale asymmetry than nonmusicians and musicians without perfect pitch (Schlaug et al. 1995). It is not clear, however, whether these differences are the cause of absolute pitch or the outcome of differences in learning or experience.

One might expect musicians who have absolute pitch to be more successful than those who do not, but this is not always true. Perfect pitch perception has circumscribed utility. For example, it makes no contribution to an individual's interpretative ability. Moreover, there is evidence that it can be learned. It is relatively common in young musicians who are given extensive musical training prior to the age of 5 or 6, perhaps because a young child pays more attention to individual notes before coming to perceive sounds as parts of larger musical structures (Ericsson and Faivre 1988). Contrary to the view that absolute pitch provides clear evidence of a talent, it is sometimes found in individuals who begin their training late (Sergent and Roche 1973), and can even be acquired by adults, although only with considerable effort (Brady 1970; Sloboda 1985; Takeuchi and Hulse 1993).

Eidetic imagery has likewise been taken to be a talent. Like absolute pitch, it is observed in some young children but not others, and it appears in the absence of deliberate learning. Eidetic imagery seems to make young children capable of recalling visual information in some detail, but the phenomenon is somewhat fleeting and hard to verify with certainty, and it conveys few, if any, practical benefits. Although the phenomenon seems genuine as a subjective experience, evidence that eidetic imagery is correlated with above average remembering has proved elusive (Haber 1979; Haber and Haber 1988). Accordingly, there is little justification for believing that eidetic imagery conveys an advantage.

2.3 Evidence of biological involvement in exceptional skills

There is a large body of mainly correlational research on the relationship between various measures of brain structure, function, and activity and behavioural data. Performance has been linked to (1) electrocortical measures such as evoked potentials (Benbow and Lubinski 1993; Hendrikson and Hendrikson 1980) and their components (McCarthy and Donchin 1981), (2) hemispheric laterality (Gazzaniga 1985), (3) brain images (see Eysenck and Barrett 1993), and (4) saccadic eye movements.

A number of correlates of high ability have been identified, including left-handedness, immune disorders, myopia (see Benbow and Lubinski 1993), blood flow measures (Horn 1986), neurohistology (Scheibel and Paul 1985), prenatal exposure to high levels of testosterone (Geschwind and Behan 1982), allergy, uric-acid levels, and glucose metabolism rates (see Storfer 1990), and laterality (Eysenck and Barrett 1993).

Gender differences in spatial abilities (Humphreys et al. 1993) appear to contribute to gender differences in mathematical performance and are probably based on biological differences. Information-processing parameters involved in a number of human abilities, such as response speed, are at least moderately heritable (Bouchard et al. 1990). Hereditary factors underlie various other individual differences in competence, such as working memory (Dark and Benbow 1991). Enhanced ability to manipulate information in short-term memory has been observed in young people who are unusually successful in mathematics (Dark and Benbow 1990). Moreover, because there are modest positive correlations between measures of special skills and heritable basic abilities such as general intelligence (Ackerman 1988; Howe 1989b), it is likely that some of the innate influences that contribute to variability in intelligence test scores also contribute to individual differences in special skills.

In general, the correlational evidence linking performance to brain characteristics suggests that innately determined biological differences contribute to the variability of expertise in specific areas of competence. There is a large gulf between identifying neural correlates of behavioural differences and finding a neural predictor of talent, however. The relations between neural and performance measures are too weak to warrant conclusions about talent. Moreover, the correlations diminish as tasks become more complex (Sternberg 1993).

To provide support for the talent account, neural correlates of exceptional skills would have to (1) be accompanied by clarity about the direction of causality, (2) include evidence that the neural measure is innately determined (rather than the outcome of differences in experience), (3) be specific to an ability, and (4) selectively facilitate expertise in a minority of individuals. We are unaware of any neural measures that come close to meeting these criteria. Nor has firm alternative evidence of early physical precursors of specific abilities emerged from studies of either prenatal capacities or postnatal cognition (Hepper 1991; Lecanuet 1995; Papousek 1995; Trehub 1990).

Ericsson (1990) and Ericsson and Crutcher (1988) argue that apparent indicators of structural precursors of ability may need to be interpreted with caution. Ericsson (1990) points out that individual differences in the composition of certain muscles are reliable predictors of differences in athletic performance and that this fact has been widely held to demonstrate genetic determinants of athletic excellence. He notes, however, that differences in the proportion of the slow-twitch muscle fibres that are essential for success in long-distance running are largely the *result* of extended practice in running, rather than the initial *cause* of differential ability. Differences between athletes and others in the proportions of particular kinds of muscle fibres are specific to those muscles that are most fully exercised in athletes' training for a specific specialization (Howald 1982).

Some individual differences in brain structure and function are the outcome of differences in experiences rather than a primary cause. Experience can lead to changes in various parts of the mammalian brain, including the somatosensory, visual, and auditory systems (Elbert et al. 1995). For example, in violinists and other string players the cortical representation of the digits of the left hand (which is involved in fingering the strings) is larger than in control subjects. The magnitude of the difference is correlated with the age at which string players began instruction. Differences in early musical learning experiences may also account for the atypical brain asymmetries observed in musicians by Schlaug et al. (1995).

Although the evidence of a genetic contribution to human intelligence is consistent with the talent account, there are only weak correlations between general intelligence and various specific abilities (Ceci 1990; Ceci and Liker 1986; Howe 1989c; 1990b; Keating 1984). General intelligence need not limit final levels of achievement (Ackerman 1988), and may have little or no direct influence on specific abilities (Bynner and Romney 1986; Horn 1986; Howe 1989c). Moreover, there is no evidence of specific gene systems affecting high-level performance of special skills in the predictive and selective manner required by the talent account. Psychological traits are more likely to be influenced indirectly by genes in a probabilistic way (Plomin and Thompson 1993). Even in the case of general intelligence, most of the research addresses the aetiology of individual differences in the normal range of ability. Relatively little is known about the genetic origins of high-level ability.

Knowledge about the genetic basis of specific high-level abilities is particularly limited (Plomin 1988; Thompson and Plomin 1993). In the Minnesota Study of Twins Reared Apart, self-ratings of musical talent correlated 0.44 among monozygotic twins reared apart, considerably less than the correlation of 0.69 for monozygotic twins reared together (Lykken, in press), suggesting that family experience makes a substantial contribution to self-ratings of musical ability. Similarly, in a study of musical abilities in twins, Coon and Carey (1989) concluded that among young adults musical ability was influenced more by shared family environment than by shared genes. On a number of measures the correlations between dizygotic twins, which ranged from 0.34 to 0.83, were not much lower than those between monozygotic twins (0.44 to 0.90).

The importance of general processing constraints diminishes as levels of expertise increase (Ackerman 1988; Krampe and Ericsson 1996); and some differences in basic skills are predictive of unskilled performance but less so of skilled performance (Ericsson et al. 1993b). In Coon and Carey's study all eight relevant estimates of the heritability of musical ability were lower for participants who had taken some music lessons than for those who took no lessons at all; the average was less than 0.20 in the former group. Genetic differences that are initially relevant to expertise may be less important when large amounts of training and practice have been provided.

2.4   Evidence of unusual capacities in autistic savants

In most case histories of idiot savants it is apparent that the emergence of special skills is accompanied by obsessive interest and very high degrees of practice (e.g., see Howe 1989a; 1989b; Howe and Smith 1988; Sloboda et al. 1985; Treffert 1989). However, there a few reports of mentally handicapped children who display remarkable specific skills that seem to have been acquired without deliberate training or instruction. Among the well-documented cases are those of two child artists and a young musician; all three were described as being autistic.

From the age of 4, one of the artists, a girl named Nadia, was unusually slow, clumsy, and unresponsive, and spoke hardly at all, but drew many remarkable pictures, usually of horses, birds, and other animals. These pictures used advanced techniques to represent perspective, proportion, foreshortening, and the illusion of movement; they also showed impressive manual dexterity (Selfe 1977). The drawing skills of the other child artist, Stephen Wiltshire, are equally impressive (O'Connor and Hermelin 1987; Sacks 1995).

A 5-year-old autistic boy was described in Miller's (1989) study of musical abilities in the mentally handicapped. Like the artist Nadia, this boy was largely unresponsive to his physical environment and severely retarded in language development, with practically no speech. When confronted with a piano keyboard, however, he could not only reproduce a heard melody but also transform the piece by transposing it to a different key. He could improvise in ways that conformed to the conventions of musical composition. The abilities Miller observed seem to be based on a capacity to encode the fundamental units quickly and efficiently and to represent musical items in a complex knowledge system that incorporated sensitivity to harmonic relationships, scale or key constraints, melodic structure, and stylistic norms.

The remarkable capacities of autistic musicians and artists may seem to call for something close to the talent account. At least in the cases of Nadia and the 5-year-old boy described by Miller, their observed level of performance was beyond anything encountered in nonautistic children of comparable ages. Exactly why these children could do things that others could not remains largely a matter for speculation, although it is noteworthy that in many documented cases the autistic individuals spent many hours each day concentrating on their special interests. There is no direct evidence that the causes are innate, and if they do have an innate component, its main direct effect may be to augment the individuals' obsession rather than their specific skills as such.

3   Evidence Appearing to Contradict the Talent Account

Section 2 examined various kinds of evidence that appears to be consistent with the talent account. This section cites a variety of findings in the opposite direction. Other reasons for questioning the innate talent viewpoint are also introduced.

3.1   Lack of early signs

As noted in section 2.1, much of the evidence pointing to very early indications of unusual abilities is either retrospective or based on records supplied by parents whose claims to have played no active role in stimulating their children's progress are belied by other information. Except in the case of a small number of autistic children mentioned in section 2.4, there is no firm evidence of exceptional early progress without above-average degrees of parental support and encouragement. This is not to say that parental support or special opportunities and training account for all instances of excellence.

Innate influences might operate in ways that do not produce early signs, but to predict progress early evidence of talent is necessary.

Unidentifiable early influences cannot be regarded as instances of talent, for the reasons given in section 1.1.

We will first consider some studies of whether children identified as unusually able by mid-childhood or later had displayed any early signs of special qualities other than those induced by early parental training or special encouragement.

It is important to keep in mind that early ability is not evidence of talent unless it emerges in the absence of special opportunities to learn. For example, it was once thought that the ability of infants in certain parts of Africa to sit and walk appreciably earlier than European children must have a genetic basis, but Super (1976) showed that this inference was wrong. Studying infants in a Kenyan tribe, he confirmed that they did indeed display motor capacities such as walking, standing, and sitting without supprt a month or so earlier than children in other continents, but he also discovered that the only skills these infants acquired earlier than others were those that their mothers deliberately taught them. When genetically similar infants from the same tribe were brought up in an urban environment in which parents did not provide the special training given in traditional villages, the infants displayed no motor precocity. Super reported a correlation of −0.9 between the age at which a baby began to crawl and a measure of the extent to which parents encouraged crawling. These findings do not rule out the possibility that some early differences have biological bases (Rosser and Randolph 1989), but they do show that this cannot be automatically assumed.

Retrospective interview studies of the early progress of individuals who eventually excel have provided little evidence of early signs of promise. Sosniak (1985; 1990) interviewed at length 21 outstanding American pianists in their mid-30s, who were on the brink of careers as concert pianists. She also talked to their parents. There were few indications of the musicians displaying signs of future excellence while they were still very young. In most cases, unusually fast progress followed rather than preceded a combination of good opportunities and vigorous encouragement. Even by the time the young pianists had received approximately six years of relatively intensive training, it would have been possible to make confident predictions about their eventual success in only a minority of the cases. Similarly, a biographical study of 165 professional musicians in Poland produced very few reports of any preschool behaviour predictive of unusual musicality

(Manturzewska 1986). A longitudinal study of elite German tennis players likewise found no early capacities that predicted tennis performance in early adulthood (Schneider 1993; see also Monsaas 1985). Interview studies of the childhood progress of accomplished artists (Sloan and Sosniak 1985), swimmers (Kalinowski 1985), and mathematicians (Gustin 1985) reported very few early signs of exceptional promise prior to deliberate parental encouragement.

Howe et al. (1995) studied the form and frequency of early signs of musical ability in 257 children, only some of whom made superior progress as performing musicians. The investigators asked the parents to indicate whether specific indicators of musical promise had occurred, and if so, when. The parents were asked when their children first sang, moved to music, showed a liking for music, were attentive to music, or sought involvement in a musical activity. Only with the first of these behaviours, early singing, did those who were eventually most successful display (slightly) earlier onset than the other children. In most of these cases a parent regularly sang to the infant well before any singing by the infant was observed (see also Howe and Sloboda 1991a; 1991b; 1991c; Sloboda and Howe 1991).

Some authors have suggested that early interest and delight in musical sounds may indicate innate musical potential (Miller 1989; Winner and Martino 1993), but a questionnaire found that these indicators failed as predictors of later musical competence (Howe et al. 1995). In any case, the assumption that even very early preferences must be innate rather than learned is questionable. Small differences in the amount of attention infants give (for any of a number of reasons) to different kinds of stimuli may elicit increasingly different actions and responses, which eventually produce marked preferences and contribute to differences between young children in their patterns of abilities (Renninger and Wosniak 1985; see also Slater 1995).

3.2 Evidence pointing to an absence of differences in ease of learning between "talented" individuals and others

Differences in rate or ease of acquisition of a capacity could reflect a specific talent, but only if other influences are ruled out. This is not easy to do. Confounding variables such as the degree of familiarity with task items may influence performance even in simple memory tasks based on highly familiar numbers (Chi and Ceci 1987; Miller and Gelman 1983).

Investigations of long-term practice effects provide some relevant evidence. Sloboda et al. (1996; see also Sloboda 1996) found no significant differences between highly successful young musicians and other children in the amount of practice time they required to make a given amount of progress between successive grades in the British musical board examinations. Group differences in average progress were no greater than would have been expected from the differences in the amount of time spent practising. Consistent with these results, Hayes (1981) and Simonton (1991) found that all major composers required long periods of training (see also Ericsson and Lehmann, in press; Howe 1996a; 1996b; 1997). Hayes (1981) concludes that at least 10 years of preparation are necessary. Simonton (1991) considers this an underestimate of the amount of time required. He estimates that, on average, prominent composers produced the first of their compositions to gain a secure place in the classical repertoire between the ages of 26 and 31, having begun music lessons around the age of 9 and started composing at around age 17. Chess players likewise need at least 10 years of sustained preparation to reach international levels of competitiveness (Simon and Chase 1973) and those who begin in early childhood take even longer (Krogius 1976). Comparable periods of preparation and training are essential in various other areas, including mathematics (Gustin 1985), X-ray and medical diagnosis (Patel and Groen 1991), and sports (Kalinowski 1985; Monsaas 1985; see also Ericsson et al. 1993b).

3.3   Exceptional levels of performance in "untalented" people

A body of findings hard to reconcile with the talent account comes from experiments on ordinary adults who are given large amounts of training at skills that make heavy demands on memory (Ceci et al. 1988; Chase and Ericsson 1981) or perception (Ericsson and Faivre 1988). In some instances, the trained subjects achieved performance levels far higher than what most people (including experts in the psychology of learning and memory) had believed possible. Uninformed observers assumed that the participants must have had a special innate aptitude. There have been similar findings in studies of job-related skills in waiters

(Ericsson and Polson 1988) and bar staff (Bennett 1983). The cocktail waitresses in Bennett's study could regularly remember as many as 20 drink orders at a time: their performance was considerably better than that of a control group made up of university students. It is conceivable that people who are employed as waiters and bar staff gravitate to such jobs because of an inborn memory skill, but the Chase and Ericsson findings make it far more likely that employees excel in recalling orders because of on-the-job practice.

Accomplishments that are rare in one culture but relatively common in another also implicate learning rather than innate aptitude. In certain cultures very high levels of skill (by Western standards) have been observed in children swimming and canoeing (Mead 1975), in land navigation over apparently featureless terrains (Lewis 1976), and in maritime navigation across open water. Certain musical accomplishments are also considerably more widespread in some non-Western cultures than in our own (Blacking 1973; Feld 1984; Marshall 1982; Merriam 1967; Messenger 1958; Sloboda et al. 1994a; 1994b), and Australian desert aboriginal children perform better than white subjects on certain visual memory tasks (Kearins 1981). The fact that such precocious development of some skills in infants disappears when parents do not apply traditional training customs (Super 1976, see section 3.1) suggests that cultural variability in performance is caused by differences in opportunities to learn.

3.4 Conceptual difficulties with the notion of talent

There are certain conceptual and logical problems with the idea that talent contributes to exceptional human abilities. In everyday discourse reasoning about talent is often circular, for example: "She plays so well because she has a talent. How do I know she has a talent? That's obvious, she plays so well!"

Even among researchers who use the concept of talent for explanatory purposes, the supporting evidence is based on its alleged *effects*. Like many scientific constructs, talent is not observed directly but is inferred. There is nothing wrong with this, but one must be certain that the findings cannot be accounted for more plausibly without introducing the talent concept (Howe 1988a; 1988b; 1990b; 1990c; 1996b; Sloboda et al. 1994a; 1994b).

4   Alternative Influences Contributing to the Phenomena Attributed to the Effects of Talent

The causes of exceptional abilities may not be qualitatively different from those of less exceptional abilities in ordinary people. The links between high abilities and experiences that promote learning have been extensively discussed elsewhere (e.g., Berry 1990; Howe 1990a). Here we will consider the contribution of training and practice to various kinds of expertise.

Many dimensions of human variability may influence an individual's learning experiences and that person's eventual patterns of ability. These include: (1) relevant prior knowledge and skills; (2) attentiveness, concentration, and distractibility; (3) interests and acquired preferences; (4) motivation and competitiveness; (5) self-confidence and optimism; (6) other aspects of temperament and personality; (7) enthusiasm and energy level; (8) fatigue and anxiety.

Variations in opportunities and experiences, and in the appropriateness of training and the effectiveness of learning, practice, and testing procedures, are also influential.

4.1   Evidence from studies of practising

Dramatic effects of training and practice on ordinary people were discussed in section 3.3. Even those who are believed to be exceptionally talented, whether in music, mathematics, chess, or sports, require lengthy periods of instruction and practice (Charness et al. 1996; Ericsson and Charness 1994; Ericsson et al. 1993b; Starkes et al. 1996). Music is an area of competence thought to be especially dependent on talent (Davis 1994; O'Neill 1994); hence practice effects in other areas of competence are likely to be at least as strong as in music.

Ericsson and his coworkers (Ericsson et al. 1990; 1993a) have found strong correlations between the level of performance of student violinists in their 20s and the number of hours that they practised. By the age of 21 the best students in the performance class of a conservatory had accumulated approximately 10,000 hours of practice, compared with less than half that amount for students in the same institution who were training to be violin teachers. Differences of similar magnitude were found in a study comparing expert and amateur pianists (Krampe

1994). Measures of the accumulated number of practice hours since instrumental lessons began were good predictors of within-group as well as between-group differences in performance. Studies of expert musicians by Manturzewska (1990), Sloboda and Howe (1991), and Sosniak (1985) provide further evidence that regular practice is essential for acquiring and maintaining high levels of ability. Furthermore, considerable help and encouragement is required by all young players, even those thought by their teachers and parents to be highly talented, if they are to maintain the levels of practice necessary to achieve expertise (Sloboda and Howe 1991; see also section 4.2).

Sloboda et al. (1996) supplemented retrospective data on practice with concurrent diary-based information. They confirmed the strong positive correlation between practice and achievement, which was largest for the more formal and deliberate kinds of practice activities, such as scales and exercises. Achieving the highest level (grade 8) of the British Associate Board examinations in performing music required an average of approximately 3,300 hours of practice irrespective of the ability group to which the young people in the study were assigned. This suggests that practice is a direct cause of achievement level rather than merely a correlate of it.

Correlations between measures of performance and amounts of practice by music students range from approximately +0.3 to above +0.6 (Lehmann 1997). It is likely that these figures substantially underestimate the real magnitude of the relationship between performance and practice, for the following reasons: (1) the performance measures provided by grade levels are inexact indicators of attainment; and (2) global measures of practice time take into account neither the effectiveness of the particular practice strategies nor the role of other potentially influential factors such as the student's level of alertness, enthusiasm, and determination to do well. Kliegl et al. (1989) have confirmed that the intensity and quality of practice are as important as the sheer amount of it. Of course, the finding that practice is a major determinant of success does not rule out inherited influences; some traits that affect practising, such as the capacity to persist, may have innate components, but such components would not constitute "talents," as required by the talent account.

To summarize, there may be little or no basis for innate giftedness for the following reasons: (1) the lack of convincing positive evidence (section 2); (2) the substantial amount of negative evidence (section 3);

(3) the finding that even crude retrospective measures of practice are predictive of levels of performance (section 4.1); (4) the observation by both Hayes (1981) and Simonton (1991) that "talented" individuals do not reach high levels of expertise without substantial amounts of training (section 3.2); (5) the evidence of Ericsson and others (Ericsson and Faivre 1988) that people who are assumed to possess no talent are capable of very high levels of performance when given sufficient opportunities for training (section 3.3); and (6) the apparent absence of differences in the amount of practice time required by the most and least successful young musicians to make an equivalent amount of progress (sections 3.2 and 4.1). The conclusion is reinforced when some of the other measurable factors known to contribute to variability in performance are taken into account: opportunities, preparatory experiences, encouragement, support, motivation, self-confidence, perseverance, and single-minded concentration (Howe 1975; 1980). To these influences must also be added differences in quality of instruction, effectiveness of practice strategy, and degree of enthusiasm.

4.2 Criticisms and counterarguments

There has been considerable opposition to the suggestion that the influence usually attributed to talent can be accounted for by the many known determinants of performance levels (including hereditary ones) that fall outside the definition of talent (Davidson et al. 1996; Ericsson et al. 1993a; Sloboda and Howe 1991; 1992; Sloboda et al. 1994a; 1996). A first objection is that the evidence linking practice to progress is largely correlational. Most of the findings take the form of data showing that the more a person trains and practices, the higher that individual's level of performance. These correlations could merely indicate that individuals who are successful in and committed to a field of expertise are likely to spend more time practising than those who are less successful.

One counterargument is that the findings closely parallel those obtained in training studies in which amounts of practice have been deliberately manipulated (Ericsson et al. 1990). Also relevant is the finding by Sloboda et al. (1996) that the rate of progress of young musicians in a given year is most highly correlated with the amount of practice and teacher input in that same year, whereas if the correlation simply reflected differing lifestyles of more and less successful performers, the amount of progress in one year would be more highly correlated with the amount of practice in the following year.

It is conceivable that some children practice more than others because they have some kind of innate potential that encourages them to do so. However, as Sloboda and Howe (1991) and Howe and Sloboda (1991b) discovered, even among highly successful young musicians, the majority freely admit that without strong parental encouragement to practise they would never have done the amounts of regular practising needed to make good progress. Strong and sustained parental encouragement to practise was evident in virtually all successful young musicians (Davidson et al. 1996). It is conceivable that the parents who gave the most support did so because they detected signs of special potential, but that seems unlikely in view of the failure to find early signs of excellence in those children who later excelled (section 3).

Of course, a parent's beliefs about a child's putative talents can affect parental behaviours; hence such beliefs may indirectly affect a child's performance (e.g., Brophy and Good 1973). As noted in section 1, it is also true that self-beliefs can predict future performance (Dweck 1986; Sloboda et al. 1994a; Vispoel and Austin 1993). However, the question at issue is whether talent as such, as distinct from an individual's beliefs about its presence, influences a child's attainments.

A second objection is that although differences in training, practice, and other aspects of an individual's experiences can go a long way toward accounting for differences in technical skills, they fail to account for those differences in less tangible traits, such as expressivity or creativity, that separate the most exceptional performers from others. This objection represents a certain shifting of the goalposts when it is introduced as an argument for the existence of talent. Nevertheless, it needs to be considered. Expressivity in music has been discussed by Sloboda (1996), who argues that although *technical* skills must be acquired *ab initio* by extensive instrument-specific practice, some *expressive* accomplishments may occur rather early through an application of existing knowledge (such as emotional signals, gestures, and other bodily movements) to the domain of music. People might differ in musical expressivity in the absence of any differences in music-specific practice for a variety of reasons, one being that people differ in their levels of nonmusical expressivity. Expressive ability may thus appear to arise in the absence of overt evidence of practice or teaching, but this does not mean it is innate.

A third possible objection is that although practice, training, and other known influences may jointly account for performance differences in the majority of people, there could be a small number of individuals to whom this does not apply. Evidence to support this objection is lacking, however.

The fourth criticism is that, although comparisons between more and less successful groups of people may not have revealed differences in the amount of practice needed to achieve a given amount of progress (Sloboda et al. 1996), this does not demonstrate that such differences do not exist at an individual level, and there is some evidence that they do (Charness et al. 1996). In future research on practising it would be desirable to pay more attention to individual differences. However, as reported in section 3.2, no case has been encountered of anyone reaching the highest levels of achievement in chess-playing, mathematics, music, or sports without devoting thousands of hours to serious training.

5 Summary and Conclusion

We began this target article by describing the widespread belief that to reach high levels of ability a person must possess an innate potential called talent. Because the belief in talent has important social and educational consequences that affect selection procedures and training policies, it is important to establish whether it is correct. Belief in talent may also act as a barrier to further exploration of the causes of excellence in specific domains of ability.

To ensure that our use of the term coincided with that of scientific researchers as well as teachers and practitioners, we suggested that: (1) a talent has its origin in genetically transmitted structures; (2) there are early indicators of talent; (3) talent provides a basis for estimating the probability of excelling; (4) only a minority of individuals have special talents; and (5) the effects of a talent will be relatively specific.

In examining the evidence and the arguments for and against the talent account, we began in section 2 by considering positive findings. We examined evidence that certain young children excel without special encouragement and that some children are born with special capacities that facilitate the acquisition of particular abilities. There proved to be little evidence of early accomplishments that could not be explained by other known determinants of early progress. We also found no evidence of innate attributes operating in the predictable and specific manner implied by the talent account, apart from autistic savants whose exceptional skills appear to stem from an involuntary specialization of their mental activities.

Section 3 surveyed evidence contrary to the talent account. The absence of early signs of special ability was discussed. Where early precocity is encountered, it is invariably preceded by ample opportunities and encouragement. In addition, when prior differences in knowledge, skills, motivation, and other factors known to affect performance are controlled for, there is little evidence of individual differences in ease of learning. High levels of accomplishment invariably require lengthy and intensive training, and even people who are not believed to have any special talent can, purely as a result of training, reach levels of achievement previously thought to be attainable only by innately gifted individuals (section 3.3). There are also logical and conceptual arguments against the notion that talent is explanatory (section 3.4).

Section 4 examined alternatives to the talent account. Large amounts of regular practice were found to be essential for excelling. Studies of long-term practice and training suggest that individual differences in learning-related experiences are a major source of the variance in achievement.

The evidence we have surveyed in this target article does not support the talent account, according to which excelling is a consequence of possessing innate gifts. This conclusion has practical implications, because categorizing some children as innately talented is discriminatory. The evidence suggests that such categorization is unfair and wasteful, preventing young people from pursuing a goal because of the unjustified conviction of teachers or parents that certain children would not benefit from the superior opportunities given to those who are deemed to be talented.

We do not claim to have a full or precise answer to the question: "If talents do not exist, how can one explain the phenomena attributed to them?" However, we have listed a number of possible influences, and evidence of their effects.

Innate talents are inferred rather than observed directly. One reason for assuming that they exist at all has been to explain individual differences, but these can be accounted for adequately by experiential ones such as training and practice, as well as biological influences that lack the specificity and predictable consequences associated with the notion of talent.

It could be argued that the talent account is not totally wrong, but simply exaggerated and oversimplified. In our list of the five defining attributes of innate talents (section 1.1), two are relatively unproblematic: (1) individual differences in some special abilities may indeed have partly genetic origins, and (4) there do exist some attributes that are possessed by only a minority of individuals. In this very restricted sense, talent may be said to exist.

One might argue for retaining the concept of talent even though the other three criteria are not met. If the underlying issues were exclusively academic this would be reasonable. "Talent" would be the place-holder for the as yet unmapped influence of biology on special expertise. In practice, however, the other three attributes – (2) being identifiable before the emergence of high ability, (3) providing a basis for predicting excellence, and (5) being domain-specific – are crucial, because it is precisely these attributes that are the ones regarded by practitioners as justifying selectivity and discrimination.

References

Ackerman, P. L. (1988). Determinants of individual differences during skill acquisition: cognitive abilities and information processing. *Journal of Experimental Psychology: General,* **117**: 299–318.

Benbow, C. P., and Lubinski, D. (1993). Psychological profiles of the mathematically talented: some sex differences and evidence supporting their biological basis. In: *Ciba Foundation Symposium* **178**: The origins and development of high ability, eds G. R. Bock and K. Ackrill, Wiley.

Bennett, H. L. (1983). Remembering drink orders: the memory skills of cocktail waitresses. *Human Learning: Journal of Practical Research and Applications,* **2**: 157–70.

Berry, C. (1990). On the origins of exceptional intellectual and cultural achievement. In: *Encouraging the Development of Exceptional Abilities and Talents,* ed. M. J. A. Howe, British Psychological Society.

Blacking, J. (1973). *How Musical is Man?,* Faber & Faber.

Bouchard, T. J., Lykken, D. T., McGue, M., Segal, N. L., and Tellegen, A. (1990). Sources of human psychological differences: the Minnesota Study of Twins Reared Apart. *Science,* **250**: 223–8.

Brady, P. T. (1970). The genesis of absolute pitch. *Journal of the Acoustical Society of America*, **48**: 883–7.

Brophy, J., and Good, T. (1973). *Individual Differences: Toward an Understanding of Classroom Life*, Holt, Rinehart & Winston.

Bynner, J. M., and Romney, D. M. (1986). Intelligence, fact or artefact: alternative structures for cognitive abilities. *British Journal of Educational Psychology*, **56**: 13–23.

Ceci, S. J. (1990). *On Intelligence ... More or Less: A Bio-Ecological Treatise on Intellectual Development*, Prentice Hall.

Ceci, S. J., and Liker, J. (1986). A day at the races: a study of IQ, expertise, and cognitive complexity. *Journal of Experimental Psychology: General*, **115**: 255–66.

Ceci, S. J., Baker, J. G., and Bronfenbrenner, U. (1988). Prospective remembering, temporal calibration, and context. In: *Practical Aspects of Memory: Current Research and Issues*, eds M. M. Gruneberg, P. Morris, and R. Sykes, Wiley.

Charness, N., Krampe, R. Th., and Mayr, U. (1996). The role of practice and coaching in entrepreneurial skill domains: an international comparison of life-span chess skill acquisition. In: *The Road to Excellence: The Acquisition of Expert Performance in the Arts and Sciences*, ed. K. A. Ericsson, Erlbaum.

Chase, W. G., and Ericsson, K. A. (1981). Skilled memory. In: *Cognitive Skills and their Acquisition*, ed. J. R. Anderson, Erlbaum.

Chi, M. T. H., and Ceci, S. J. (1987). Content knowledge: its role, representation, and restructuring in memory development. *Advances in Child Development*, **20**: 91–142.

Coon, H., and Carey, G. (1989). Genetic and environmental determinants of musical ability in twins. *Behavior Genetics*, **19**: 183–93.

Dark, V. J., and Benbow, C. P. (1990). Enhanced problem translation and short-term memory: components of mathematical talent. *Journal of Educational Psychology*, **82**: 420–9.

Dark, V. J., and Benbow, C. P. (1991). The differential enhancement of working memory with mathematical versus verbal precocity. *Journal of Educational Psychology*, **83**: 48–60.

Davidson, J. W., Howe, M. J. A., Moore, D. G., and Sloboda, J. A. (1996). The role of parental influences in the development of musical performance. *British Journal of Developmental Psychology*, **14**: 399–412.

Davies, J. B. (1994). Seeds of a false consciousness. *Psychologist*, **7**: 355–6.

Davis, M. (1994). Folk music psychology. *Psychologist*, **7**: 537.

Detterman, D. K. (1993). Discussion (p. 234). In: *Ciba Foundation Symposium* **178**: The origins and development of high ability, eds G. R. Bock and K. Ackrill, Wiley.

Dweck, C. S. (1986). Motivational processes affecting learning. *American Psychologist*, **41**: 1040–8.

Elbert, T., Pantev, C., Wienbruch, C., Rockstroh, B., and Taub, E. (1995). Increased cortical representation of the fingers of the left hand in string players. *Science*, **270**: 305–7.

Ericsson, K. A. (1990). Peak performance and age: an examination of peak performance in sports. In: *Successful Aging: Perspectives from the Behavioral Sciences*, eds P. B. Baltes and M. M. Baltes, Cambridge University Press.

Ericsson, K. A., and Charness, N. (1994). Expert performance: its structure and acquisition. *American Psychologist*, **49**: 725–47.

Ericsson, K. A., and Charness, N. (1995). Abilities: evidence for talent or characteristics acquired through engagement in relevant activities. *American Psychologist*, **50**: 803–4.

Ericsson, K. A., and Crutcher, R. J. (1988). The nature of exceptional performance. In: *Life-Span Development and Behavior. Vol. 10*, eds P. B. Baltes, D. L. Featherman, and R. M. Lerner, Laurence Erlbaum.

Ericsson, K. A., and Faivre, I. A. (1988). What's exceptional about exceptional abilities? In: *The Exceptional Brain*, eds L. K. Obler and D. Fein, Guilford Press.

Ericsson, K. A., and Lehmann, A. C. (in press). Expertise. In: *Encyclopedia of Creativity*, eds M. A. Runco and S. Pritzer, Academic Press.

Ericsson, K. A., and Polson, P. G. (1988). An experimental analysis of a memory skill for dinner-orders. *Journal of Experimental Psychology: Learning, Memory and Cognition*, **14**: 305–16.

Ericsson, K. A., Krampe, R. Th., and Heizmann, S. (1993a). Can we create gifted people? In: *Ciba Foundation Symposium* **178**: The origins and development of high ability, eds G. R. Bock and K. Ackrill, Wiley.

Ericsson, K. A., Krampe, R. Th., and Tesch-Römer, C. (1993b). The role of deliberate practice in the acquisition of expert performance. *Psychological Review*, **100**: 363–406.

Ericsson, K. A., Tesch-Römer, C., and Krampe, R. Th. (1990). The role of practice and motivation in the acquistion of expert-level performance in real life. In: *Encouraging the Development of Exceptional Abilities and Talents*, ed. M. J. A. Howe, British Psychological Society.

Eysenck, H. J. (1995). *Genius: The Natural History of Creativity*, Cambridge University Press.

Eysenck, H. J., and Barrett, P. T. (1993). Brain research related to giftedness. In: *International Handbook of Research and Development of Giftedness and Talent*, eds K. A. Heller, F. J. Mönks, and A. H. Passow, Pergamon.

Feld, S. (1984). Sound structure as a social structure. *Ethnomusicology*, **28**: 383–409.

Feldman, D. H. (1980). *Beyond Universals in Cognitive Development*. Ablex.

Feldman, D. H. (1988). Creativity: dreams, insights, and transformations. In: *The Nature of Creativity*, ed. R. J. Sternberg, Cambridge University Press.

Feldman, D. H., with Goldsmith, L. (1986). *Nature's Gambit: Child Prodigies and the Development of Human Potential*, Basic Books.

Fowler, W. (1981). Case studies of cognitive precocity: the role of exogenous and endogenous stimulation in early mental development. *Journal of Applied Developmental Psychology*, **2**: 319–67.

Freeman, J. (1990). The intellectually gifted adolescent. In: *Encouraging the Development of Exceptional Skills and Talents*, ed. M. J. A. Howe, British Psychological Society.

Gagné, F. (1993). Constructs and models pertaining to exceptional human abilities. In: *International Handbook of Research and Development of Giftedness and Talent*, eds K. A. Heller, F. J. Mönks, and A. H. Passow, Pergamon.

Gardner, H. (1984). *Frames of Mind: A Theory of Multiple Intelligences*, Heinemann.

Gardner, H. (1993a). Early giftedness and later achievement. In: *Ciba Foundation Symposium* **178**: The origins and development of high ability, eds G. R. Bock and K. Ackrill, Wiley.

Gardner, H. (1993b). *Multiple Intelligences: The Theory in Practice*, Basic Books.

Gardner, H. (1995). Why would anyone become an expert? *American Psychologist*, **50**: 802–3.

Gazzaniga, M. S. (1985). *The Social Brain: Discovering the Networks of the Mind*, Basic Books.

Geschwind, N., and Behan, P. (1982). Left-handedness: associations with immune disease, migraine, and developmental learning disorders. *Proceedings of the National Academy of Science*, **79**: 5097–100.

Goldsmith, G. (1990). The timing of talent: the facilitation of early prodigious achievement. In: *Encouraging the Development of Exceptional Skills and Talents*, ed. M. J. A. Howe, British Psychological Society.

Gross, M. U. M. (1993a). Nurturing the talents of exceptionally gifted individuals. In: *International Handbook of Research and Development of Giftedness and Talent*, eds K. A. Heller, F. J. Mönks, and A. H. Passow, Pergamon.

Gross, M. U. M. (1993b). *Exceptionally Gifted Children*, Routledge.

Gustin, W. C. (1985). The development of exceptional research mathematicians. In: *Developing Talent in Young People*, ed. B. S. Bloom, Ballantine.

Haber, R. N. (1979). Twenty years of haunting eidetic imagery: where's the ghost? *Behavioral and Brain Sciences*, **2**: 583–94.

Haber, R. N., and Haber, L. R. (1988). The characteristics of eidentic imagery. In: *The Exceptional Brain*, eds L. K. Obler and D. Fein, Guilford Press.

Hargreaves, D. J. (1986). *The Developmental Psychology of Music*, Cambridge University Press.

Hargreaves, D. J. (1994). Musical education for all. *Psychologist*, **7**: 357–8.

Hayes, J. R. (1981). *The Complete Problem Solver*, Franklin Institute Press.

Heller, K. A. (1993). Scientific ability. In: *Ciba Foundation Symposium* **178**: The origins and development of high ability, eds G. R. Bock and K. Ackrill, Wiley.

Hendrikson, A. E., and Hendrikson, D. E. (1980). The biological basis for individual differences in intelligence. *Personality and Individual Differences*, **1**: 3–33.

Hepper, P. G. (1991). An examination of fetal learning before and after birth. *Irish Journal of Psychology*, **12**: 95–107.

Hollingworth, L. S. (1942). *Children Above IQ 180: Origin and Development*, World Books.

Horn, J. L. (1986). Intellectual ability concepts. In: *Advances in the Psychology of Human Intelligence. Vol. 3*, ed. R. J. Sternberg, Erlbaum.

Howald, H. (1982). Training-induced morphological and functional changes in skeletal muscle. *International Journal of Sports Medicine*, **3**: 1–12.

Howe, M. J. A. (1975). *Learning in Infants and Young Children*, Macmillan.

Howe, M. J. A. (1980). *The Psychology of Human Learning*, Harper & Row.

Howe, M. J. A. (1982). Biographical information and the development of outstanding individuals. *American Psychologist*, **37**: 1071–81.

Howe, M. J. A. (1988a). Intelligence as an explanation. *British Journal of Psychology*, **79**: 349–60.

Howe, M. J. A. (1988b). The hazards of using correlational evidence as a means of identifying the causes of individual ability differences: a rejoinder to Sternberg and a reply to Miles. *British Journal of Psychology*, **79**: 539–45.

Howe, M. J. A. (1989a). *Fragments of Genius: The Strange Feats of Idiots Savants*, Routledge.

Howe, M. J. A. (1989b). The strange achievements of idiots savants. In: *Psychology Survey* **7**, eds A. M. Colman and J. G. Beaumont, British Psychological Society/Routledge.

Howe, M. J. A. (1989c). Separate skills or general intelligence: the autonomy of human abilities. *British Journal of Educational Psychology*, **59**: 351–60.

Howe, M. J. A. (1990a). *The Origins of Exceptional Abilities*, Blackwell.

Howe, M. J. A. (1990b). Does intelligence exist? *Psychologist*, **3**: 490–3.

Howe, M. J. A. (1990c). Gifts, talents, and natural abilities: an explanatory mythology? *Educational and Child Psychology*, **7**: 52–4.

Howe, M. J. A. (1993). The early lives of child prodigies. In: *Ciba Foundation Symposium* **178**: The origins and development of high ability, eds G. R. Bock and K. Ackrill, Wiley.

Howe, M. J. A. (1995). What can we learn from the lives of geniuses? In: *Actualizing Talent: A Lifelong Challenge*, eds J. Freeman, P. Span, and H. Wagner, Cassell.

Howe, M. J. A. (1996a). The childhood and early lives of geniuses: combining psychological and biographical evidence. In: *The Road to Excellence: The*

Acquisition of Expert Performance in the Arts and Sciences, ed. K. A. Ericsson, Erlbaum.

Howe, M. J. A. (1996b). Concepts of ability. In: *Human Abilities: Their Nature and Measurement*, eds I. Dennis and P. Tapsfield, Erlbaum.

Howe, M. J. A. (1997). Beyond psychobiography: towards more effective syntheses of psychology and biography. *British Journal of Psychology*, **88**: 235–48.

Howe, M. J. A., and Sloboda, J. A. (1991a). Young musicians' accounts of significant influences in their early lives: 1. The family and the musical background. *British Journal of Music Education*, **8**: 39–52.

Howe, M. J. A., and Sloboda, J. A. (1991b). Young musicians' accounts of significant influences in their early lives: 2. Teachers, practising and performing. *British Journal of Music Education*, **8**: 53–63.

Howe, M. J. A., and Sloboda, J. A. (1991c). Early signs of talents and special interests in the lives of young musicians. *European Journal of High Ability*, **2**: 102–11.

Howe, M. J. A., and Smith, J. (1988). Calendar calculating in "idiots savants": How do they do it? *British Journal of Psychology*, **79**: 371–86.

Howe, M. J. A., Davidson, J. W., Moore, D. G., and Sloboda, J. A. (1995). Are there early childhood signs of musical ability? *Psychology of Music*, **23**: 162–76.

Humphreys, L. G., Lubinski, D., and Yao, G. (1993). Utility of predicting group membership and the role of spatial visualization in becoming an engineer, physical scientist, or artist. *Journal of Applied Psychology*, **78**: 250–61.

Kalinowski, A. G. (1985). The development of Olympic swimmers. In: *Developing Talent in Young People*, ed. B. S. Bloom, Ballantine.

Kearins, J. M. (1981). The visual spatial memory in Australian Aboriginal children of desert regions. *Cognitive Psychology*, **13**: 434–60.

Keating, D. P. (1984). The emperor's new clothes: the "new look" in intelligence research. In: *Advances in Human Intelligence. Vol. 2*, ed. R. J. Sternberg, Erlbaum.

Kliegl, R., Smith, J., and Baltes, P. B. (1989). Testing the limits and the study of age differences in cognitive plasticity of mnemonic skill. *Developmental Psychology*, **25**: 247–56.

Krampe, R. Th. (1994). *Maintaining Excellence: Cognitive–Motor Performance in Pianists Differing in Age and Skill Level*, Max-Planck-Institut für Bildungsforschung.

Krampe, R. Th., and Ericsson, K. A. (1996). Maintaining excellence: cognitive–motor performance in pianists differing in age and skill level. *Journal of Experimental Psychology: General*, **125**: 331–68.

Krogius, N. (1976). *Psychology in Chess*, RHM Press.

Lecanuet, J. P. (1995). Prenatal auditory experience. In: *Perception and Cognition of Music*, eds I. Deliege and J. A. Sloboda, Erlbaum.

Lehmann, A. C. (1997). The acquisition of expertise in music: efficiency of deliberate practice as a moderating variable in accounting for sub-expert performance. In: *Perception and Cognition of Music*, eds J. A. Sloboda and I. Deliege, Erlbaum.

Lewis, D. (1976). Observations on route finding and spatial orientation among the aboriginal peoples of the western desert region of central Australia. *Oceania*, **46**: 349–82.

Lykken, D. (in press). The genetics of genius. In: *Genius and the Mind*, ed. A. Steptoe, Oxford University Press.

McCarthy, G., and Donchin, E. (1981). A metric for thought: a comparison of P300 latency and reaction time. *Science*, **211**: 77–9.

Manturzewska, M. (1986). Musical talent in the light of biographical research. In: *Musikalische Begabung Finden und Förden*, Bosse.

Manturzewska, M. (1990). A biographical study of the life-span development of professional musicians. *Psychology of Music*, **18**: 112–39.

Marshall, C. (1982). Towards a comparative aesthetics of music. In: *Cross Cultural Perspectives in Music*, eds R. Falck and T. Rice, University of Toronto Press.

Mead, M. (1975). *Growing Up in New Guinea*, Morrow.

Merriam, A. P. (1967). *The Ethnomusicology of the Flathead Indians*, Aldine.

Messenger, J. (1958). Esthetic talent. *Basic College Quarterly*, **4**: 20–4.

Miller, L. K. (1989). *Musical Savants: Exceptional Skill in the Mentally Retarded*, Erlbaum.

Miller, K., and Gelman, R. (1983). The child's representation of number: a multidimensional scaling analysis. *Child Development*, **54**: 1470–9.

Monsaas, J. (1985). Learning to be a world-class tennis player. In: *Developing Talent in Young People*, ed. B. S. Bloom, Ballantine.

O'Connor, N., and Hermelin, B. (1987). Visual and graphic abilities of the idiot savant artist. *Psychological Medicine*, **17**: 79–90.

O'Neill, S. (1994). Factors influencing children's motivation and achievement during the first year of instrumental music tuition. *Proceedings of the Third International Conference on Music Perception and Cognition*, University of Liege, Belgium.

Papousek, H. (1995). Musicality and infancy research. In: *Perception and Cognition of Music*, eds I. Deliege and J. A. Sloboda, Erlbaum.

Parncutt, R. (1993). Prenatal experience and the origins of music. In: *Prenatal Perception, Learning and Bonding*, ed. T. Blum, Leonardo.

Patel, V. L., and Groen, G. J. (1991). The general and specific nature of medical expertise: a critical look. In: *Toward a General Theory of Expertise*, eds K. A. Ericsson and J. Smith, Cambridge University Press.

Perkins, D. N. (1981). *The Mind's Best Work*, Harvard University Press.

Plomin, R. (1988). The nature and nurture of cognitive abilities. In: *Advances in the Psychology of Human Intelligence*, ed. R. Sternberg, Erlbaum.

Plomin, R., and Thompson, L. A. (1993). Genetics and high cognitive ability. In: *Ciba Foundation Symposium* **178**: The origins and development of high ability, eds G. R. Bock and K. Ackrill, Wiley.

Radford, J. (1990). *Child Prodigies and Exceptional Early Achievers*, Harvester Wheatsheaf.

Radford, J. (1994). Variations on a musical theme. *Psychologist*, **7**: 359–60.

Renninger, K. A., and Wozniak, R. N. (1985). Effect of interest on attentional shift, recognition and recall in young children. *Developmental Psychology*, **21**: 624–32.

Revesz, G. (1925). *The Psychology of a Musical Prodigy*, Kegan Paul, Trench & Trubner.

Rosser, P. L., and Randolph, S. M. (1989). Black American infants: the Howard study. In: *The Cultural Context of Infancy. Vol. 1: Biology, Culture and Infant Development*, eds J. K. Nugent, B. M. Lester, and T. B. Brazelton, Ablex.

Sacks, O. (1995). *An Anthropologist on Mars*, Picador.

Schlaug, G., Jäncke, L., Huang, Y., and Steinmetz, H. (1995). In vivo evidence of structural brain asymmetry in musicians. *Science*, **267**: 699–701.

Scheibel, A. B., and Paul, L. (1985). On the apparent non-adhesive nature of axospinous dendritic synapses. *Experimental Neurology*, **89**: 279–83.

Schneider, W. (1993). Acquiring expertise: determinants of exceptional performance. In: *International Handbook of Research and Development of Giftedness and Talent*, eds K. A. Heller, F. J. Mönks, and A. H. Passow, Pergamon.

Selfe, L. (1977). *Nadia: A Case of Extraordinary Drawing Ability in an Autistic Child*, Academic Press.

Sergent, D., and Roche, S. (1973). Perceptual shifts in the auditory information processing of young children. *Psychology of Music*, **1**: 39–48.

Shuter-Dyson, R., and Gabriel, C. (1981). *The Psychology of Musical Ability*, 2nd edition, Methuen.

Simon, H. A., and Chase, W. D. (1973). Skill in chess. *American Scientist*, **61**: 394–403.

Simonton, D. K. (1991). Emergence and realization of genius: the lives and works of 120 classical composers. *Journal of Personality and Social Psychology*, **61**: 829–40.

Slater, A. (1995). Individual differences in infancy and later IQ. *Journal of Child Psychology and Psychiatry*, **36**: 69–112.

Sloan, K. D., and Sosniak, L. A. (1985). The development of accomplished sculptors. In: *Developing Talent in Young People*, ed. B. S. Bloom, Ballantine.

Sloboda, J. A. (1996). The acquisition of musical performance expertise: deconstructing the "talent" account of individual differences in musical expressivity. In: *The Road to Excellence: The Acquisition of Expert Performance in the Arts and Sciences*, ed. K. A. Ericsson, Erlbaum.

Sloboda, J. A., and Howe, M. J. A. (1991). Biographical precursors of musical excellence: an interview study. *Psychology of Music*, **19**: 3–21.

Sloboda, J. A., and Howe, M. J. A. (1992). Transitions in the early musical careers of able young musicians: choosing instruments and teachers. *Journal of Research in Music Education*, **40**: 283–94.

Sloboda, J. A., Davidson, J. W., and Howe, M. J. A. (1994a). Is everyone musical? *Psychologist*, **7**: 349–54.

Sloboda, J. A., Davidson, J. W., and Howe, M. J. A. (1994b). Musicians: experts not geniuses. *Psychologist*, **7**: 363–4.

Sloboda, J. A., Hermelin, B., and O'Connor, N. (1985). An exceptional musical memory. *Music Perception*, **3**: 155–70.

Sloboda, J. A., Davidson, J. W., Howe, M. J. A., and Moore, D. G. (1996). The role of practice in the development of performing musicians. *British Journal of Psychology*, **87**: 287–309.

Sosniak, L. A. (1985). Learning to be a concert pianist. In: *Developing Talent in Young People*, ed. B. S. Bloom, Ballantine.

Sosniak, L. A. (1990). The tortoise, the hare, and the development of talent. In: *Encouraging the Development of Exceptional Abilities and Talents*, ed. M. J. A. Howe, British Psychological Society.

Starkes, J. L., Deakin, J., Allard, F., Hodges, N., and Hayes, A. (1996). Deliberate practice in sports: what is it anyway? In: *The Road to Excellence: The Acquisition of Expert Performance in the Arts and Sciences*, ed. K. A. Ericsson, Erlbaum.

Sternberg, R. J. (1993). Procedures for identifying intellectual potential in the gifted: a perspective on alternative "metaphors of mind." In: *International Handbook of Research and Development of Giftedness and Talent*, eds K. A. Heller, F. J. Mönks, and A. H. Passow, Pergamon.

Storfer, M. D. (1990). *Intelligence and Giftedness: The Contributions of Heredity and Early Environment*, Jossey-Bass.

Super, C. (1976). Environmental effects on motor development: the case of "African infant precocity." *Developmental Medicine and Child Neurology*, **18**: 561–7.

Takeuchi, A. H., and Hulse, S. H. (1993). Absolute pitch. *Psychological Bulletin*, **113**: 345–61.

Thompson, L. A., and Plomin, R. (1993). Genetic influence on cognitive ability. In: *International Handbook of Research and Development of Giftedness and Talent*, eds K. A. Heller, F. J. Mönks, and A. H. Passow, Pergamon.

Torff, B., and Winner, E. (1994). Don't throw out the baby with the bath water. *Psychologist*, **7**: 361–2.

Treffert, D. A. (1989). *Extraordinary People*, Harper & Row.

Trehub, S. E. (1990). The perception of musical patterns by human infants: the provision of similar paterns by their parents. In: *Comparative Perception. Vol. 1: Basic Mechanisms*, eds M. A. Berkeley and W. C. Stebbins, Wiley.

Usher, J. A., and Neisser, U. (1993). Childhood amnesia and the beginnings of memory for four early life events. *Journal of Experimental Psychology: General*, **122**: 155–65.

Vispoel, W. P., and Austin, J. R. (1993). Constructive response to failure in music: the role of attribution feedback and classroom goal structure. *British Journal of Educational Psychology*, **63**: 110–29.

Winner, E. (1996). The rage to master: the decisive role of talent in the visual arts. In: *The Road to Excellence: The Acquisition of Expert Performance in the Arts and Sciences*, ed. K. A. Ericsson, Erlbaum.

Winner, E., and Martino, G. (1993). Giftedness in the visual arts and music. In: *International Handbook of Research and Development of Giftedness and Talent*, eds K. A. Heller, F. J. Mönks, and A. H. Passow, Pergamon.

Subject Index